WOOD ETERNAL

Other books by Fred Tarpley

Place Names of Northeast Texas

From Blinky to Blue-John: A Word Atlas of Northeast Texas

1001 Texas Place Names

Jefferson: Riverport to the Southwest

Jefferson: East Texas Metropolis

Interjections for Aggies with Dale Talkington

Wood Eternal

The Story Of Osage Orange, Bois d'Arc, etc

Fred Tarpley

Tarpley Books
4540 FM 1568
Campbell, Texas 75422

Copyright

Tarpley Books

4540-FM1568, Campbell, Texas 75422

All rights reserved. Published 2010

Printed in the United States of America

All rights reserved.

First Edition, 2010

Library of Congress Control Number

ISBN:9781453740613

Cover Watercolor by Walt Davis

Back cover portrait by Dave Walvoord

Book design by Joe Shipman, Michael Lewandowski, Jessica Martin

Dedication

To everyone who has ever hugged a Maclura pomifera,

rolled horse apples down a sidewalk,

pulled the string of an Osage orange bow,

admired the tree's stunning heartwood,

stared in wonder at a sprouting hedge seed,

or collected bois d'arc memories.

And especially to my extraordinary family

and to all who reside in the Bois d'Arc

Capital of Texas.

Acknowledgements

To all of the individuals and institutions listed below, I express my deepest gratitude for assistance in providing the information and services that brought *Wood Eternal* to its present form:

Libraries and librarians. Especially the Gee Library at Texas A&M University-Commerce; the Library of Congress; Thomas Jefferson Collection, University of Virginia; the Center for American History at the University of Texas at Austin; the Botanical Research Institute of Texas; Dallas Public Library; Fort Worth Public Library; Waldrop Harrison Public Library, Greenville, Texas; libraries of New York City and Philadelphia; the British Museum; Mexico City Public Library; interlibrary loan and special collections of Gee Library, Texas A&M University-Commerce.

Walt Davis. Watercolor of a Hunt County bois d'arc tree for the cover of *Wood Eternal*.

Dave Walvoord. Back cover portrait.

Joe Shipman, Michael Lewandoski, and Jessica Martin. Cover design and book design.

Proofreaders. Jim Ainsworth, Walt and Isabel Davis, Jack Gray, Dr. Jerry Hutton, Shirley Moore, Dr. Arthur Pullen, Carolyn Trezevant.

Arlan and Bobbie Purdy. Field research at Bois d'Arc Springs and photography.

Dale Talkington. Research assistance, location of information sources in Oklahoma.

Dr. Frank Newhouse. Research assistance, travel arrangements.

Supporters of the annual Bois d'Arc Bash in Commerce, Texas.

Table of Contents

Introduction
1. Anatomy of an American Tree 1
2. Native Habitat 25
3. Escape from Indian Lands 37
4. Horse High, Bull Strong, Pig Tight 55
5. Ascent of Barbed Wire 103
6. Windbreaks and Shelterbelts 114
7. Favored Wood of Archery 125
8. Food for Silk Worms 131
9. Famous Osage Orange Trees 135
10. Celebrating Osage Orange 143
11. Famous Folks and Osage Orange 149
12. Other Uses of Osage Orange 163
13. Global Range of Osage Orange 219
14. A Tree by Any Other Name. 249
15. What's Next for Osage Orange. 255
Afterword. 259
Works Cited. 263
Index. 309

Introduction

The greatest service which can be rendered any country is to add a useful plant to its culture
—Thomas Jefferson 1800

The charismatic tree known in botanical science as *Maclura pomifera* and commonly called Osage orange, bois d'arc, hedge, bow wood, and three score other names invites investigation. What other tree has a wider variety of regional names, more intriguing fruit, a more clearly defined timeline after its introduction beyond Native American tribes, a better record of durability and survival in earth and water, a more restrictive native habitat with dispersion to other locales, or more uses and potential adaptations?

The ability of Osage orange to outlast other timber as fence posts, house foundation blocks, and archery bows earned the tree the nickname of "wood eternal." In the eye of the beholder, the Osage orange evokes ecstatic praise for its unique beauty or an equally strong disdain for its messy fruits and vicious thorns. Its popularity throughout the United States has ebbed and waned as technical developments overshadowed its practical uses. Somehow the tree has endured. Osage orange has the reputation for withstanding bitter cold and drought and evolutionary replacement.

Some 1,200 forest trees have been identified on the North American continent. None can surpass the historic role and fascinating story of *Maclura pomifera*.

1
Anatomy of an American Tree

In 1804 Meriwether Lewis, in his letter to President Thomas Jefferson about the explorer's discovery of a new species of tree, called it the Osage apple (Jackson 109-10). When William Dunbar, a Scottish gentleman, wrote the earliest public account upon seeing the tree in 1804 near Natchitoches, Louisiana, during an expedition on the Red River, he used the name of bois d'arc, which he had encountered locally. In 1806, President Jefferson made what is thought to be the first public announcement of the important discovery of Dunbar and Hunter's expedition, identifying the tree as bois d'arc (*Debates and Proceedings* 1036-37: 1142).

Constantine Rafinesque, a recognized American botanist, assigned the first scientific name of *Ioxylon pomiferum* in 1817 (Rafinesque, *American Manual* 13*)*. He changed the name to *Toxylon pomiferum* in 1818 and then to *Joxylon pomiferum* in 1819 (Morton 449). *Toxylon* was of Greek derivation, referring to the Indian use of the wood for bows (Keeler 258).

Thomas Nuttall, studying a stand of the species in 1818, named the tree *Maclura aurantiaca* in honor of his friend William Maclure (Peattie, *Western Trees* 481). Nuttall's prestige gave general acceptance to the name he chose (Morton 449). The currently accepted name, *Maclura pomifera,* is the standard name although *Maclura aurantiaca* is still used. Other names given to this species are *Broussonetia tinctoria, Toxylon aurantiacum,* and *Toxylon Maclura* (Sargent, *Silva*).

David Landreth, an early promoter of Osage orange, claimed for his father the honor of having planted in Philadelphia and in the East the first Osage orange hedge about 1828 (Danhof 181). *Maclura pomifera* is now listed in the category of an endemic genus of the North American Atlantic Region, Appalachian Province (Takhtajan 79).

Names—Common and Scientific

Common names abound for *Maclura pomifera*, the current universal scientific name for this member of Moraceae, the mulberry family. In every locale where the tree is known, common names have been given. By far the most frequently used common name is Osage orange, which is consistently employed by libraries as the term in subject headings for books. In printed lists of common names, Osage orange is most likely to be the primary term in frequency. In printed sources the name Osage orange is often accompanied by one or more of the common names, especially if other names are used in the specific state or region being discussed.

In past geological eras, Maclura had many species, but now all are extinct except one. And this monotypic genus is restricted to the narrow range of the native habitat for Osage orange (Peattie 479). In the 1979 *Checklist of United States Trees,* Little noted under Maclura, "If the related genus *Chlorophora* Gaud. of tropical America and

Africa is united, total, about 12 (165)". Most modern botanists list the genus as monotypic.

From Applewood to Yellow Wood

The following alphabetical list of common names for *Maclura* represents those gathered from printed and oral sources: applewood, arrow-wood, boardarc, bodarc, bodark, bodeck, bodock, bois d'arc boudoix, bowdarc, bowwood, boxwood, brass wood, Chinese orange, geelhout, green ball, hedge, hedge apple, hedge orange, hedge plant, Indian orange, ironwood, milkball, mock orange, mockorange, monkey ball, monkey brain, North American bow wood, Osage, Osage apple, Osage apple-tree, Osage bow wood, Osage orange, Osage orange thorn, prairie hedge, prairie hedge plant, rabbit hedge, rootwood, stinking wood, wild orange, woodhedge, and yellow wood.

The listing above does not include capitalization and hyphenated variants of a common name. For example, Osage orange also appears in edited publications as Osage Orange, osage orange, osage-orange, Osage-orange, and Osage-Orange. Other common names also have alternate forms of capitalization and hyphenation.

In Schele de Vere's *Americanisms* (1872), the language auditor reported that on the lips of English-speaking hunters, bois d'arc became "bowdark" on the Western frontier before it finally settled into the still shorter "bodok" (Cassidy 1:325).

Suggestions have been made for alterations of some of the common names reported above. In a letter to the *Republican Daily Journal* in Lawrence, Kansas, a reader recommended shortening Osage orange to Maclura, the first word of the scientific name (Elliott, R. S., *Kansas* 20). Not enough readers agreed with the proposal in the letter to forsake the popular name. Objections have been raised about the name mock orange, which is also the common name of two different species of flowering shrubs (Kieran 45). The ill-chosen name of mock orange is more appropriate for *Philadelphus L.*; and yellow-wood is more properly called *Cladrastis Intea* (Burton 4).

Pronunciation Variants

Pronunciation differences are also heard, especially for the French sound sequence of bois d'arc. The French pronunciation of "bwa dark" is rarely heard in the United States although "boys dee arc" may be the spoken rendering by non-Francophiles. As folk etymologies, "bowed arc" (rhyming with "mowed arc," not "loud arc)"and "board arc" (both derived from bois d'arc) are attempts to bring meaning to a foreign name, whose French words are meaningless to most Americans. Those who choose "bowed arc" reason that the wood of the tree can be "bowed": thus "bowed arc" is a reasonable pronunciation. Those who choose "board arc" are bringing meaning to bois d'arc by extending their reasoning process from the fact that they are referring to a tree, to the general knowledge that trees produce wood, and to the obvious conclusion that the wood can be cut into boards. Thus, why not deduce the pronunciation of "board arc"?

This researcher experienced personally the rival pronunciations of bois d'arc. He was born in Leonard, Fannin County, Texas, where everyone he knew called the tree "board arc." His father had explained to him that the tree produced wood sometimes cut into boards. Thus it was logical to call the tree "board arc." At age sixteen the researcher took his pronunciation of "board arc" twenty-six miles southeast of Leonard to adjacent Hunt County and enrolled in East Texas State Teachers College (now Texas A&M University-Commerce). Here he met head-on the question of how to say bois d'arc. Almost all the natives of Hunt County said "bowed arc," but some of the students preferred "board arc," especially those from Fannin County. Later, after receiving a doctorate in linguistics with a specialization in dialectology, he was able to draw dialect boundaries between areas favoring "board arc" and those championing "bowed arc."

By 2010, pronunciation had shifted in Fannin County, where the majority of residents now seems to be favoring "bowed arc" while a minority clings to "board arc." The Graves brothers of Dodd City in Fannin County were asked how they determined the pronunciation of "bowed arc" for their documentary film, "Bois d'Arc Goodbye." In anticipation of the creation of a reservoir on the creek with construction scheduled to begin in 2013, they wanted to preserve on film the domain of their youth. Russell and William Graves replied that there was no hesitation in going with "bowed ark" because that was the way they had pronounced the word since their childhood days of hunting and fishing along the creek.

When this researcher became founding director of the Commerce Bois d'Arc Bash in 1986 to celebrate the heritage of the remarkable tree, he surrendered his birthright pronunciation of "board arc" to appease the staunch natives of Commerce insisting on "bowed arc" Even the mayor of Commerce and a leader of the Chamber of Commerce had converted to "bowed arc." That person was Dr. Jack Bell, head of the Department of Journalism at the local university and a transplanted Kansan, who had grown up among the tree where it was known as hedge.

Additional information about multiple common names of the tree and its appellation in other countries will be explored in Chapter 14, "A Tree by Any Other Name."

Introducing Osage Orange

The first known public mention of the tree in the English language has been credited to Thomas Jefferson in his message to Congress in 1806. He was quoting from a report about the tree called bois d'arc by two explorers who had seen it two years before at a post on the Washita River in Arkansas. The description by Dunbar and Hunter recognized the tree's potential usefulness as a hedge plant (Peattie 481; *Debates and Proceedings* 1036-37).

Moraceae

The system of biological nomenclature emerged from the inventive mind of Carolus Lineaeus (1707-1778), who adopted Lineaeus as a family name from a large linden tree growing near his home. The Swede created one of the great achievements of the human intellect. Uniform plant nomenclature dates from *Species Planaterum* compiled in 1753 (Bates, Marston 11-13).

Classifications range from kingdom to subspecies, with family, genus, and species in between (Pimentel). The botanical family of the Osage orange is Moraceae, to which the mulberry belongs. The Moraceae family membership includes about fifty-five genera with an estimated 2,000 species. These trees or shrubs are widely distributed in the warmer parts of the earth (Womack 1).

Maclura Pomifera

The scientific name of the Osage orange reveals more about honoring patrons of American botany and perpetuating misconceptions about the tree than providing information about this monotypic genus in a branch of the Moraceae family. The tree represents a solitairy genus in the most primitive subfamily, Moroideae.

In past geologic times, there were several species of Maclura but now botanists generally recognize only one throughout the world (Peattie 479). Maclura is related to *Maclura tinctoria* (L) D. Don., commonly known as mora or fustic, and it is sometimes classified in the genus with *Maclura pomifera* (Little, Woodbury, and Wadsworth 108).

Maclura

The first component of the scientific name refers to William Maclure (1763-1840), a Scot who became an American citizen and a distinguished patron of the natural sciences in North America. He accepted a diplomatic appointment from Thomas Jefferson and surveyed much of the territory east of the Mississippi River, making an important geological map and earning the title of "father of American geology." The promoter of an agricultural school at the communal colony in New Harmony, Indiana, (Lembke 195; Lewis, John 156), was also known as a librarian and philanthropist. He founded the Academy of Natural Science in Philadelphia in 1812 and later became its president. A few years after Thomas Jefferson told congress about the unnamed tree, Thomas Nuttall, ornithologist and botanist from Yorkshire, England, was among the first Europeans to report the Osage orange when he saw a luxuriant stand in the rich bottom lands of the Red River. Nuttall also forwarded seed to England, where the plant became an object of some curiosity (Winberry 35).

Rules of biological nomenclature required that the scientific names be Latinized (Pimentel 97), as in Maclure becoming Maclura.

Pomifera

The second component of the scientific name means "pome" or "apple-bearing," The word perpetuates the same inaccuracy found in the regional names of Osage orange, horse apple, and hedge apple, all incorrectly identifying the fruit as a familiar fruit (Pimentel).

Rafinesque, Nuttall, etc.

As the final component of a scientific name, the name of the botanist who proposed the scientific name is appended, as in Homo sapiens L., with the L. abbreviating Linaeus, who proposed the scientific name (Pimentel 97).

In *Maclura aurantiaca*, Nutt., Thomas Nuttall is acknowledged for assigning the name *Maclura aurantiaca* when he first saw the species in 1818. The name gained wide acceptance because of Nuttall's prestige as a botanist Smith, Jeffrey 2)

Likewise *Ioxylon*, Rafin. and *Toxylon*, Rafin. recognize Constantine Rafinesque for choosing those names. Meriwether Lewis, who had been shown the Osage orange in 1804 just before embarking on the Lewis and Clark Expedition, had sent seed and cuttings of the tree to Philadelphia, where a later shipment grew into trees. Some years later Rafinesque identified trees he saw in Philadelphia and gave them the botanical name of *Toxylon pormiferum*, *Toxylon* referring to bow wood. Lewis and Clark introduced many other plants to the eastern United States, but for lack of names at the time, some were credited to later explorers (Eifert 176).

The standard name used today is Maclura pomifera (Schneid.), adding an abbreviation for Schneider, who contributed the word meaning "apple-bearing.

Osage Orange

The most frequently used common name and the generic name for research in libraries and scansion of book indexes is Osage orange. Most sources attribute the name derivation to the Osage Indians, now living in Oklahoma and one of the tribes using the wood for their bows. The name has also been traced to the Osage River, the largest tributary of the Missouri River, according to the *Oxford Dictionary of Trees of the World* (Hora). The second part of the common name, orange, has been called "a delusion and a snare, being only a globular, yellowish-green mass, from four to five inches in diameter, produced by the aggregation of ripened pistils . . . " (Parkhurst 122). The resemblance of the fruit to an orange is the supposed source of the second part of the name although the fruit actually looks more like a grapefruit and is regularly called a hedge apple or a horse apple (Grace 52).

Osage apple was the name used by Pierre Chouteau in St. Louis when he made Lewis aware of the tree, and that name was reported in Lewis' letter to Jefferson on March 24, 1804 (Jackson 109-10). At that time, Chouteau, a former Indian agent, had been growing the trees he had obtained from an Osage Indian village for about five years (Munger 19).

Bois d'Arc

Another favored common name is bois d'arc, still dominant among Texans and Louisianans. In the lumber trade, bois d'arc is the standard name used in reference to fence posts (*Tree Planting in the Great Plains Region* 13). The name was chosen by French-speakers who first came upon the tree near Natchitoches, Louisiana. Knowing that the Indian tribes valued the tree for providing wood for their bows, they translated "wood of the bow" into their native language as bois d'arc. That name, however, is not the nomenclature used in France in reference to the tree. If a speaker of French hears bois d'arc, he or she will translate it as "wood of the bow" but will not associate the translation with *Maclura pomifera* unless there already is an acquaintanceship with the name bestowed upon the tree by Frenchmen in America. In France the tree that Americans call by the common name of bois d'arc is identified by other common names. Thus bois d'arc remains an American French designation unused for the tree by French speakers in other parts of the world.. Common names of the *Maclura pomifera* in languages other than English are reported in Chapter 14, "A Tree by Any Other Name."

Because Indians were known to make their bows from the tree and use the wood as a valuable trading commodity, French-speakers in Louisiana gave the tree a name meaning "wood of the bow." Bois d'arc is responsible for the name *Ozark*, applied to the Missouri and Arkansas hills (Steyermark 564). A French trading post established in that region in the 1700s was called "Aux Arc" for the abundant bois d'arc trees. The phrase *aux arc* ("to the bow") evolved into Ozark (Burton and Barnett 1).

Through folk etymology the bois d'arc tree came to be considered the wood used by Noah to construct his biblical ark. Because the tree of this name provided wood that was strong and durable, and because the name included *arc*, the assumption was sometimes made in the United States that Noah chose this material for building an "arc" to offer flood refuge to his family and to pairs of each animal (Spiegelman 365). Biblical scholars have determined that Noah's arc was built of cypress wood.

General Description

Before an examination is made of the Osage orange's history, important role as a living fence on the prairies, economic values, and various other uses, a botanical dissection of the tree and a description of its wood, leaves, fruits, and other component parts will be beneficial. "From fruit to root," as the folk saying goes, the tree is worthy of a meticulous dissection.

Drought resistant, tolerant of pollution, and not alienated by poor soil, the tree is native to a small habitat but nevertheless the most planted tree in the nation. In most climates and soils, Osage orange grows rapidly and matures at a relatively low height of from 20 to 66 feet. In the cold temperatures of New England and upstate New York or in soils of the alkaline plains of the Midwest, the tenacious tree may survive but be stunted to a dwarfish ten feet or fewer (Baumgardt 26). The crown of the tree forms a silhouette with irregular, ragged, but round contour (Collingwood and Brush 266). It has won favor with urban horticulturalists because it satisfies many of the standards that street trees must meet (Aker H07).

Commenting on the strong visual impact made by the Osage orange, a botanist in 1855 wrote, "At all times it strikes the beholder as something remarkable in the northern forest by the beauty and splendour of its dark and shining foliage."

Sex

Each tree is of a single sex, male or female, with only the female trees bearing fruit (Polunin, Oleg 65). Some fundamental sex education will explain why fruit is never found on some of the trees, why the flowers are different on male and female trees, and why female trees need the wind-blown pollen of a nearby male. After botanists encountered the Osage orange, it took decades for them to fully understand the sexual secrets of the tree. In 1835, *Gardener's Magazine* reported, "Botanists have not concurred in deeming the sexes of the Maclura . . . ." One of the earliest explanations of the barren male tree and the female tree producing fruit with perfect seeds appeared in *Trees of America* in 1846. The book reported that at Beaver Dam, Virginia, a female tree in 1835 had borne 150 fruits weighing eighteen or nineteen ounces each (Browne 466).

Bark

Osage orange radiates character with its somewhat ribbed, deeply furrowed muscular trunk. Rising only a few feet before breaking into a tangle of gnarled branches, a mature tree has moderately thick bark of about one inch, described as "thick, dark orange brown, deeply and irregularly furrowed with coarse, interlacing, edges." On old trees the bark is "brown-shreddy" (Barnes and Wagner, Jr. 252; "Tree with Eye-Catching Bark: 4G). The bark peels in longitudinal strips (Baerg 109). Yielding yellow dye, the bark has also been used in tanning leather (Phillips, Roger 30). Indians used the outer layers of the roots to make a paper-like product.

Trunk

Cut into slices, the trunk of an Osage orange tree reveals annual growth rings, the dark golden heartwood, the white sapwood, and the bark (Hutchins, *Tree* 30-31).

Dividing a few feet above the ground, the trunk separates into stout, upward branches (Baumgardt).

In the trunk, as well as in the branches, the wood seasons with some irregularities and occasionally warps. The ever-present knots create problems for wood craftsmen. On the positive side, the grain is pronounced and attractive, and the wood takes a fine polish. The wood shrinks or swells very little in comparison to the wood of other trees (Van Der Linden and Farrar).

Branches

While the slender branching is erect on young trees, it becomes very crooked and irregular on older trees (Moore 70). Tinted with gray to tan hues, the branches are smooth and shiny on the top side (Clark 49). Twigs are browsed by cattle when other more palatable food is not available (Miller 59).

Sapwood

Osage orange has one of the thinnest bands of sapwood found in trees, with only one or two sapwood increments (Shigo 296) and generally not more than two centimeters wide (Brown, Panshin, and Forsmith). Living cells of sapwood serve multiple functions for the tree. Among trees, Osage orange and locust have only a few rings of sapwood. In contrast, birch and maple may have as many as one hundred rings of sapwood but very little heartwood (Moll and Ebenreck 74). The appearance of the sapwood has been described as "lemon colored" (Otis, *Michigan* 133).

Osage orange wood is distinctive for its high luster, but both odor and taste are absent (Smith, Jeffrey 5).

Heartwood

Osage orange heartwood is usually yellow with red streaks but sometimes orange to dark golden-brown. It is enclosed in white sapwood. The elastic wood takes a luxurious polish (Platt, *Discover* 111). The heartwood invites attention because of its high resistance to decay and insect attacks. Research in Michigan has concluded that the avoidance of decay is credited to the chemical pentahydroxystilbene. Among fifty trees listed as having heartwood that resisted decay, only Osage orange, black locust, and red mulberry showed exceptionally high resistance (Panshin and Zeeuw 353).

The root yields colored matter that gives a yellowish hue when it is placed in warm water (Core, Cote, and Day 156). Annual rings are distinct, made up of comparatively dark, thin bands of summerwood and lighter colored, frequently narrower bands of springwood. Although the heartwood cells are dead, healthy Osage orange trees are sound, contributing support and protection to the tree (Moll and Ebenreck 74). Exposed, the heartwood turns brown, and after aging, its color has been described as purplish or chocolate.

Leaves

The lustrous, waxy leaves of the deciduous tree widen toward the base, with pronounced, branched veins tapering to a long pointed tip. The toothless leaves turn yellow in autumn (Hunter, Carl 66). Their contour is almost heart-shaped to some observers but oval or egg-like to others. Size of the leaves is three to six inches long and two to three inches wide (Collingwood and Brush 266). Deep dark green and very glossy on the upper surface, the leaves are light green underneath. In the fall leaves turn clear yellow (Li 141). The entire margin of each thick, firm leaf is shiny green and smooth (Palmer 147). Black-tailed deer have been observed browsing on the leaves (Elias 257).

Thorns

Single thorns zigzag from thorn to thorn on a twig. The thorns, scientists have discovered, are actually transformed leaves (Rehder, *Manual* 89-90). The Russian olive, although much different in appearance, is the only other similar tree which combines entire leaves and thorny twigs in the manner of the Osage orange (Van Der Linden and Farrar). The Osage orange was added to the list of poisonous plants in *The Gazette* in 1894 after Hershberger, a botanist of that era, wrote a note to the periodical to that effect. One of the editors added that one of his friends had confirmed the report by which the thorns had pierced his skin, and they seemed to leave a poison in the wound (Coulter, Barnes, and Arthur 200).

Pigs were known to fear hornets, bees, and Maclura thorns. It was said of the animals, "Pigs, if not thin-skinned, are sensitively skinned" (*Prairie Farmer* 14 (Nov. 1851): 309).

The Osage orange branches have been classified as armed twigs. One collateral bud often produces a thorn on vigorous twigs. As early as 1934, botanical publications were reporting that a thornless variety of Osage orange (*Maclura pomifera inermis* (Schneid.) was being planted occasionally (Harrington 419). Before 1969, Albert B. Ferguson at an Iowa nursery had succeeded in grafting scions from a staminate tree selected for its upright branches to propagate trees that remained thornless for as long as three years. The trees first developed a few short thorns but were expected to be complexly thornless soon. Root grafts, however, yielded trees that immediately became very thorny (McDaniel 45).

In 1973, Kansas State University released altered Osage orange trees that are thornless and male, thus bearing no fruit, under the cultivar names of Pawhuska and Chetopa. These new specimens fulfilled the wishes of urban gardeners exclaiming, "If only we could eliminate the unwanted fruits and thorns!" These propagations descended from two trees found growing in the wild. A profitable future was predicted for these declawed and non-littering trees in the urban landscape and on city streets

(Whitcomb 89). Horticulturalists had earlier suggested propagation from scions or cuttings taken high enough in an old tree, where the twigs are thornless (McDaniel 45).

Thorns are used in field guides to identify the Osage orange with a tree clue, "If the thorns are single, on a twig that zig-zags from thorn to thorn, it is Osage orange." Some old Osage orange trees also have warty growths on the twigs (*Master Tree Finder* 29).

Flowers

By far the most complex element of the Osage orange tree is the flowers, male and female growing on separate trees. Most profiles of the tree omit a technical exploration of the sexual nature of the flowers. When an explanation is given, the technical terms resemble a foreign language that only seasoned botanists can decipher. In the words of Peattie, the male flowers grow "in spikes 1 to 1 ½ inches long, green with 4 stamens opposite the 4 lobes of calyx." The female flowers are "dense spherical heads dropping on short anxilary stalks on the new shoots, the calyx divided to the base into 4 green, unequal-sized sepals which invest the compressed green ovary that bears a slender stile covered with white stigmatic hair" (Peattie, *Natural History* 179).

Clarence Hylander gives less information: "Male and female flowers appear in June on separate trees; the female flowers develop into green knobby fruits. . ." (*Trees and Trails* 103).

Of the flowers, Julius King reveals only that "The male tree carries seed-bearing flowers, the female small round fuzzy seeds. These latter grow into a hard round 'orange,' light green in color, 3 to 5 inches diameter" (King, *Telling Trees* 67. Other botanists explain the necessity of wind-blown male pollen reaching the female flowers.

In Nuttall's *Genera of North American Plants* in 1818, he added a footnote, "Dedicated to William Maclure,

Esq. of the United States, a Philosopher, whose devotion to the geology of North America has scarcely been exceeded by Ramond or Saussure in Europe." Reflecting the lack of understanding at the time of male and female flowers on Osage orange trees, he wrote, "Male flowers unknown" (232-34).

Pollen

The pollen grains of Osage orange are round and smooth, usually containing two, three, or four pores. Wind pollination achieves the fertilization of female flowers (Smith, Jeffrey 3). The male pollen is vital to the creation of female fruit, for without the pollen, there would be no fruit containing the seeds responsible for future propagation of the species.

Fruit

Female trees begin to bear fruit at ten years of age. The staminate in racenes and the pistillate in spherical heads each develops into a multiple fruit maturing in the fall. The inside of the fruit has a texture compared to "compact cauliflower. . . . No child who has ever tasted it is eager for a second helping" (Kieran 45). Rich in resins, protein, fat, and starch, the yellowish-green fruit is a short-stemmed and wrinkled syncarp (several carpels growing together), with formations often compared to the human brain. A Texas botanist pointed out that no other tree in the state "bears a fruit as large, that green, or that corrugated." It is an aggregate of many small fruits. The remarkable fruits are borne high up in the female tree (*Trees Every Boy and Girl Should Know* 134).

The fruit is formed from pistillate clusters suspended from stalks in the axils (the upper angle yielding a leaf, twig etc.). The compound fruit is comprised of scores of the ripened flowers, and the calyxes enter into the composition of the structure. Their size is believed to be enhanced by long white stiles of the flowers, "which sometimes cover the inflorescence so completely that it could pass for a ball of coconut shreds. The stiles are shed after fertilization, but the remainder of the flower persists into fruit, the compound structures often reaching a diameter of four or five inches" (Rogers, Walter 218). The fruit turns yellow at full ripeness and exudes a milky sap, when penetrated, is compared to the "pungent fragrance of oriental lacquer" (Platt, *Discover* 111). The dried portion of the fruit was described as smelling like "the scent of honeycomb, but in a fainter degree" (*Gardener's Magazine* 11 (1835): 315).

Trees may begin to bear fruit at ten years of age. Osage orange female trees between twenty-five and seventy-five years old have been found to bear the largest crop of fruits. Reports from northern locales indicate that the fruit does not mature in colder climates.

The estimate for the number of fruits per bushel is 80 (Schopmeyer 526). Exuding milky juice when cut or punctured, the fruit can cause dermatitis on sensitive skin (Muenscher 9, 62; Hicks and Stephenson 218). The milky juice of the Osage orange is listed in a comprehensive study as one of the native or cultivated plants causing dermatitis (Hardin and Arena 14). The juice is also blamed for hay fever (Stephens, H. A., *Poisonous Plants* 150).

Printed reports on whether the Osage orange fruit is edible take many conflicting positions. Two botanists proclaimed, "When the heavy fruits of the Osage orange drop to the ground and soon decay, apparently no bird or native mammal ever eats them or disperses their seed" (Gleason and Cronquist, *Natural Geography* 44).

Contrary reports confirmed that the fruit and leaves are part of the diet of several animals. Occasionally an ambiguous statement is made, such as, ". . . sometimes eaten by livestock though may be poisonous (Duncan and Duncan 251). In 1849 a Texan who moved to Illinois reported, "I will also state that the Osage Orange plants produce a most beautiful fruit, which I have seen wild horses fatten on in Texas. I have also known our tame horses to eat the fruit and seem to do well on it. . . (Hancock, John). In 1912 a botanist reported, "The fruit is eaten by cattle but is not good for them (Keeler 262).

The fox squirrel shows no hesitation in eating the fruits (Miller 59). Squirrels use their sharp teeth to slice open a fallen fruit, and, defying the adhesive latex, gnaw the tiny nut-like seeds buried deep inside. They leave a heap of fruit pulp under the tree. Rabbits are reported having been seen tearing into the fruits for seeds in Kansas (Stephens, H. A., *Trees . . . in Kansas* 91). The crossbill and fox squirrel, as well as quail, raccoons, and skunks, have been observed devouring the seeds. Stomach records of black-tailed deer give evidence of digestion of seeds (Odenwald and Turner 343).

Opinion is divided about the appeal of Osage orange fruit to cows and horses. Some observers claim that hungry horses will sometimes eat the fruit after it has dried, and the very name of "horse apple" suggests that the animals had developed a fondness for their namesake.

Belief that fresh fruit of Osage orange will cause dairy animals to "dry up" is possibly due to the low molecular weight resins present in the latex, causing some inflammatory action in the digestive tract. The fruit has been used successfully as feed for horses, mules, and steers (Womack 142).

Although distasteful to humans and generally uninviting to animals, the fruit of the Osage orange, except for the seeds and leaves, is not a substantial part of the diet of cattle, horses, and wildlife. Deaths of horses and cattle attributed to Osage orange are usually the results of choking on the sticky fruits, not actual toxicity (Smith and Perino 34).

Cows attempted to swallow the fruit often enough to motivate a Midwestern veterinarian to devise a pronged spear on the end of a stick that could be pushed into a cow's esophagus to remove lodged Osage oranges. Horses and cows have also been observed eating the fruit and grazing on the leaves when nothing better is available.

Usually declared inedible for humans, the fruit is reported to have been eaten by the Indians, "but it is a very inferior food" (Coker and Totten 172).

Historically inaccurate myths maintain that the most famous teeth to bite into an Osage orange belonged to George Washington. Hearing that his dentures were made of tough wood, subscribers to the myth assumed that Washington wore false teeth made of Osage orange wood. However, Washington died before Osage orange was introduced to the eastern United States.

Side Effects of Milky Juice and Pollen

The milky juice of the Osage orange fruit, leaves, and branches has been identified as a toxic substance, causing dermatitis and hay fever in sensitive individuals (Stephens, H. A. *Poisonous Plants* 150). A culprit for hay fever has been identified as wind-blown pollen from the flowers (Steyermark, *Missouri* 564; Wodhouse 91).

Seeds

Pale chestnut-brown jackets cover seeds contained within sections of the fruit in an arrangement similar to that of seeds found in oranges, only in several concentric circles instead of just one *(Prairie Farmer.* 14 (29 Jan. 1864):40). Only the seeds of the fruit are eaten by squirrels splitting the grapefruit-size spheres with their sharp teeth. For humans the seeds are difficult to remove, and during the decades that Osage orange seed for living fences was a valued commodity on the prairies, residents of the area where the tree was a native sought ways to remove the seeds efficiently. Botanists claim that the seeds are also part of the diet of quail (Miller 59), but no explanation was given as to how the birds free the seeds from their secure home. Hemagglutinins are known to be toxic to man mammals, birds, and some insects, but researchers suspect that some of the toxicity reported for mammals came from the injection of the hemagglutinins rather than from ingestion (Smith, Jeffrey 17).

The number of cleaned seeds to a pound ranges from a low of 7,000 to a high of 16,000, averaging 14,000. From a bushel basket of fruit, 24,500 seeds or 2 ¼ pounds may be extracted. Purity of 96 percent and soundness of 95 percent have been determined (Schopmeyer 526).

Roots

Osage orange roots run deep and are wide spreading (Barnes and Wagner, Jr. 232). The roots contain tannin substances used in tanning hides and for making yellow dye. Warnings have been issued that chemicals extracted from the roots are highly toxic to goldfish and mosquito larva. These pigments are thought to protect the roots from decay and attacks by pests, much like the antifungal agent found in the Osage orange wood (Smith, Jeffrey 16).

As the long, voracious roots spread at a shallow depth, they become a threat to sewers, drains, and other underground installations (Maino and Howard 52). The tap root is so deep that farmers, noting that the root has warmed enough to send signals for the branches to bud, proclaim, "Winter is over; the Osage orange is budding." The tree buds after all of its neighbors have started the process. Botanists generally classify the Osage orange as having a tap root system (Bernatzky 29).

Weight

Recognized as the heaviest wood native to North America, Osage orange, when air dry, yields approximately forty-eight pounds to the cubic foot (Collingwood 509). The weight, combined with the strength and durability, makes Osage orange a preferred wood for many uses that require the qualities it affords.

Durability

Among the species rated naturally durable and giving good service in contact with the ground without treatment, the Osage orange is one of the seven trees rated most durable (Anderson and Smith). Certain natural oils and other materials in Osage orange are credited with warding off attacks of organisms causing decay (Sharpe, Hendee, and Allen 305).

During the 1960s when a new school building was being constructed in Celeste, Texas, excavations of the previous structure unearthed heavy bois d'arc slabs that had been sunk into the ground to support the foundation seventy years earlier. The *Greenville Herald Banner* reported that the wood was found to be "solid as a rock" when it was dug up, and it was put to use in other construction projects.

Osage orange has been called "the most durable of all North American woods" (Everett, Thomas 140). Its survival in earth, water, and mud is easily observed.

Strength

For strength and toughness, Osage orange ranks in the first tier of trees. It is two and a half times as strong as white oak (Collingwood 509; Preston 229).

Hardness

While the wood of the Osage orange is twice as hard as white oak, it is not nearly so stiff (Palmer 147). Driving a nail into a dried fence post to string barbed wire is a difficult feat, and saw blades with carbide tips are quickly dulled in sawing seasoned Osage orange.

Longevity

The Osage orange has the potential for a long life. A specimen mentioned by Sargent in 1947 was 134 years old. Estimates of Osage orange longevity are now reported at 150 years or more (Smith, Jeffrey 6). Increment borings of five trees on the campus of Miami University at Oxford, Ohio, sometime before 1967 yielded ages of 140-175 years, ranking them as some of the oldest in Ohio since the species was noted by historians before 1806. It is probable that the Osage orange was not seen by white men until the Dunbar and Hunter expedition of 1805 (Morton 431-39). The life span of Osage orange is given as exceeding two hundred years according to an encyclopedia of American woods (Harrar and Harrar 80).

In Texas there is a saying that "oak posts last a long time, mulberry lasts still longer, cedar lasts one hundred years, bois d'arc lasts forever" (MacMillan 2).

Descriptors

The undemanding Osage orange is a rough but interesting tree that is a tough, rugged-looking specimen and a healthy, dangerous tree with barby branches and wonderful wood. A sampling of statements from scientists and casual observers dramatizes the diversity of views surrounding the Osage orange.

One botanist declared the Osage orange "a rarity in Europe; after all, there is little about it that is of much interest." In Europe it is a connoisseur's tree, only occasionally obtainable in a nursery and not generally considered a gracious tree (Peattie).

Osage orange fruit have a not-unpleasing spicy odor but a flavor which is distasteful even to hungry animals (Hylander, *Trees and Trails* 103).

"God designed Osage orange especially for the purpose of fencing the prairies" (Steavenson, Gearhart, and Curtis).

"A fully grown Osage orange is a beautiful sight and quite desirable for ornamental purposes" (Robinson 425).

"It has warty fruit and stiff, spiny interlacing branches." (Dirr 182).

" . . . small tree with straggling branches." (Darby 504).

" . . . ugly, hairy, sticky apple." (Harris).

"The buttressed base, the short heavy twigs, fierce spines, and the leathery green leaves are the picture of strength (Baumgardt 26).

"It [Osage orange] makes a piece of growing sculpture for the garden (Smith, Alice).

"It is not a gracious tree; it sends out, unless carefully tended, long sprawling shoots that render it shapeless and unsightly. The foliage is very tardy, not appearing until mid-May in the latitude of Chicago, and the unattractive flowers, which bloom in June and July, are wind-pollinated and cause some hay fever . . . (Peattie 410).

"[Osage orange] is in Europe a connoisseur's tree. The tree is obtainable only in a nursery" (Boom and Kleijn 62).

"The Osage orange is a handsome round-headed tree" (Rogers, Julia *Trees Worth Knowing* 99).

"In the neighborhood of Philadelphia, I saw, in the Autumn of 1839, some fine specimens of this tree, several of which were loaded with fruit. I have rarely seen an object in the vegetable world more strikingly beautiful (Emerson 317).

"Osage orange is one of our 'dirty dozen' landscape trees" (Michigan State University horticulturists).

A particularly appealing description of Osage orange appears in *Some American Trees*: "One may like to think of a tree having a will of its own; in this case one may easily imagine that the Osage Orange tree has taken yellow as its favorite color; the inner bark is dark orange, the sapwood lemon-colored and the heartwood brilliant orange with so much color that a damp blotter, laid on it for a few minutes, will show a yellow strain. The ripe fruit is yellowish-green, and the leaves in autumn turn a lovely clear yellow; even the roots, when exposed, will be found covered with a startlingly bright orange bark that makes them look as if they have been dipped in ocher paint" (Werthner 193).

Appeal

So intriguing is the Osage orange among all the trees catalogued in North America that it was included as one of the eighty-three species featured in *Trees Every Boy and Girl Should Know*. The tree Osage orange is characterized as "very hard, strong, tough, and durable." (American Forestry Association).

The Maclura Orange
Prairie Farmer, 1853

2
Native Habitat

Knowledgeable plant geographers agree that the Osage orange has one of the most restricted native habitats of all American trees, but the exact boundaries of that domain have not been determined with universal acceptance. Problems in delimiting the habitat have been created by attempts to indentify native trees as opposed to planted trees. One thing is certain among botanists: Osage orange is the most frequently planted in the nation. Its dominance as the favored plant for living fences and for windbreaks established its premier position among trees naturalized beyond their native range.

Most stands of native Osage orange trees have long been removed by total cutting to satisfy demands for its wood. Because of the excellent quality of Osage orange wood and its ease in carving, many useful objects were made with it, and after a few decades of demands for fence posts and foundation blocks, concentrations of the trees practically disappeared (Bloom and Klejin 62). The areas of their abundant growth in rich river bottoms have become farm lands (Rogers, Julia, *Trees* 99).

The native limits of Osage orange are traditionally described as the Red River Valley or, more specifically, both sides of the Red River Valley from Fouke, Arkansas, as the eastern edge to Gainesville, Texas, as the western edge, with a narrow spur following the blackland prairie southward from the Red River in Fannin County for two hundred miles toward Austin. Some skepticism has always existed about extending the native range to southwestern Arkansas and northwestern Louisiana because of suspicions that the Osage orange had been naturalized in those locations by Native Americans.

A second habitat, tiny and discrete, began to appear on some botanical maps during the past forty years. The locale is an isolated grove of Osage orange trees near Marathon in the Big Bend of Texas. Residents in that region insist that these trees grew from seeds brought from afar by Comanche Indians eager to produce a source for bow wood closer to their homeland. Nevertheless, some botanical maps continue to identify the detached grove as part of the native habitat more than five hundred miles from the Red River Valley range.

Bois d'Arc Springs

Of particular interest to plant geographers is one of the most scenic and historical sites in Fannin County, Texas. Bois d'Arc Springs has attracted travelers seeking a ford across Bois d'Arc Creek, as well as thirsty folk, hikers, and campers. At the bottom of a twenty-foot bluff overlooking the spring-fed bulge in Bois d'Arc Creek, large sandstone blocks preserve the names of those who wanted to leave a lasting record of their visit (Tolbert, "Old Inscriptions"). Today, many residents of the area, as well as most of the current staff members of the Caddo National Grasslands, are unaware of Bois d'Arc Springs. A retired Grasslands employee remembered the springs and agreed to guide this researcher, who had visited the springs two decades ago, and friends who would see the springs for the first time. The site is about four miles south of Red River and a mile north of Crockett Lake and Coffee Mill Lake, both government reservoirs in the Caddo National Grasslands.

The springs would no doubt remain a popular destination for hikers visiting the Grasslands except for the fact that they are on private land. Springs still flow from the bluff, and massive segments of stone at the base of the bluff and on the banks of the creek offer fascinating deciphering of inscriptions dating to 1840.

Bois d'Arc Springs is not far from the stand of bois d'arc trees mentioned in the 1808 journals of Anthony Glass. Other concentrations of the tree in the area are described in historic diaries and more recently in archaeological reports about Indian bow wood trading and about the native habitat of bois d'arc.

Native or Naturalized

The traditional native habitat in the Red River Valley covers only about 10,000 square miles, and probably half of that area now produces no trees of merchantable size (Burton 3).

Some printed sources include southwestern Arkansas, northern Louisiana, and southwestern Missouri as part of the native habitat, and travel accounts from the early nineteenth century testify that Osage orange trees were growing in these areas, but it cannot be proved that the trees had not been planted earlier when seeds and cuttings were brought from other locales.

Several states acknowledge that Osage orange trees are now thriving within their borders with the exceptions of Maine, Minnesota, the Dakotas, Idaho, Montana. Arizona,

Utah, and Oregon. Only a few carefully tended naturalized specimens are listed by Nevada, California, and Washington.

Even in the northern tier of states from Iowa eastward to Pennsylvania, agricultural publications alerted the planters about winter-kill of Osage orange as the nineteenth century farmers tried desperately to grow living fences on the prairies. The tree inventories of many states explain that Osage orange is not native to the state but is an imported tree. A book on Florida trees comments that the Osage orange is rare in that state because it needs a winter chill to mature (Haehle 31).

Specimens of the Osage orange, all imported, have been identified in the British Isles, France, Germany, Italy, the Netherlands, Portugal, Romania, Russia, Switzerland, and Australia (Smith and Perino 30). Perhaps no other North American tree has such a small native habitat and so wide a naturalization range.

Reports verify that Osage orange is hardy as far north as Massachusetts (Fett 258). Even in northern areas where the Osage orange survives the winter, profiles written about trees growing in those states usually mention that the Osage orange did not mature as much, did not reach heights or circumferences as great, did not flower as early, and did not bear fruit as large as trees in the south. The naturalized range has been described as far north as New England and upstate New York and all the way westward into the alkaline plains, where the tree survives although often dwarfed to ten feet and shorter (Baumgardt 26).

Tree scientists have reconstructed an ice age migration that defined the native zone of the Osage orange. The theory is supported by evidence of pre-ice age pollen discovered near Toronto, Canada, and augmented by the hypothesis that after the giant wooly mammals disappeared during one of the glacial periods, no bird or other mammal remained that was large enough to eat the fruit and carry the seeds to deposit elsewhere. The explanation for the shrinking of the native habitat is expressed in these words: "During one of the glacial periods which affected the eastern United States, part of Pennsylvania, almost all of Ohio, Indiana, and Illinois, all the lands north of these states were deeply covered by ice. Osage orange must have been living at the time somewhere south or more likely southwest of this ice field. The glacial advance was followed by an interglacial period, probably warmer than the present time, and during that time the Osage orange migrated north or northeast as far as Toronto. How much farther north or east it may have gone is not known, nor do we know when it started or the route it followed. The tree made a journey of at least 300 miles and probably considerably more" (Gleason and Cronquist, *Natural Geography* 44).

Fossils of pollen from the last interglacial period when climate was warmer than that of the present time attest to Osage orange growing as far north as Toronto in Ontario, Canada. Pollen of the tree's flowers now preserved from 120,000 years ago in fossil form was found in sediments from the Don Valley Brickyard in Ontario (Morgan, Alan V.).

Recent research has been conducted at trade centers where Indians bartered for Osage orange wood for making bows. Written accounts by non-Indian visitors survive, and relics of ancient Osage orange Indian bows have been found as far as 1,000 miles from the traditional habitat of the tree in northeastern Texas, southeastern Oklahoma, and southwestern Arkansas.

Studies of Bois d'Arc Creek Habitat

Two significant accounts published in 1996 and 2000 have reduced the native habitat of Osage orange in Texas to twelve counties in Northeast Texas on either side of Bois d'Arc Creek, which flows northeastward across

Fannin County to the Red River. The stream is said to have been a translation of the Indian name (Hodge 13), but details have not been found about the tribe involved or the Native American word translated as bois d'arc. Prominent historians believe it was the first American stream to be named for the tree.

Frank F. Schambach of the Arkansas Archeological Survey wrote in 2000 about the Sanders archaeological site near the mouth of Bois d'Arc Creek south of the Red River in Fannin County. He hypothesized that "Spiroans established their entrepot [a place for the storage of goods] on a bluff overlooking Bois d'Arc Creek because the creek bottoms supported a major and possibly unique stand of the best bow wood available to the peoples of the Southeast and the Plains." Schambach believes that among the many creeks and bayous with variations of the name Bois d'Arc, this one is the original (8). The creek's name was given for the bois d'arc trees growing along its course in large quantities. Here the Spiroans had access to, and perhaps some control over, a major stand of superb bow wood, for which the Red River Valley was famous at the time.

Schambach argues that the Spiroans chose the mouth of Bois d'Arc Creek as their trading point rather than the mouth of the Kiamichi Creek twenty miles to the east, where they would have found an easier departure over a water route to their home in what is now northeastern Oklahoma. Their choice of the Bois d'Arc Creek site was, in Schambach's opinion, because of the bois d'arcs growing there, he concludes. The concentration of trees, Schambach's study states, was "not just a first-rate stand of trees. It was probably the northeasternmost significant stand during the Mississippi period, if not the only significant one" (10). From the accounts in early journals of Indian traders, the very best growths of Osage orange seldom occupied more than one hundred acres (Womack 9-10).

The tiny range of the bois d'arc is attributed to a neotropical anachronism that barely survived the cold weather and the animal extinctions of the Pleistocene era. Bois d'arc trees had an ideal environment along Bois d'Arc Creek because prairies, not forests, lined either side of the stream, and the tree would not have tolerated forests shading the watercourse. The bois d'arc would not have fared well in the presence of other trees blocking the sun and casting shade over its turf (Schambach 10).

Furthermore, there were horses in the area to consume the horse apples of the trees and pass their long seeds through their digestive system intact. And beaver along Bois d'Arc Creek built beaver ponds. Bois d'arc seeds would float to the ponds to propagate (Schambach 10)

French trappers traveling up the Red River during the latter decades of the first half of the eighteenth century had seen the Caddo taking bow staves from the long, dense three-to-six mile stand of bois d'arc. The historic period of trade for the prized bow wood, according to Schambach's research, had a span of four hundred to six hundred years, beginning soon after 1000 A.D. (8).

Schambach believes that horses "relish the fruit of the Osage orange, sometimes called horse apples. . . . Horses were inadvertently reintroduced to the Blackland Prairie in 1691 by the Texan expedition to the Upper Nasoni village on the Red River, the result being the enormous herd of feral horses that American 'mustangers' discovered in the area in the early 1800s" (27-28).

Schambach proposes that these horses spread the Osage orange beyond the extraordinarily limited ecological niche more than one hundred years before Meriwether Lewis brought the tree to the attention of science in his letter of 1804 to Thomas Jefferson. In 1819, Thomas Nuttall saw what he believed were the northernmost native stands of Osage orange on the north side of the Red River fifteen or twenty miles east of the Sanders site and the mouth of Bois d'Arc Creek. The trees Nuttall mentioned, Schambach asserts, "were probably not native plants but the result of seed dispersal by horses returning to the Blackland Prairie 128 years earlier" (27-28).

Study of Texas Witness Trees

In another important study of the native range of the Osage orange, Del Weniger in 1996 used "witness trees" from records of the Texas Land Office to establish the native habitat of the Osage orange in Texas. The evidence analyzed led to the conclusion that the native range of Osage orange in Texas was probably limited to twelve Northeast Texas counties. Weniger examined the field notes of the pre-1860 surveys in the general file in the records division of the Texas General Land Office in Austin. Data on 53,030 witness trees, including Osage orange, were described in 22,879 early Texas land surveys. The species found growing before 1860 were presumed indigenous. For Osage orange the counties forming its native habitat in Texas were Bowie, Red River, Lamar, Fannin, Grayson, Collin, Dallas, Rockwall, Kaufman, Hunt, and Delta (Weniger 235). Declared "one of the classic examples of an endemic species in North America" by Smith and Perino, the Osage orange was avowed by Weniger to be endemic, without doubt, in Texas.

An article published on June 13, 1987 in the *Los Angeles Times*, without indicating a source, reported, "It's [Osage orange is] a Southerner, originally found in only 57 counties of East Texas and in tiny corners of Arkansas and Oklahoma" (Associated Press, "Osage Orange . . . in Illinois"). Thus, varying opinions continue about the native habitat of Osage orange trees.

The reason for any uncertainty about the original range of bois d'arc is "that even before the time for first botanizing in this region, bois d'arc had already been introduced into new areas far outside its original range.

How very early this process was going on is attested to by the remarkable statement by Custis in his catalog of plants he found in 1806 on the Red River: "bois d'arc, of this tree you have already had a description—it is probably a new Genus . . . it is said first to make its appearance about the 2nd Little river and is very abundant on a creek called Bois d'arc. The tree which I saw was one growing within a mile of Natchitoches" (quoted in Weniger 237).

Weniger reasoned that any tree having attained by 1806 the size described by Custis must have been transplanted long before, perhaps when there was no one present at the site to do the job except Indians. Bois d'arc shows up in many places in the Trans-Pecos—always at Indian campgrounds or caves, indicating that Indians had brought seeds from the east and planted them near their Trans-Pecos homes. The records used in Weniger's study were written by 290 explorers, soldiers, adventurers, settlers, and other pioneers, who experienced and observed the Texas wilderness before 1860 and left a valuable legacy in their writing (237).

Only fourteen pre-1860 written records listed bois d'arc trees growing in Texas. The researcher, comparing the small number of these early bois d'arc reports to more than 600 separate written records of mesquites, concluded that a healthy skepticism is supported about the hypothesis that the bois d'arc was native to any wide area of the state. Tabulated data on 152,030 witness trees of many species located and named in the early Texas surveys isolated only 123 that were bois d'arc. This number is insignificant, Weniger believes, in portraying the species as having statewide coverage (237).

While there is agreement on the certainty of its endemic status, no consensus has been reached about the tree's natural range in Texas (Weniger 237). Naturalization of the tree to other areas of the United States makes it impossible for field work to rediscover the limits of the natural range of the species. The testimony of the early surveyors is that the species was then growing wild before 1860 in areas that are now identified as the twelve counties in the native range. Because in each of these counties, some of these trees were described as having been large, mature specimens, they most certainly were indigenous (Weniger, 219).

When Charles deMorse, publisher of the Clarksville *Northern Standard*, was traveling down the East Fork of the Trinity River in 1853, his party had to stop for the night because "the creeks upon both sides of the river were overflown, and although there was a ferry flat in the river, there were none at the creeks, and so we concluded to wait a few hours, as we were told that swimming the creeks might be dangerous from Bois d'Arc brush in them full of thorns—so we waited till morning, and the water rose during the night" (Weniger 240).

That the thorny branches of this species would be a real hazard and could form impenetrable thickets is further emphasized by the description of one curious episode. The traveler made a journal entry that he was struggling to get from the western wilderness to the comparative civilization of Louisiana in 1843 when he experienced the situation which he recalls as " . . . after traveling some six or eight miles, we found our further progress cut off by a deep and precipitous chasm, lined with impassable briars" (Weniger 240).

Nuttall, who first provided the scientific name for this tree species, attested to its growing in just such thickets as described in Texas. He wrote that when almost directly across the Red River from Bois d'Arc Creek in the Choctaw country of western McCurtain County, Oklahoma, ". . . along the margin of all the rivulets we met with abundance of the Bow wood (Maclura), here familiarly employed as yellow dye" (Weniger 241). Weniger concludes his arguments for the limited native habitat of bois d'arc in Texas by stating, "So I think that we have to make the effort to imagine at least the center of the 12 county range already outlined as a vicious, thorny, almost impassable thicket of bois d'arc instead of the open expanse it is today" (241).

Bois d'Arc Creek Homeland Center

Maps showing the native habitat of the Osage orange should give pause to those who want to probe more deeply into the continuing research regarding where the tree is a native and where it is an invited or a fugitive guest. There is no question that Osage orange was found in Oklahoma, Arkansas, Louisiana, and Missouri in the early 1800s. But were those trees naturalized from the restricted native habitat of twelve Northeast Texas counties with Bois d'Arc Creek exactly in the middle of its homeland? Furthermore, another clue to the importance of Bois d'Arc Creek as a possible center of the Texas native habitat is the belief of a significant number of botanists that the stream was the first anywhere to be named for the valuable bow wood tree.

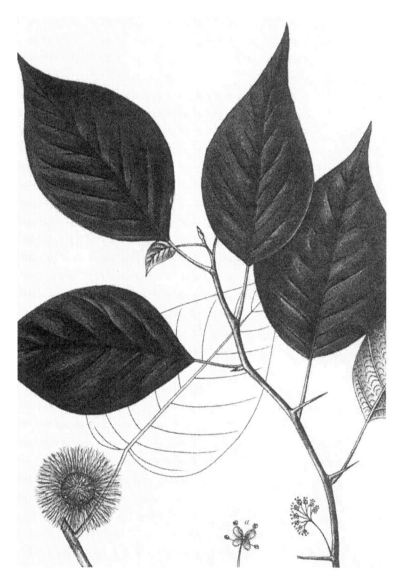

Maclura Aurantiaca
Michaux, 1835

3
Escape from Indian Lands

Radiocarbon-dated ages of Indian bows made of Osage orange establish their existence at least seven hundred years before Meriwether Clark's letter on March 26, 1804 to President Thomas Jefferson stating that he had seen a remarkable tree growing in a St. Louis garden. A well-preserved Osage orange bow from the Mounds Plantation site in northwest Louisiana, crafted with recurved tips and draw weights in the seventy-pound range, was judged to date from around 1050 A.D. (Schambach 9).

With the first shipment of Osage orange cuttings to President Jefferson, Lewis gave this information:
St. Louis
March 26th 1804
Dear Sir,
    I send you herewith inclosed some slips of the Osage Plums, and Apples. I fear the season is too far advanced for their success. Had I earlier learned that these

fruits were in the neighbourhood, they would have been forwarded at a more proper time. . . . I obtained the cuttings, now sent you, from the gardens of Mr. Peter Chouteau, who resided the greater portion of his time for many years with the Osage nation. . . ."

The Osage Apple is a native of the interior of the continent of North America, and is perhaps a nondescript production, the information I have obtained about it is not so minute as I would wish, nor such as will enable me to describe it in a satisfactory manner. Mr. Peter Chouteau . . . obtained the young plants at the great Osage village from an Indian of that nation. The general contour of this tree, is very much that of the black haw, common to most parts of the United Sates. . . . so much do the savages esteem the wood of this tree for the purpose of making their bows, that they travel many hundred miles in quest of it. The particulars with respect to the fruit, are taken principally from the Indian description; my informant having never seen but one specimen of it, which was not full ripe, and much shriveled and mutilated before he saw it. The Indians give an extravagant account of the exquisite odour of this fruit when it has obtained maturity, which takes place the latter end of summer, or the beginning of autumn. They state, that at this season they can always tell by the scent of the fruit when they arrive in the neighbourhood of the tree, and usually take advantage of this season to obtain the wood. . . . An opinion prevails among the Osages, that the fruit is poisonous tho' they acknowledge that they have never tasted it. They say that many animals feed on it, and among others, a large species of Hare which abounds in that country. This fruit is the size of the largest orange, of a globular form, and a fine orange colour. . . .

I have the honour to be with sincere esteem Your Obt. Servt.
Meriwether Lewis (Jackson 109-110).

It appears that no one has ventured a guess about the date when Indian tribes first began to fashion bows from Osage orange staves or when the first non-Indian made contact with the Native Americans and came under the spell of the exotic tree and its peculiar fruit. Only when early travelers and traders ventured into Indian lands west of the Mississippi and felt compelled to mention the Osage orange in their journals did America and the world have a lasting record of their encounter with the tree. Many accounts of the Osage orange were stored in family and public archives or never published, but fortunately some of the representative written descriptions did make their way into print.

Prehistoric Times

In a study of prehistoric man on the Great Plains, the wood of the Osage orange, designated a native tree to the southern plains of Texas and Oklahoma, "was widely traded for the manufacture of bows" (Wedel 40).

Early European Explorers in America

Before the tree had been assigned common names, the writers could give only a description, and whether or not a reference was made to an Osage orange is still being debated. Specifically, in April 1520 Cabeza da Vaca was traveling among the aboriginals west of the mouth of the Mississippi, and he later wrote of his observation of a tree. He noted that members of an aboriginal tribe procured poison from the twigs of a certain tree the size of the apple tree. The Indians dipped the tips of their arrows in the poison, da Vaca reported. Notes by editors of da Vaca's account sometimes leave the tree unidentified, but others attempt to name the tree with the parenthetical notation (Maclura?) within the text or in their footnotes and editorial comments (Pickering 869). The tree has been identified as the Osage orange although no reliable botanical report has classified any part of the tree toxic to humans, cattle, or wildlife.

Early Spanish explorers recognized that the Caddo Indians had two articles of trade for which they were noted: Osage orange bow wood and salt (Swanton 37). In Swanton's *Source Material on the History and Ethnology of the Caddo Indians,* he quotes Robbins, Harrington, and Faeire-Marreco, who had written, "The wood of this shrub is considered better for making bows than any which grew in the Tewa country. It was brought from the east by the Tewa, or obtained from the Comanche or other eastern tribes" (Swanton 37).

The DeSoto expedition is reported to have encountered bow wood (Osage orange) being traded by Caddo Indians in 1542 (Swanton 192). In 1562, members of the LaSalle expedition, according to a journal entry, had met two Cahinnio Indians who came to engage in trade for Osage orange bows. Members of LaSalle's party traveled with the Indians back to their own people encamped somewhere near the Ouachita River (Swanton 91). Historians have speculated that the expedition was traveling at a point in the locale of present Arkadelphia, Arkansas.

A note for a journal entry from the LaSalle Expedition to Texas involving the Osage orange tree suggests that this tree is the one being referred to without being named in the journal of Henri Joutel (248). The English translation of the original French entry reads, "Because our plan was not to linger long in this place, we asked the chief for someone to guide us to the village named Cahaynohoua. Fortunately, it happened that two men from that village were there who had come to the Cadodaquis to procure bows." The editor adds that "the party would travel fifty to sixty leagues round trip for this purpose because they had excellent wood for making bows." The note states that the bow wood was probably bois d'arc, which the Osage and other Indians used to make bows (Joutel 248).

Colonial Times

Claims have been made that Osage orange was used for cattle enclosures in Virginia in colonial times (Taylor, Raymond 63), but if the colonial period ended in 1776, as most historians agree, the livestock corrals enclosed by Osage orange would have been in existence at least twenty-eight years before Jefferson received the first shipment of cuttings for that tree from the Lewis and Clark Expedition. In colonial times and for three decades thereafter, landowners such as George Washington were seeking living fence plants and even ordering saplings of trees from England that had been successful hedges there.

On October 25, 1750, Benjamin Franklin of Philadelphia wrote to Jared Eliot for information about planting a particular hedge: "I request you to procure for me a particular Account of the manner of making a new kind of Fence we saw at Southhold on Long Island, which consists of a Bank and Hedge. I would know every Particular relating to this Manner of erecting it; the best Time for the Work; the best Way of planting the Hedge; the Price of the Work to Labourers per Rod or Perch, and whatever may be of Use for our Information here, who begin in many Places to be at a Loss for Wood to make Fence with" (Franklin 90).

The 1750 letter indicates an interest in hedge fences fifty-four years before Osage orange was introduced to the East Coast.

Early American Hedge Fences

By the beginning of the nineteenth century, hedges symbolized gentility, wealth, and status for gentleman farmers in America. Particularly in northern Delaware, the desire for agricultural innovation was led by farmers from England or those who had been influenced by English hedges in the state. In 1798 John Spurrier of Brandywine, Delaware, became the first in New Castle County to disseminate information nationally about the hedge through a book (Bourcier 547-48; Spurrier).

Caleb Kirk and practitioners of agrarian ideology admonished others that "the appearance of a farm fence indicated the virtue of the farmer who constructed it." In the early nineteenth century, society recognized properly practiced farming as "the most ancient, innocent, pleasing, noble, honorable, healthy, and independent activity of man." Osage orange hedges gained prominence in Delaware after the apple borer killed hedge in the area, and news was circulated that the living fences on the Midwest prairies using that plant had resisted the insect (Bourcier 552, 562).

Explorers after the Louisiana Purchase

The Osage orange had been described by Meriwether Lewis and others in 1804, but the first published details of the tree, with the assertion that it was a genus new to science, was written in 1806 by Peter Custis (Flores, *Jefferson and Southwestern Exploration*). T. Freeman and Peter Custis were leading a party up the Red River as one of the three expeditions Thomas Jefferson had planned as early as 1783 (Barton and Barnett 1). Jefferson's inquisitive mind desired knowledge of the domain beyond the Mississippi River, which remained the western boundary of the country until the Louisiana Purchase was completed in 1803. Specific information about plants was required by President Jefferson of his explorers. He wanted "the dates at which particular plants put forth or lose flowers, or leaf," especially those unknown in the United States (Munger 10-11).

The earliest written account of the Osage orange tree was recorded by a traveler from Scotland, William Dunbar, in his narrative of a journey made in 1804 to St. Catherine's Landing on the Mississippi and then westward to the Washita River (Keeler 260). Dunbar and G. Hunter had led an expedition up the Red, Black, and Ouachita rivers into Arkansas in October 1804 as one of three explorations Thomas Jefferson had envisioned twenty years before (Barton and Barnett 1).

It is probable that the Osage orange was not seen by white men until the Dunbar and Hunter expedition of 1805 (Smith, Jeffrey 8). Although they described the tree in some detail, their short botanical list was never published in their official report or in newspapers (Flores, *Jefferson*, 200). Dunbar and Hunter have been credited with recommending to President Jefferson cultivation of Osage orange as a hedge plant (Smith, Jeffrey 8; Peattie 481).

Lewis Sends Osage Orange to Jefferson

The Osage orange obtained from Pierre Chouteau, a former Indian agent living in St. Louis, has been called the most significant botanical discovery of the Lewis and Clark Expedition. The Osage orange would become one of 226 plants documented by Lewis and Clark across what is now the western United States ("Common to This Country," *Science* 303).

For many Americans Osage orange was the most important revelation of the Lewis and Clark trek from Missouri to Oregon. Lewis provided the name of a St. Louis resident who would send more specimens to the East if his did not survive. The first shipment of Osage orange saplings in 1804 did not survive, but samples Lewis collected in 1807 ("Osage Oranges Take a Bough" 35) thrived on the East Coast in Philadelphia and at the University of Virginia (Sudol 69). In later written accounts by Jefferson and Bernard McMahon, a Philadelphia gardener, they verified that the Osage orange cuttings referred to had been viable.

McMahon was one of several men trusted by Jefferson to care for the plants and seeds he received from the Corps of Discovery. Described as Jefferson's gardening mentor, McMahon had provided plants for the gardens at Monticello over the years. Two decades after he received plants from Lewis for planting in his gardens at Monticello, Jefferson corresponded with a friend about two trees he thought quite beautiful. One was Osage orange. The irony no doubt occurred to Jefferson that instead of being named for Lewis, the Osage orange tree was given a scientific name by Nuttall to immortalize McClure, primarily a geologist (Munger 20).

Osage orange had been described to Jefferson by both John Sibley and Meriwether Lewis in 1804. Sibley's letter was sent in March 1804 from the Red River near Natchitoches. Describing himself as a physician who had lived for the past six months at Natchitoches, Sibley told the president that he was interested in two of his avocations: botany and Indian ethnology. In his first letter, Sibley discussed what he called the French bois d'arc, or bow wood, and he sent some samples of dyes he had extracted. Jefferson would soon receive a letter and cuttings of Osage orange from Meriwether Lewis in St. Louis (Flores, "Ecology" 33).

The first published details of the tree were written by Peter Custis. He asserted that the tree represented a genus never before known to science (Flores. "Ecology" 33). Custis would probably win recognition as the first non-Indian to discover the exotic tree had he offered a name. Because the tree was not in flower when he saw it, he could not name it. Scientific protocol required that a description of a tree in bloom be submitted for formal registration of a name. Custis described the tree as a cultivated rather than a wild tree, a detail arguing perhaps that the natural range should be confined to the Blackland Prairies and Cross Timbers, centering on Bois d'Arc Creek in Fannin County. The trees found scattered farther east near Caddo settlements were possibly transplanted by the Indians (Flores, *Jefferson*).

Evidence that Osage orange seeds were being circulated in the eastern United States soon after the Meriwether Lewis discovery comes from a letter written by William Hamilton to Jefferson on February 5, 1808. Hamilton remarked, "I have nevertheless obtained plants of the yellow wood, or Osage apple . . ." (*Thomas Jefferson's Garden Book* 363).

The sharing of seeds and information with national leaders was demonstrated in a letter from Richard F. Simpson, a U.S. representative from South Carolina, to John C. Calhoun on January 15, 1833. He wrote, "Judge [Edward] Cross [Representative from Arkansas], a particular friend of yours from Arkansas, handed to me some seed of the osage orange & desired me to send them to you which I now enclose. He will write to you soon and give you whatever discription [sic] of its uses you have desire. I understand however from him that it is a beautifull [sic] evergreen yard tree and that when trim[m]ed makes an excellent hedge, with this peculiarity, that if a part of the hedge dies, as it may, the dead stalk will dry up and stand for years as strong, as when alive" (Wilson 17:708).

Journals of Anthony Glass

On August 1, 1808, Anthony Glass, age thirty-five, wrote his impressions of chancing upon "large quantities of bois d'arc" for the first time while crossing two creek bottoms near Natchitoches, Louisiana. He observed, "The tree resembles an Apple tree and the fruit an Orange. The wood is yellow like. The tree is hard, takes a brilliant polish and [is] the most Elastic of long wood known The Indians make their bows of it from which the French have given it the names of Bois d'Arc or Bow Wood" (Flores, *Glass* 43).

On August 3, 1808, Glass wrote, "We made about seven miles WNW [and crossed] Bois d'Arc Creek or River we supposed near 75 miles from its mouth where it falls into Red River, the Bed of the River about thirty feet wide but affords but little water except in rainy seasons. Here we Saw great numbers of Wild horses" (Flores, *Glass*).

The Glass party had traversed the prairie near present-day Paris and the present Fannin County line. As the group approached the area that is now Bonham, they forded Bois d'Arc Creek, a favorite beaver stream for the early French hunters. Glass made a journal entry about "observing great numbers of bisons and mustangs" (Flores, *Glass* 44).

On September 14, after the party led by Glass had reached the Taovaya-Wichita villages located on the Red River north of the Brazos River, Glass reported, "I have seen an Indian with a bow of the Bois d'Arc wood, the most elastic wood in the world, that drives an arrow entirely through a Buffalo with more force than a rifle would have sent a ball" (Flores, *Glass* 60). In a note on page 114, Glass helps his readers visualize his perception of the original range of the Osage orange tree. His note characterizes the limitations of the native range as a narrow endemic, the center of its range extending from the Red River and extending two hundred miles both north and south, and westward from the Blackland Prairie to the Eastern Cross Timbers" (Flores, *Glass* 114).

Glass's journal is also useful in clarifying the original habitat of the Osage orange. The trees growing farther east seem to be the result of Indian transplanting (Flores, *Glass* 114).

Indian Traders and Other Travelers

John Bradbury undertook extensive travel in the interior of North America in 1809, 1810, and 1811, telling how he saw two Osage orange trees growing in the garden of Pierre Chouteau, the St. Louis resident who had shown Meriwether Lewis the species in 1804 (Keeler 260).

Science Recognizes a New Tree

The scientific name of the Osage orange, *Maclura pomifera*, was bestowed by Thomas Nuttall, who first explained in 1818 that he was honoring "William Maclure, Esq. of the United States, a philosopher, whose devotion to natural science, and particularly to the geology of North America, has been exceeded by Ramond or Saussure in Europe." He described Osage orange as "A small lactescent tree, producing wood similar to fustic; leaves alternate, entire, destitute of stipules, furnished with superaxillary simple spines, armaments axillary; berry vertucose and large, at first latescent, yellow. Male flowers unknown" (Nuttall, *Genera* 234*)*. . . . It is worthy of note that Nuttall had no understanding that fruit was borne only by the female and that female and male flowers were different. A French botanical dictionary in 1823 was able to describe the female flowers but the male flowers were dismissed as "unknown" (*Dictionnaire des Sciences Naturelles* 518). Nuttall reveals to the reader that "The above account was based on observation of living plants in the garden of M. Shoutou [Chouteau] at St. Louis." He added, "Plants of this interesting tree are now cultivated in the garden of the late Mr. M'Mahon of Philadelphia, but have not yet flowered."

Nuttall's comments mention Bernard McMahon, a botanist and nurseryman in Philadelphia who was born in Ireland about 1775. He arrived in America in 1796, becoming one of the first successful gardeners in the country. This friend of Thomas Jefferson is thought to be have hosted a meeting in his home to plan the Lewis and Clark Expedition. Botanists think that McMahon was the first East Coast gardener to promote the Osage orange tree discovered in St. Louis in 1804. The botanist settled in Philadelphia and founded a botanical garden there in 1811 three miles of Philadelphia. He is credited with being the first to introduce the Osage orange seed and cuttings brought back by Lewis and Clark (Harshberger, *Botanists* 117-18).

Osage orange seeds crossed the Atlantic to England about 1818, delivered from America by Senhor Correa de Serra, a Portuguese botanist and diplomat (Browne 467).

Later, trees of both sexes arrived in Paris at the delight of French nurserymen. By 1836, Osage orange leaves had been fed to silkworms with partial success (Browne 467).

In 1837 Nuttall had written in the supplement to Michaux's *Trees of North America* that Osage orange "was first noticed" by Hunter and Dunbar in their voyage up the Red River, on the banks of the Little Missouri of the Washita River, also near Natchitoches and upon the banks of the Arkansas, in Major Long's expedition along the banks of the Arkansas and the Canadian, etc. But the whole history as developed here and the first discovery of the Osage orange should be credited to the Lewis and Clark expedition"("Early History of Osage Orange" (*Meehans' Monthly* 4*)*.

John D. Hunter Among the Indians

In 1823 John D. Hunter recorded his observations of the Osage orange from his travels, published later as *Manners and Customs of Several Indian Tribes Located West of the Mississippi*. Hunter wrote, "I will close . . . with a few observations on the Osage orange, or bow wood tree, . . . of which very little appears to be known. The Osage orange is found in abundance on the St. Francis, White [rivers], some parts of the Arkansas, Vermillion, Canadian, and Osage rivers, and there are a few scattering ones on the Kansas. I do not recollect to have seen them farther north, though they may exist on the Missouri, and in many other places, without my knowledge. The tree delights in a fertile, or rather dry, soil, and attains to a height of fifteen to thirty feet, with a trunk proportionally large" (41).

Hunter continues with a typical description of the tree, with the following excerpts of special interest: "In May or June, the male, or tree not bearing fruit, is covered with numerous pale yellow flowers. . . . [The ripened fruit] is slightly pulpy, an acid, and by many of the Indians esteemed as an agreeable esculent. . . . The wood . . . is held in high estimation by the Indians, on account of its great elastic properties. They manufacture it into bows, which become articles of commerce . . . I knew a Sioux to give his horse for a single [bow]; and among the upper tribes they frequently bring three or four beaver skins each" (181).

Hunter recognizes the difference between the flowers of male and female, a distinction not previously pointed out by earlier writers. He also makes one of the earliest observations in print that the fruit was valued by Indians as edible food. This observation probably inspired later references to the fruit as an Indian food source. He also gives some idea of the value of the Osage orange at that time in the trading for bows and bow wood.

Between 1823 and 1827, David Douglas made journal entries about his visits in the northeastern United States to inquire about Osage orange trees. On August 23 he visited botanist and nurseryman McMahon three miles north of Philadelphia. Douglas wrote, "I here saw a fine plant of Maclura about twenty feet high, very rustic, leaves large, ovate, at the stalk of which is a large thorn, a few fine fruits on the tree; stands perfectly well the winter in a poor, light, sandy soil; the shoots of this year are in length five feet. He had a few stout plants propagate from cuttings last season, two of which I am glad to have the pleasure of carrying to England from this place (8).

A week later on Staten Island, Douglas wrote, "This morning I put the Osage apple in spirits; afterwards I waited on Mr. Floy for the purpose of selecting specimen trees from his grounds. On November 1, Douglas was in

Pennsylvania writing entries in his journal. "I waited on Mr. William Dick, janitor of the University of Pennsylvania. ... I had the pleasure of meeting here Mr. Nuttall, whom I found very communicative. ... We looked round Mr. Dick's garden. I am again pleased to see *Maclura aurantiaca*. The night's frost had made them drop their leaves, and the tender shoots were injured a little (24)

Still in Philadelphia on November 23, Douglas wrote, "Got two fruits of *Maclura* and I shall put them with the other one; I shall pack in charcoal (26).

Constantine Rafinesque-Schmaltz, leading botanist of the early nineteenth century and a professor of botany at Transylvania University, Lexington, Kentucky, recalled his earlier experiences with the Osage orange in one of his publications of 1830 (Rafinesque, *Atlantic Journal* 146). Using his invented term of *Toxylon* instead of Nuttall's *Maclura*, Rafinesque began by stating, "The genus *Toxylon* published by myself in 1817 and again by Nuttal [sic] in 1818 as *Maclura*; name already employed, differs from *Moras* and two other Genera by flowers. . . . Only one species *Toxylon* native of Texas, Arkansas and Missouri now introduced to our gardens but only one sex, the fruit bearing tree that produces seedless fruit as large as Oranges, but not edible. The wood is valuable for making bows and implements and the bark also may produce Silk. It is easily propagated from cuttings like all the above, and is said to make very good hedges" (Rafinesque, *American Manual* 2).

In this entry Rafinesque makes clear that Osage orange differs from three other genera often confused and placed in the Osage orange genus at that time. He mentions that only one species has been introduced to his gardens, revealing this failure to recognize, as later botanists have verified, that only one species of Osage orange exists. His pronouncement that the fruit is not edible disagrees with statements by earlier observers of Indians eating it or by botanists supporting that opinion, His repeating of the belief that Osage orange would make good hedges, while not the earliest statement about the trees as a plant for living hedges, precedes the promotion of Osage orange for hedges a few years later by Jonathan Baldwin Turner, a professor at Jacksonville College in Jacksonville Illinois, and by John S. Wright, editor of the *Prairie Farmer* in Chicago.

Dispatching Misinformation

In his 1846 publication, *Trees of America: Native and Foreign,* D. J. Browne contributed to the mounting misinformation being repeated that the fruit of Osage orange was somehow "nutritious and pleasant to the taste" and in the same natural order belonging to the Jamaica breadnut (*Brosium alicastrum*). His statement that "Boiled with fish or flesh, they [the fruits] are also eaten as food in times of scarcity, by the poor" (59) was perhaps the erroneous link of Jamaica breadnut to Osage orange that contributed to the later belief in England that Osage orange fruit was eaten by Americans. Browne's statement could also have supported belief in reports circulating in the United States after the Civil War to explain a shortage of Osage orange seeds because Southerners had consumed the fruit during food shortages.

In 1855, John Darby erroneously recorded in *Botany of the Southern States* that Osage orange belonged to the same interesting family of plants "as the famous breadfruit of India and the islands of the Pacific and the deadly Upas of Java, whose inspissated juice is found to contain the most virulent of all poisonous principles, strychnia. It is, however, somewhat doubtful what the real affinities of this plant are, as it is acknowledged to be an anomaly in the family" (127-31). This report was retained by many readers as the scientific truth although other botanists soon corrected the membership of Osage orange in the same family as breadfruit.

Before botanists understood the difference between the male tree and the fruit-bearing female, several misconceptions about the sexual nature of the plant were circulated. On November 9, 1832, *The American Farmer* of Baltimore reported, ". . . the female tree bears fruit, to all appearance perfect without the assistance of a male tree." Later the necessity of wind-blown pollen from the male tree would be recognized.

In *Botany of Western Trees* from *Contributions from the U.S. National Herbarium,* the Osage orange habitat was located from eastern to central and southern Texas, but no other source consulted has ever identified southern Texas as a habitat (Coulter, 2:408). A 1971 publication on Western trees identified Osage orange as a native of the central states (Baerg 109).

In defining the native regions of Osage orange in 1838, Rafinesque had used the phrase "south of the Missouri, near the Arkansas river and the neighborhood of New Mexico (*American Monthly* 1833). That the range included "regions south of the Missouri, near the Arkansas River and the neighborhood of New Mexico was repeated in 1955 (Jones and Fuller 174). This repetition illustrates how misinformation that has once gained permanence in print is likely to be replicated for centuries in the minds of unsuspecting readers.

Public uncertainty about the native habitat of Osage orange continued in 1862 when a printed guide to Canadian flora identified the native habitat of Osage orange as Arkansas (*Flore Canadienne,* 2:523). A comparison of other printed statements about the Osage orange original range multiples the confusion about the tree's specific native habitat.

British, European First Impressions

Browne, giving details of the naturalization of Osage orange in Britain, reported, "About the year 1818, seeds of this tree were sent to Lord Bagot in England by

Senhor Correa de Serra, a Portuguese botanist and diplomat, and subsequently trees of both sexes were imported by English nurserymen" (Browne 58; *Gardner's Magazine* 1826). Another source stated that Osage orange had been introduced to England when a correspondent for the *London Journal of Horticulture* arrived with an apple from St. Louis. "Delicious scent but quite uneatable," the journalist reported. "Indians did not eat them."

Elsewhere in Europe, Browne wrote, there was an Osage orange tree in the Jardin des Plantes in Paris. In ten years after planting, it had attained the height of eighteen feet. In the nursery of M. Sidy in Lyons, another specimen had grown to a height of twenty-five feet and borne fruit. Since 1836, Browne stated, "Its leaves have been employed in France . . . with partial success as a food for silkworms." Because he admired the beautiful finish of Osage orangewood, Browne predicted possible success of Osage orange for inlaying fine furniture (58).

As early as 1823, the Osage orange was being listed under *Maclura* in a comprehensive checklist of trees in a French volume. Osage orange was reported as a plant growing on the banks of the Missouri River and in the Louisiana region (*Dictionnaire des Sciences Naturelles*, 7:517-18).

In a personal testimonial to the beauty of the tree, rare in early manuals describing plants, Browne said of the Osage orange, "A beautiful deciduous tree. But at all times it strikes the beholder as something remarkable in the northern forest by the beauty and splendour of its dark and shining foliage . . . The tree deserves a place in every collection wherever it will grow" (58-59).

Naturalists and Promoters

The journals of S. W. Woodhouse from his travels in Indian Territory in 1849 and 1850 mention the first sighting of an Osage orange tree on the east bank of the North Canadian River about two miles east of present-day,

Eufaula, McIntosh County, Oklahoma, now covered by Lake Eufaula. He wrote, " . . . for the first time on this tramp I saw the Osage Appl growing" (Tomey and Brodhead 249).

In Edward Smith's *Account of a Journey Through North-Eastern Texas. Undertaken in 1849 for the Purposes of Emigration,* the era of traders with Indians and expeditions into uncharted regions had ended, and journals with comments about the Osage orange tree were appearing in travel accounts intended to attract new residents to the United States. Texas had been a member of the union of states for five years when Smith's account was published in London. Bonham, the county seat of Fannin County in Northeast Texas, was a center of bois d'arc logging. Bonham was mentioned as a commercial center with prices lower than Jefferson, Texas, or Shreveport, Louisiana. The Osage orange was identified as a tree native to the region that was used for wagons, articles of furniture, knife handles, and walking canes (98, 136).

In his listing of twenty-one trees growing in Northeast Texas prairies and woodland, Smith placed an adjective before only one species, calling it the "beautiful bois d'arc."

Over the span of forty-five years, from 1804, when Meriwether informed East Coast government officials and friends that he had encountered Osage orange, until 1849, when Edward Smith was luring emigrants to Northeast Texas and touting the activity of a Fannin County logging center for the tree, Osage orange had been gaining national and international attention. Would the tree remain a curiosity, or would it become an important economic boon?

4
Horse High, Bull Strong, Pig Tight

"Fences rank right behind air, water, food, and shelter as necessities of life." These sage words of Hank Burchard, a *Washington Post* writer, clearly delineate the dilemma of American farmers on the vast fertile prairies. They had livestock and crops to enclose but no timber to build the rail fences they had relied upon back East. Without fences, herds of cattle grazed wherever they pleased, and feral hogs made feasts of unprotected crops (Burton and Barnett 3). These pioneers would have agreed with Philosopher Jean Jacques Rousseau, who called fences the foundation of civilization (Burchard N51).

Hedges and Fences before Osage Orange

Ancient hedges were prestigious symbols of property owners marking their land boundaries and protecting their possessions. In the narratives and parables of scriptures, the hedges marked boundaries of prominent plantations and vineyards (*The Fence. Facts, Figures and*

Opinions), representing pride in ownership but also symbolizing thorny entanglements impeding the righteous life. Although Osage orange first appeared in living fences in nineteenth century America, similar thorny barriers have an ancient history and were mentioned in the Bible, usually with metaphorical significance. In Proverbs 15:19, "The way of the slothful man is as a hedge of thorns." In Lamentations 3:7, "He hath hedged me about, that I can not get out; he hath made my way crooked." In Job 1:10, "Hedge around them whom God hath hedged in."

The use of hedges to enclose parcels of land is a practice mentioned regularly in the documents of medieval Europeans. Hedges appeared frequently in medieval documents in Europe. Most of the barriers reported m medieval records had been in existence for some time, but occasionally new plantings were made. For example, in 1325, St. John's Abbey in Colchester, England, accepted an obligation to plant a hedge "from the first gate to the second, so that a lane may be made between the said gates . . . . taking branches from the trees growing in the said hedge to maintain the hedge" (First International Arboricultural Conference 11).

When emigrants from England first settled on American farm land, their memories were filled with pleasing images of green hedgerows adding distinction to their motherland. But in North America, hedges were little known until civilization reached the treeless prairies (Martin, George 67).

As American botanists became acquainted with the Osage orange, they recognized its potential as a likely plant for living fences. Colonial farmers sought ways to enclose their property, keeping current about successful hedges in England. George Washington, who died in 1799, five years before Meriwether Lewis sent the first cuttings of the tree to President Jefferson, never lived to see an Osage orange tree or to hear reports about its use as a hedge. Hedge plants successful as fences were being imported from England, and species of trees growing in America were being cultivated as living fences along the East Coast in the eighteenth century. Before a qualified fence plant appeared on the American landscape, all potential barriers underwent experimentation: cactus, running roses, ditches, and sod fences.

Washington's Quest for Hedge

If citizens of Williamsburg, Virginia, had read the correspondence of George Washington between 1776 and 1797, they could have become well aware that Osage orange hedges were unknown in Virginia at that time. However, George Washington, as well as many other gentleman farmers, was searching for such a hedge plant.

The *Writings of George Washington*, edited by John C. Fitzpatrick, provides, from 1776 until two years before his death, a continuous desire for living hedges on his properties. His passion for thriving hedges was relentless, patient, but ever hopeful.

An early reference to hedges appears in a letter written to Lund Washington from New York on August 19, 1771. Opening with news of the revolution, the general was anticipating an attack upon the city, where he commanded a force of about 23,000 against as many as 17,000 enemy troops awaiting the arrival of another 5,000 Hessians. After three and one-half pages, Washington shifts abruptly to the subject of hedges: "These Trees to be Planted without any order or regularity (but pretty thick, as they can at any time be thin'd) and to consist that the North end, of locusts altogether, and that at the South, of all the clever kind of Trees (especially flowering ones) that can be got, such as Crab apple, Poplar, Dogwood, Sasafras, Laurel Willow (especially yellow and Weeping Willow). . . . There is no doubt but that the Honey locust if you could procure enough, and that would come up, will make (if sufficiently thick) a very good hedge; so will the Haw, or

Cedar or any kind of ever green, would look better; however, if one thing will not do, we must try another, as no time ought to be lost in rearing of Hedges, not only for Ornament but use" (5:457-59).

Seventeen years later regular correspondence began with William Pearce, Washington's new superintendent at Mount Vernon, and concluded with Pearce's retirement in 1796. At times the president was writing far more letters giving instructions for the care of his farms than he was for matters of state. In the agreement culminating with the employment of Pearce written at Mount Vernon on September 23, 1793, Washington included among the many responsibilities that obligated his superintendent "to substitute live in place of dead fences where it is practicable" (33:98). Thus began a record of Washington's active interest in hedges, his attention to details of hedge cultivation, his keeping abreast of hedge publications, and his even-handed leadership styles.

Writing from Philadelphia on January 12, 1794, Washington communicated these instructions to Pearce: "And I would have the thorn berries, Cedar berries, honey locust seed and such other things as may be intended for hedges raised first in nurseries; that, when transplanted they may receive the cultivation. As the case has been, they are sowed, or planted along the ditches and for want by the weeds" (33:239-40).

Writing from Philadelphia to Pearce on April 20, 1794, Washington reported that Mr. Lear, then in London, had communicated the following information: "I have engaged 5000 of the white thorn plants which will be put on board the ship Peggy bound to George Town, she will sail by or before the 10th of February and is addressed to Colo. Deakins." Washington instructed Pearce to "make diligent enquiry for the Vessel if she is not already arrived, as the Season is advanced and the plants will be much injured if not lost, if not soon got into the ground" (33:337).

Writing from Philadelphia on April 27, 1794, Washington asked Pearce, "How does the White thorn, and the cuttings of the Willow and other sets which have been put out this Spring, look? And appear to have taken, and to be in a thriving condition? (33:344).

Writing from Philadelphia on May 4, 1794, Washington alerted Pearce, "I am sorry to find by the first that the Ship Peggy had not arrived at George Town from London. I fear the White thorn plants (5,000 in number) which I have on board, together with Mr. Lears fruit Trees, will suffer very much, if they are not entirely destroyed, by the advanced season. Let the ground (wherever the first are to go) be prepared for their reception, that no time which can be avoided may be lost in getting them into it. . . (33:351).

Writing from Philadelphia to Pearce on July 13, 1794, Washington reminded his superintendent that, as the landowner had often repeated, one of his goals was "to substitute as fast as possible hedges and live fences in place of dead ones, and of anything that will make them" (34:440).

Writing from Philadelphia to Pearce on January 11, 1795. Washington stated, "I shall send you by the first Vessel at least a bushel and half of clear honey locust seed which I would have raised in a nursery for the purpose of hedging. By an experiment I have made a (large) quart containing 4,000 seeds; this, allowing ten Seed to a foot, would sow, or plant, four rows of 100 feet each; at this rate, 40 quarts 160 rows. For which I would have you prepare whenever you shall find most convenient, that the Seed may be put in as soon as it arrives; two feet apart will be enough for the rows. . . (34:85).

Writing from Philadelphia to Pearce on February 1, 1795, Washington stated, "I have no doubt of Ceder making a good hedge, but I have very great ones of your getting them to live, when transplanted; and if they should not, your labour as well as the plants will be lost" (34:108).

Writing from Philadelphia to Pearce on February 8, 1795, Washington again mentioned "making live fences (especially where hogs are not suffered to run) (34:112).

Writing from Philadelphia on April 5, 1795, Washington remarked, "I hope the Honey locust seed are in the ground, that they may vegetate and get above ground before the weather may become hot and dry" (34:171).

Writing from Philadelphia to Pearce on May 24, 1795, Washington stated, "If you have transplanted any of the Honey locust plants (in the manner before directed) and find they succeed, continue the practice as long as the season will allow it. I sent a book for your perusal between this and my next visit to Mount Vernon, which contains many useful experiments, and observations on Hedging &ca. At that time it may be returned to me after information is got from it. This book is written by a man of established character, of course, except what may proceed from difference of climate is to be depended upon, and followed by us (34:205).

Writing from Philadelphia to Pearce on May 31, 1795, Washington asked, "How does the honey locust stand transplanting? If well, follow it up as long as the season will answer" (34:209).

Writing from Philadelphia to Pearce on October 19, 1795, Washington instructed, "Do not delay gathering (before the birds thin them) all the berries of the white thorn and lay up a large store of Cedar berries in due Season. On this subject, and hedging, I shall write to you more fully after I get to Philadelphia; but mention them now that the white thorn berries (which I fancy are rather scarce) may be got while they are in being" (34:338).

Writing from Philadelphia to Pearce on November 22, 1795, Washington stated, "At least 15 years have I been urging my managers to substitute live fences in lieu of dead ones, which, if continued upon the extensive scale my farms require, must exhaust all my timber; and to this moment I have not one that is complete; nor never shall, unless they are attended to in the manner before mentioned; and if plants die, to replace them the next season; and so on, until the hedge is close, compact, and sufficient to answer the purpose for which it is designed" (34:370).

Writing from Philadelphia to Pearce on December 6, 1795, Washington gave these instructions: "Make good the hedges as you proceed, in this business; otherwise you will have incomplete ones, that will render no service. Anxious as you perceive I am, to substitute hedges instead of dead fences, I have full confidence in your exertion to raise them; and as I have observed in a former letter, those for inner and cross fences, where no hogs are suffered to run, may, in the first instance, be made of anything that suits the soil, and will grow quick; altho' they should be doubled hereafter" (34:382-83).

Writing from Philadelphia to Pearce on January 17, 1796, Washington mused, "It was always my intention, and is my earnest wish, to get a hedge of the honey locust, or some plant of quick and stubborn growth upon the outer ditch as soon as possible" (34:422).

Writing from Philadelphia to Pearce on May 2, 1796, Washington acknowledged a report that had reached him: "It is much to be regretted, and I do regret exceedingly, that the Honey locusts which have been set out, should have perished. It would seem I think as if I never should get forward in my plan of hedging" (35:66).

In a memorandum dated November 5, 1796, in Philadelphia, Washington "communicated such directions as have occurred to me since I left Mount Vernon, and are necessary to be followed in this way; that such of them as may not be executed, or executed in part only by Mr. Pearce may be consigned over and completed, or attempted to be completed by his Successor, Mr. Anderson."

Within the ten-page document, Washington wrote, "All the hedges which were planted last Spring or Autumn, should be made good at the proper Season; otherwise the labour and materials which have been applied that way, will have stood for nothing; as an imperfect hedge forms no inclosure, and would be little better than a nuisance. The ground should be well prepared for this purpose. In truth, it is idle to put either plants or Seeds in to it without; for there is no better chance of their succeeding without cultivation, (until they arrive to a certain strength to protect themselves) that there is to expect a crop of Corn from merely putting the Seed in the ground and giving it no attendance thereafter" (35:263).

Writing from Philadelphia on December 18, 1796, Washington sent a Certificate to William Pearce beginning: "Mr. William Pearce having Superintended the Farms, and other business appertaining to my estate of Mount Vernon, during my absence as President of the United States for the last three years (ending the 31st of the present month) It is due to him to declare, and I certify it accordingly, that his conduct during that period has given me entire satisfaction; and that I part with him reluctantly, at his own request, on account of a Rheumatic affection which he thinks would prevent him from giving that attention to my business which from laudable motives he conceives would be necessary (35:338).

Writing from Philadelphia on January 29, 1797, Washington gave instructions to James Anderson, successor to William Pearce. Telling the superintendent to attend to necessary matters until Washington could return to Mount Vernon, he added, "Afterwards, I can converse with you on the subject more fully, and on that of hedging and ditching also, than which, nothing, in that line, is more desirable" (35:376).

Writing to William Strickland from Mount Vernon on July 14, 1797, Washington stated in a nine-page letter,

"I am not surprised that our mode of fencing should be disgusting to a European eye; happy would it have been for us, if it had appeared so in our own eyes; for no sort of fencing is more expensive or wasteful of timber. I have been endeavouring for years to substitute live fences in place of them, but my long absences from home has in this, as in everything else frustrated all my plans that required time and particular attention to effect it. I shall now (although it is too late in the day for me to see the result) being in good earnest to Ditch and hedge, the latter I am attempting with various things but believe none will be found better than Cedar; although I have several kinds of white thorn growing spontaneously on my own grounds" (35: 504).

In the final mention of hedging in his correspondence, Washington keeps the faith he had in living fences but laments that planting them comes "too late in the day for me."

This selection of letters, concluding with one written two years before Washington's death, demonstrates the firm determination of the Revolutionary general and first American president to grow living fences on his properties. The letters also illustrate his continuous supervision of his overseers, his attention to detail, and his willingness to import hedge plants from England, home of his recent enemies. Although the Osage orange tree was not known beyond Indian lands at the time, Washington's frantic pursuit of live fencing conjures an image of Osage orange as a messiah preparing to make its appearance only a few year's after Washington's death. Lively imaginations can portray the Father of His Country embracing the Osage orange as the realization of his visions. But, alas, Washington missed the tree by less than a decade.

In 1807, three years after Lewis Meriwether first sent Osage orange samplings to President Jefferson, Thomas Main, a resident of Washington, D.C., published a book of *Directions for the Transplantation and Management of Young Thorn and Other Hedge Plants*. Although he mentioned pyracantha, hawthorn, honey locust, red cedar, holly, and other hedge plants (33-35), there was no reference to any plant that resembled the yet-unnamed Maclura pomerifa. The scientific name would not be bestowed until Nuttall recorded it in 1819. Although the Osage orange had reached the East Coast in 1804, it was known only to a few members of Jefferson's circle at the time of the hedge publication, and its potential as a hedge plant had not been fully recognized. Like Washington, readers of this book in 1807 could only sustain their quest for the ideal hedge plant.

Population of the Prairies

With the westward movement, settlers began to populate the plains and look for viable fences. In Kansas, Nebraska, and other states on the Great Plains, the rail fences they had known in their previous homes required wood that was being depleted in the prairie region. Wood that could be brought to them from the forests of Michigan was too costly.

The first significant enthusiasm for hedging in America had been identified in the early 1800s in the region including New Castle County, Delaware and adjacent southeastern Pennsylvania. Local farmers recommended the adoption of Virginia thorn and New Castle, or Delaware, thorn hedges. Decline in the popularity of these hedges began in the 1840s. After 1857, the year that the apple borer killed many hedges in the area, the living fences began to fall into disrepute (Burnett 11; Bourcier 517).

Until the advent of Osage orange, farmers in the Midwest faced a future resembling the European plan of small, fenceless farms. Vast areas of the Midwest lacked the stone for New England-style fencing and the timber for the rail fences popular in Ohio and Indiana. Then by the

1860s, the planting of Osage orange seed for hedges reached a fever pitch (Iowa State College 256).

Jonathan B. Turner and John S. Wright

Osage orange received its most enthusiastic endorsement as a hedge plant from Jonathan Baldwin Turner, who arrived at Illinois College in Jacksonville to teach the classics in 1833, and from John S. Wright, editor of *The Prairie Farmer,* whose first issue published in Chicago in 1841, addressed the Osage orange more than any other topic. Both of these men are credited as the leaders most responsible for establishing Osage orange as the premier hedge plant. With editorial offices in Chicago, the largest city in Illinois, *The Prairie Farmer* expected its location in the state that was arousing national interest in Osage orange hedges to create a clearing house for information about living fences (Lewis, Lloyd).

In 1847 Turner issued his first public circular recommending Osage orange as the best-qualified hedge plant when he initially offered the plant for sale (Merris papers; Turner papers). Turner contributed articles on Osage orange not only to *The Prairie Farmer* but to several other agricultural journals throughout the East and South.

Jonathan Turner's "Folly"

Turner, born on December 7, 1805, grew up in Worcester County, Massachusetts. His older brother, Asa, was a member of the Yale University "Illinois Association," a group pledging themselves in February 1827 to go to Illinois as missionaries. Although Asa remained in New England, Jonathan Turner, as a senior, was recommended by the Yale president, who had been invited by the Illinois College president to find a teacher for him. Turner began his journey to Illinois in September 1833 to start his teaching career there. He would return to the East in September 1835 and embark again to Illinois in

March 1836 with his bride, Rhodolphia Kibbe (Mcrris papers; Turner papers).

"What can public schools do for families so widely scattered over the uncultivated prairies?" Professor Turner asked himself soon after he first arrived from the East. He decided that in an area where there was not enough timber to construct fences to protect crops or corral livestock, he set his first goal on finding something for fences that would be "horse high, bull strong, and pig tight." He experimented with barberry, box, hawthorn, and many other plants, even going to the considerable expense of ordering additional hedge varieties from England and other countries (Carriel 59).

A contemporary account of Turner's motivations in promoting Osage orange hedges in Illinois has been interpreted as being intended, in part, to allow close settlement on the prairie, encouraging the building of churches and New England-type schools. Thus the New Englander's objectives sought multiple benefits, not only for farmers but for all prairie residents (Hewes and Jung (184).

At a church meeting in Pisgah, Illinois, in the summer of 1835, Professor Turner met the Rev. Dr. David Nelson, who was preaching along his multiple-state circuit including Illinois, Kentucky, Tennessee, Arkansas, and Missouri. While talking to the minister, Professor Turner mentioned his experiments to find a plant that would make reliable fences. Dr. Nelson described to Professor Turner a thorny plant growing on the banks of the Osage River in Arkansas. He promised to bring some of the seed of the tree with him when he returned to Turner's region of Illinois (Carriel 60).

Growing impatient to become acquainted with the tree before the circuit-riding minister returned to Jacksonville, Professor Turner wrote, "He [Nelson] gave such an interesting account of this plant that I immediately determined to send for it. I wrote to every one in the Southwest I heard of that would be likely to give me any information about it; but as the Doctor had failed to give me the name bois d'arc, by which it is known farther west, these inquiries were pushed for years without any satisfactory results" (Carriel 60). For the next four years, Turner wrote many letters, making everyone he knew aware of his search for the plant Nelson had mentioned. Finally, he read in an agricultural paper an article by a Colonel MacDonald of Alabama about a hedge named Maclura. Thinking that the plant was the one described by Nelson, Turner wrote to the colonel and obtained "one simple plant." "As I remember," Turner said, ". . . I paid, I think, one dollar" (Lewis, Lloyd 155).

For all of his efforts in cultivating hedges from Osage orange saplings, Turner initially received incredulous laughter from the passers-by. For the first year or two, the experiments were called "Professor Turner's Folly." Gradually Professor Turner convinced farmers in the Jacksonville area and then readers of agricultural publications that he had found a superior plant for living fences.

If Wright had subscribed to *American Farmer* published in Baltimore, he would have read in the September 18, 1832, issue about the potential of Osage orange as a hedge plant. After mentioning failure in constructing living fences in the United States, the newspaper stated, "It is gratifying, therefore, to be assured, that in one of our native plants, namely the *maclura* or Osage Orange, we are likely to realize this desirable object [a hedge plant]" (137). The possibilities of Osage orange were also frequently explored in issues of *The Farmer and Gardener*.

After fifteen years at Illinois College, Turner left his position in 1848 because of his public support of such radical beliefs as abolition and Congregationalism, values brought from his New England youth. Nevertheless, Turner remained active in the college community, beginning his important work in education as advocate of land grant state colleges (Merris papers)..

One of the best descriptions of Turner's personality, as perceived by an Illinois resident of The Grove writing for *Horticulturist* in 1852, expressed these thoughts: "J. B. Turner is a thoughtful man, but no 'visionary'—an innovator—but no 'leveler.' He is not even an enthusiast—but an earnest scholar—a learned and pious theologian—strict in his example, and yet liberal in his views; and the most *earnest* and unselfish man I ever knew, in his desire to give the producing classes a liberal education, suiting to their wants, and to the practical requirements of their several vocations" (Kennicott 7 (1852): 374).

John S. Wright's Broad Interests

Wright, also a New Englander trained in the classics like Turner, had come to Illinois from New England in the early 1830s. It was Wright who offered the influential suggestion of the Osage orange hedge to the prairie farmers, but it was Turner who would be remembered for the fencing sensation. Turner, a passionate individual devoted to his causes, remained a poor man all his life, but Wright accumulated a fortune to allow him to endow educational projects and support other interests. Turner had a more focused frame of mind, but Wright embraced many pursuits. Turner was a more patient scientist whereas Wright did not remain with a project long enough to conquer its complex facets (Lewis, Lloyd).

On July 8, 1840, Wright was elected secretary of the Union Agricultural Society, a philanthropic corporation that would begin printing *The Union Agriculturist* under Wright's editorship (Lewis, Lloyd 57-61, 152-53).

In the fall of 1840, while John S. Wright was preparing copy for his first formal issue of *The Union Agriculturalist,* his attention turned to an article in the

Hartford Silk Culturist. Many faddists "had been caught up in the 'Silk Mania'—that the United States could become a nation of silk producers, with worms feeding on mulberry leaves all summer in the back yard and surrendering long threads of silk to farm women in attics all winter" (Lewis, Lloyd 156). What impressed Wright in the article was the statement about Osage orange trees that "when set at a distance of fifteen inches asunder, [they] make the most beautiful as well as the strongest hedge fence in the world, through which neither man nor animals can pass" (Lewis, Lloyd 156-57). Wright reprinted the article in his January 1841 issue and asked his readers to supply additional information.

From the very first issue of *The Prairie Farmer*, Wright had made this appeal to his readers for submission of testimonials about the Osage orange: "Can any one tell us more of this tree? We are desirous of having our columns made the vehicle for communicating of any material that may be made valuable for hedging" (*Prairie Farmer.* 1 (1841).

From the beginning it was Wright's intention to let his readers carry on the debate about the merits of Osage orange. While personally supporting it as the ideal hedge plant, Wright refrained from launching his private crusade.

Professor Turner, since leaving the faculty of Illinois College in 1848, had been devoting himself to the cultivation of various plants like Osage orange and the red raspberry and to the invention of agricultural implements, not to mention his continued activities in the antislavery movement and other causes (Frank 71).

When J. Ambrose Wight became editor of *The Prairie Farmer* in 1843, Wright turned his attention to writing educational news while his editor continued the search for a suitable fence. The publication continued to print long articles written by Turner about his experiments with Osage orange (Lewis, Lloyd).

Turner's Endorsement of Osage Orange

Turner moved slowly in his endorsement of the superiority of Osage orange over all other living fences, but in an article in *The Prairie Farmer* in August 1848, he wrote that he had never "been able for one moment to persuade myself that the beneficent Creator had committed the obvious blunder of making the prairies without also making something to fence them with . . . and if all men should fail for a hundred years to come to make the discovery, I should still believe that God had somewhere on this continent produced a shrub which he designed especially for the purposes of fencing the prairies" (Carriel).

The first volume of *The Prairie Farmer* stated, "The Osage Orange (its botanical name we do not know) has been highly recommended for hedging. We know nothing of it, except that it grows in Arkansas, and is said to be very beautiful (*Prairie Farmer.* 1 (1841): 55).

Opinions about Osage orange immediately became the immediate subject of discussion in *The Prairie Farmer* and other publications, with most of the respondents giving positive accounts of their experiences with Osage orange while some told the editor about their negative experiences. The merits of Osage orange touched off a constant debate from the time of its introduction. A representation of pro and con arguments is quoted below.

Aye Votes for Osage Orange

"I have been making some experiments with the Osage Orange for hedging. It satisfies me that it will prove superior to any other material known, for hedges in this country." H. F. Lodge. *(Prairie Farmer.* 2 (1842): 26).

"I have been an advocate of the Washington thorn as the best plant within my knowledge for the production of living hedges, in Illinois. I can no longer doubt that that plant [Osage orange] is destined to supersede all others as the material from which live hedges are grown." William C. Greenleaf, at the Thorn-Hedge Nursery, near Chatham, Sangamon County, Illinois. (*Prairie Farmer.* 8 (1848): 314).

"I feel safe in saying that as far as my observation goes, the Osage orange is by far the best hedge plant cultivated in the West." L. H. Robinson, Macomb, McDonough County, Illinois. (*Prairie Farmer.* 8 (1848): 337).

"I have been in the culture of Osage Orange hedge for more than five years. I have hedge of White Thorn and the English; also the Virginia Thorn, and I can say with safety, that the Osage Orange hedging is superior to any that I ever saw." John Hancock, Groveland, Tazewell County, Illinois. (*Prairie Farmer.* 9 (1849):189).

"The two-year-old Osage orange trees in our grounds are in perfect health." (*Prairie Farmer.* 10 (1850): 109).

Warnings were also shared by readers, as in the following admonition: "Do not buy Osage orange for hedges until gophers have been eliminated." George W. Seevers, Oskalosa, Iowa. (*Prairie Farmer.* (11 (July 1851): 304).

"Mr. William Neff said it [Osage orange] made a perfect hedge; he had planted it every year for the last seven years, and that he had just sent a quantity to be planted on his farm in Edgar County, Illinois. Since then I have seen some of the hedge at Cincinnati and have no doubt of its proving to be the best tree for hedging in the United States." S. Edwards, Bureau County, Illinois. (*Prairie Farmer.* 6 (1856):181).

"I have no faith in Osier willow (or anything else without thorns making a fence that will turn cattle, when breachy—but the Osage orange will turn anything." J. D. Porter. (*Prairie Farmer.* 23 (1862): 236).

In 1857 *the Kansas and Nebraska Handbook* cited ten merits of Osage orange as a hedge plant: "1. The seeds may be obtained in any desirable quantity, at a cost of ten to twenty dollars per bushel; 2. The seeds, when properly treated, are certain to produce as corn-seed; 3. The young plants are rarely, if ever, attacked by insects; 4. No plant bears removal better than the Osage orange; 5. The growth of the hedge where the land has been properly prepared and cultivated is very rapid; 6. The wood is durable; 7. When pruned, it will always throw out sprouts from the extreme points of the living wood; 8. It never throws up any suckers from the roots; 9. The spines [thorns] are strong, durable, and very offensive to all domestic animals; 10. It will grow on any soil, where any description of timber will grow" (Parker 356).

In the fall of 1865, an issue of *The Kansas Farmer* recommended the Osage orange hedge as an excellent fence for these four reasons: 1. It is easily acclimated to all sections of Kansas as it grows wild along the banks of streams in the southern part of the state; 2. It is valuable for timber—durable as black locust, and not attacked by borers; 3). Seeds are again available at a reasonable price; 4. It is next best to stone fences. (Richards, W. M. 12).

Nay Votes for Osage Orange

The first report of failure with Osage orange hedge appeared in *The Prairie Farmer* in 1843: "The Osage orange is a tree of beautiful foliage but does not seem to stand this climate. With me, it has winter-killed for two seasons. This year it looks like living through the winter." (*Prairie Farmer.* 3 (1843):35).

"The Osage Orange has with me proved a total failure. For the last four years, it has killed down to the ground in the fall and started again in the spring (*Prairie Farmer.* 5 (1845): 38).

Printing a list of objections to Osage orange from *The New York Farmer and Mechanic*, *The Prairie Farmer editor* defended the hedge plant against the attack. The negative aspects of Osage orange that had been reported were the following: "That it will not make a fence to stop swine unless thickened at the bottom by cutting is not news here. The pruning is difficult. The immense amount of brush can be removed after it is pruned off only by means of a fork, which renders it a very tedious operation. If the hedge is neglected, it soon becomes an unsightly nuisance." Wilkinson, Germantown, Pennsylvania. (*Prairie Farmer*).

Four objections to Osage orange hedges were raised by *The Kansas Farmer*: "1. The ground must be in a good state of cultivation when plants are set; 2. The plants must be cultivated for at least two years after setting; 3. Seed costs $40 a bushel and at that price it is hard to get; 4. The young plants must be protected from rodents and livestock until they develop thorns" (Richards, W. M. 11).

Coronation of a Hedge Plant

A leading authority on hedges proclaimed, "That the Osage Orange (*Maclura aurantiaca*) is THE HEDGE PLANT for the United States may now be asserted. Though some persons may have failed with it in producing the desired effect, still, I am satisfied that a thorough investigation of the facts would show that the work had not been well performed, and that the hedger, rather than the hedge-place, was to blame (Warder 85).

In 1846 and 1847, Turner was pressed by readers of *The Prairie Farmer* for confirmation that Osage orange would halt the razorback pigs migrating north to Illinois. Not yet ready to testify to the complete effectiveness of the hedge, Turner withheld his absolute endorsement.

As early as 1848, Professor Turner had written, "It is in all respects unrivalled as a hedge-plant in quickness of growth, stubbornness, and density of its branches and thorns, and the extreme beauty of its foliage, flowers, and fruit. They all agree that it will prove perfectly hardy in any climate where the Isabella grape will ripen in the open air.

An article originally published in the *Ohio Cultivator* was reprinted in the *Horticulturist* in 1848, indicating that the Osage orange had established itself as the hedge plant of choice: "In conversation with Mr. Neff, at Cincinnati, (who first introduced the Osage Orange as a hedge plant in the West), he stated that notwithstanding his large quantity of young plants he has already on hand—enough to plant nearly 20 miles of hedge—he has purchased a large quantity of seed for sowing this spring for the use of himself and others on lands in Illinois. He said to us, that, in his opinion, we could not do our readers a greater service than by urging them to plant hedges of the Osage Orange. The hedge, first planted by him on a farm seven miles from Cincinnati, he informs us, is now ten years old, and affords satisfactory proof of the perfect adaptedness of the plant for the purpose" ("Live Fences—Osage Orange," *Southern Cultivator* (6 (1848): 70).

Publicly endorsing the virtues of Osage orange as a prairie hedge, Wright declared in the October 1848 issue of *The Prairie Farmer,* "I now write with my eye resting upon a hedge four years old . . . on the public street through which thousands of mules and wild Missouri steers, hogs, and sheep are driven each year and all the stock of this village runs at large. And Pharaoh of old knew what a starved town cow was." Behind this hedge Turner grew his fruit trees and garden crops, yet "the wild Missouri steers will not throw it down or bulge over in drove . . . as they used to do every year before I had a hedge" (Lewis, Lloyd 160). At last, Turner was giving an unqualified endorsement of the hedge's ability to prevent animals from ruining crops.

In 1849, Turner went to Missouri, Ohio, Iowa, and Wisconsin to plant a hundred miles of hedge, intending to prove that it could be as useful in those regions as in Illinois (Rice, Mary 18). He wrote in *The Prairie Farmer* in 1850, "Perhaps you have wondered why I have not before written in the defence of the Osage hedge against its opponents. The fact now is that our people here are so far advanced in their hedging operations that all the world cannot stop them, and they want all the plants they can get at any price" (*Prairie Farmer,* 10.10 (1850).

Osage orange hedge crusades began in some areas, emphasizing the prospects that the burden of high-cost fencing would be overcome and that the populating and civilizing of the expansive prairies would be realized (Hewes 504).

As the search progressed for the ideal hedge plant, the Osage orange attracted the greatest intensity of attention. Around Osage orange was concentrated the hope to the dilemma of fencing through hedging. The tree was hailed as the "God-given" fencing material for the prairies (Danhof 181).

Nineteen Century Publications

The saga of Osage orange in the lives of Jonathan B. Turner and John S. Wright will resume later, but at this juncture, it seems appropriate for more voices from nineteenth publications to address concerns of the time. Better than any historical narrative, these authentic commentators can capture the dynamic energy of the past.

At the same time *The Prairie Farmer* created a forum, other agricultural publications were giving more space to the living hedge than any other subject ensnaring attention of American farmers. One reader commented that the Osage orange was occupying more column inches than important political topics.

The following quotations and summaries from agricultural publications were selected to capture the tone and topics found in print from the 1840s to the 1850s and later. The thoughts expressed reflect the search for an ideal hedge plant, the promotion of Osage orange, the dominance of Osage orange, and the beginning of the decline of the popularity of the favorite hedge tree. This sampling of the publications does not represent the columns devoted in each issue to these repeated questions: Where do I get the seed or cuttings to plant? How do I get the seed out of the fruit? When do I plant? How deep and how far apart do I plant the seed? When do I start trimming the hedge? How tall should it be? How wide should it be? Will its shoots claim valuable farm land? How do I make the bottom of the hedge a barrier to small animals?

Information was shared in print by several correspondents, and editors provided ample instructions about each phase of planting and maintenance. Eventually editors stated that in consideration of their longtime readers who had seen the questions answered repeatedly in the publications, they were going to suggest that the inquirers visit someone who had grown a successful hedge. Many books and publications from agricultural agents were being circulated with material devoted exclusively to Osage orange hedges. In these periodicals Osage orange and living fences were dominating the columns.

Assembled below is a cross section of statements quoted from periodicals other than *The Prairie Farmer*.

Farmers' Register

An editor addressed his readers directly when he made this statement about Osage orange hedges: "In answer to the question of another agricultural publication about the making of hedges, this seems to be a suitable time for again bringing to notice the plant which is but little known, though eminently adapted to that purpose. I allude to the Osage orange. During the past year or two, I have several times attempted to introduce it to the consideration of those who contemplate the construction of the fences" ("Hedges-Osage." *Farmers' Register*. 4 (1837: 37).

American Farmer, Baltimore

"Its [The Osage orange's] greatest merit consists in the spreading manner of its growth, the denseness of its branches, and the armature with which they are furnished" ("Hedges—Osage Orange," *Farmer and Gardener.* 5 (15 Dec. 1838): 29).

A review of the promise of Osage orange as a hedge fence and its recent growth in popularity concludes, " . . . its greatest merit is in its ability to spread rapidly, the denseness of its branches, and its armature of thorns" (*Farmer and Gardener.* 5 (18 Dec. 1838): 154).

Horticulturist

"A great many trials have been made in the last ten years, in various parts of the country, with the Osage Orange as a hedge plant. In New England it will probably be found too tender as a winter plant. We have no longer a doubt that it is destined to become the favorite hedge plant of all that part of the Union lying south and west of the state of New York" ("A Chapter on Hedges." *Horticulturist.* 2 (1848): 351).

"Messrs. Ely & Campbell, of Cincinnati, have done the country a service by procuring from the banks of the Red River, a large quantity of the seed of this beautiful and hitherto rather scarce tree. They have placed it for sale with the principal seedsmen in our cities: J. M. Thorn & Co., New York; William Thornburn, Albany; Dair & Co., Cincinnati, etc." (*Horticulturist.* 3 (1849): 573).

"I obtained a peck of seed from the same place this spring, poured water, heated to a degree scarcely to be borne by the hand, upon the seed, agreeably to the counsel of western cultivators, and allow it to remain in the water some forty hours, (a rain preventing me planting sooner) and then planted in good mellow soil; but not one seed ever germinated. All rotted in the ground" (*Horticulturist.* 4 (1850): 146).

"There are hundreds of miles of new Maclura, or Osage Orange hedges, through the whole of this central Illinois region—and yet, I saw but *one* that would turn stock of all kinds, and that had grown up too rapidly, and not thick enough at bottom for future use. Prof. Turner has some hedges commenced *right*—they turn chickens, and would almost turn a rat now—and hereafter they bid fair to be as impenetrable as a brick wall, and as formidable as a hedge of Cherokee rose in Louisiana. John A. Kennicott, The Grove, Illinois. (*Horticulturist.* 6 (1852): 375).

Three objections to the Osage orange were discussed in an 1852 article in *Horticulturist*: "First, the impoverishing of the land to 20 or 30 feet on either side of the hedge. . . . Second, . . . horses would not approach sufficiently near while ploughing. Third, . . . the expense in trimming." Jackson, Bryan, Bloomfield, Delaware. (*Horticulturist.* 6 (1852): 484).

"I know of no plant so likely . . . for hedges as the Osage Orange." D. T. (*Horticulturist.* 7 (1853): 437).

Reporting on a harsh winter, J. W. Fowler of Milford, Connecticut, wrote, "One quarter of the plants killed to the ground. All the growth [Osage orange] of last year was killed" (*Horticulturist* 9 (1856): 841).

"This great western prairie country, from here to the Rocky Mountains, has not one-fourth timber enough on it to fence it; and it is a matter of vast importance for people to know that there is a plant, thoroughly tested that will make a good and cheap hedge.

"You say, 'This plant [the Osage orange,] has some very good qualities for the purpose,' (of a hedge) 'but it requires *great* attention—more it has often been found than the generality of busy famers can afford to give it; if neglected, it runs wild, loses its lower branches, which at the best must be interlaced after the first cuttings, or they will admit the smaller animals another disadvantage is that it is a greedy feeder, extends its roots far and wide, and exhausts the crop of its proper food to some distance in the field. Our own opinion is, that in a vast portion of cases the Osage Orange, *without great attention,* will prove a disappointment" John Gage, Gage's Lakes, Illinois. (*Horticulturist.* 10 (1856): 501).

An article reviewed the hedge value of the Osage orange, concluding that "the answer must be ascertained from actual experiments and that experiments conquer problems and prove the hedges' reliability." J. E. Alexander, Washington, Ohio. ("An Experiment with the Osage Orange." (*Horticulturist.* 11(1858): 85-89).

"Two years or more ago, we ventured to suggest that the Osage orange hedge would rarely be successfully grown in America. The plant comes nearer to what we want than any other yet introduced, but it requires an amount of attention which it rarely receives, and hence, principally, its failure. We had, however, seen many jobs of planting it, and especially along the Illinois railroads, where the plants were set down and left to their fate; they were overgrown with weeds, and had never been trimmed or attended to; many of the plants were diseased, while those retaining life were growing up into trees." (*Horticulturist.* 13 (1862): 24).

"It will readily be acknowledged by those who have seen a prairie, that a fence is a matter of the first importance. Commercial parties have been long enforcing the value of the Osage Orange for this purpose, both on the level-prairie where wood is scarce, and for farms everywhere. Success has attended some efforts to this end, but in general the care and attention they require at the busiest season of the farmer, and other causes, have not been universally encouraged, nor do we find one examination that this plant has fully answered the expectations regarding it; indeed, we prognosticated the failure, except in careful hands, long since. It still has its advocates, however, and we would not discourage its cultivation where labor and attention can be brought to insure its success" ("Editor's Table." *Horticulturist.* 13 (1862): 237).

A consideration of the best plant for hedges reached a verdict in favor of the honey locust, not the Osage orange ("Best Plant for Hedges" (*Horticulturist.* 30 (1875): 82-83).

"Mr. Editor: . . . Of one thousand Osage hedges it would be difficult to find ten that do not look like brush heaps. It is a vile ferocious plant more dangerous to man than to animal" (*Horticulturist.* 30 (1875): 177.

Southern Cultivator, Athens, Georgia

"I noticed a communication in *Southern Communicator* about Osage orange as a hedge. I have had one growing about four years." (*Southern Cultivator.* 6 (1848): 46).

"I consider Osage orange and the Pomegranate the most valuable for this climate [Georgia]." (Nelson, Robert. *Southern Cultivator.* 6 (1848): 142).

Frances Bulkley wrote a report that "from twelve Osage oranges he got about 1,200 plants" (*Southern Cultivator.* 8 (1850): 79).

An article originally published in the *Ohio Cultivator* was reprinted in the *Horticulturist* in 1848, indicating the Osage orange had established itself as the hedge plant of choice: "In conversation with Mr. Neff, at Cincinnati, (who first introduced the Osage Orange as a hedge plant in the West), he stated that notwithstanding his large quantity of young plants he has already on hand—enough to plant nearly 20 miles of hedge—he has purchased a large quantity of seed for sowing this spring for the use of himself and others on lands in Illinois. He said to us, that, in his opinion, we could not do our readers a greater service than by urging them to plant hedges of the Osage Orange. The hedge, first planted by him on a farm seven miles from Cincinnati, he informs us, is now ten years old, and affords satisfactory proof of the perfect adaptedness of the plant for the purpose" ("Live Fences—Osage Orange." *Southern Cultivator.* 6 (1848):70).

"Enclosed I send you some Apple Seed, called by different names. The proper name is 'Bois d'Arc' vulgarly called 'Bodark,' the greatest shrubbery for Hedging that has ever been found out by any people" ("Osage Orange." *Southern Cultivator.* 10 (1852):75).

"I am astonished that one of your tastes in rural matters should prefer the Osage Orange to all other plants for a hedge. For my part I much prefer the Cherokee Rose to the Osage Orange. I have seen hedges 12 feet high of the latter in Texas, growing in the wild unpruned states, and they present an uncouth, jagged, naked appearance, not at all 'a thing of beauty,' though a very effective barrier to any kind of depredators. But so is the Cherokee Rose formidable to stock, while with its evergreen leaves and flowers of snow, it is gloriously beautiful." Jenkins, Montgomery, Alabama. (*Southern Cultivator.* 13 (1855): 301).

The Cincinnatus, College Hill, Ohio

"The conclusion of the committee [Cincinnati Horticultural Society] as to the merits of the Osage orange for a hedge is, that it has no rival in this country and that they have the greatest confidence that it will fully serve the purpose for which it has been eminently designed." (*Cincinnatus.* 1 (July 1856): 348-49).

Additional gleanings from other nineteenth century agricultural publications would broaden the panoramic view of the role of Osage orange at that time.

Osage Orange Seed Industry

In almost every issue of *The Prairie Farmer*, along with testimonials about the success and failure of Osage orange hedges, instruction was given about finding sources of seeds and cuttings, suggestions for planting, and techniques for maintaining the living fence. Column after column in *The Prairie Farmer* was devoted to ways of removing the seed from Osage orange fruit. One reader declared seed removal "a laborious, dirty job."

Meanwhile in Northeast Texas, Osage orange seed was becoming a leading export. Harry Thompson, editor of the Honey Grove, Texas, *Signal-Citizen,* reported that he had seen a bill of sale for fourteen sacks of Osage orange seed that were shipped by Vandy McBee to a firm in Jefferson, Texas, in April 1866. The seed brought $8 a bushel. The editor also wrote about a man named Fisher in nearby Bonham who had a mill for separating Osage orange seed. Another mill was operated by Houston Harrell on the North Sulphur River south of Dial in Fannin County (Neville, "Backward Glances" 11 May 1942).

Horse apples, as the fruit of the Osage orange tree were known in Texas, were purchased by the wagon load. When the fruit had rotted sufficiently, seed merchants ran them through the mill, used strainers to separate the seed from the pulp, then dried and sacked them, and eventually sold them to Fisher in Bonham or another dealer. (Neville, "Backward Glances" 11 May 1942).

So impatient were some of the Osage orange seed vendors that they tried to separate seeds from the fruit by boiling them furiously in a wash pot. After excessive boiling, the seeds were taken by wagon to the Midwestern prairies, where farmers were eager to buy them. Waldrop Harrison, a Hunt County historian, recorded an account of residents in the Greenville area who took their infertile seed to the prairies for profitable sales. When the seed did not produce plants, the buyers came to Hunt County looking for the men who had taken the sterile seed to the Midwest, but the guilty vendors were never identified (Harrison papers).

A similar story was reported in "Backward Glances" in the *Paris News* by A. W. Neville: "Years ago I was told that a man in the southwest part of the county [Lamar County] sold a lot of bois d'arc seed that did not germinate. He had boiled the apples so the seed would separate easily and of course they were ruined: (Neville, *Backward Glances.* 20 Feb. 1938).

Early on, the prairie farmers gave priority to producing their own Osage orange seed to satisfy the demand for creating living fences. Instead of relying upon suppliers from Texas, Arkansas, and other states, they would harvest their own seeds as the female trees in their hedge rows matured into fruit-bearing plants. The need for local supplies was magnified when the Civil War disrupted trade with the South. Just as the port of Jefferson had enjoyed the profits of exporting Osage orange seed, and seed mills had become popular in Northeast Texas, the Midwest witnessed a new economic source in the regional nurseries that added Osage orange seed and saplings to their inventories. An early surprising discovery that Osage orange seed from Northern trees would sprout hastened the use of regional sources to produce additional trees (Hewes 517).

William H. Mann, who lived on Bois d'Arc Creek in Fannin County, learned that bois d'arc seed brought eighty dollars a bushel in Peoria, Illinois. After he washed out thirty bushels of seed, he drove his farm wagon to Peoria with visions of making a small fortune. Once there, he learned that prices had fallen, and he sold his seed on credit for twenty dollars a bushel, the same price he had refused in Texas (Webb, *Great Plains* 292).

In 1863 a hedge planter feeling the shortage of Osage orange seeds during the Civil War wrote, "Osage orange seeds come mostly from Texas. The rebels have sent us more bullets than Osage for a few years past. No hedge plants for sale anywhere that I know of. I do not expect my plants to market until 1866, then let us try hedging" (Hewes and Jung 197).

At the end of the Civil War, the sale of Osage orange seed for hedgerows in the Midwest had become a significant money crop. A major export from the port of Jefferson in Northeast Texas was Osage orange seed. In *The Prairie Farmer* for February 17, 1866, six companies were advertising seed and plants. The Texas Osage Orange Seed Company with offices in Jefferson, Texas; Mendota, Illinois; and Chicago was offering seed at $2 a pound or $40 a bushel in quantities of more than ten pounds. A company in Towanda, McLean County, Illinois, reported that the owners' brother had been in Texas for the past three months buying Osage orange seed from his uncle and cousins. Prices were the same as those announced by the Texas Osage Orange Seed Company (*Prairie Farmer.* 17: (17 Feb. 1866).

In Texas, where residents prospered from selling Osage orange seed and blocks from the tree to support building foundations, former Gov. J. W. Throckmorton of Collin County encouraged farms to use Osage orange to create more living fences. In his article in the 1868 *Texas Almanac,* he wrote, "There is no question practically of more interest to the farmers of Texas than that of hedging. It is to be regretted that in the prairie regions of the states it has received so little consideration. It is a fact demonstrated in Texas and elsewhere that the bois d'arc or Osage orange supplies the very best material for a seedy and effective hedge ("Hedging").

On the prairies in 1864, a concentrated effort to gather local seed began to overcome the Civil War disruption of importing Southern seed. Encouragement came from *The Prairie Farmer*: "It may relieve the anxiety of the prairie farmers to know that there is a fair prospect of having a sufficiency of seed for the country grown on Prairie soil in a very few years at the farthest. Had we known on its first introduction that the seed would certainly mature and especially could we have apprehended the present emergency we should now have an abundant supply of home grown seed and the rebellion could not have in anywise interfered with the great enterprise of live fencing on the prairies" (13: 18 (1864).

Once the Civil War ended, *The Prairie Farmer* would carry a dramatic headline: Osage Orange Seed from Texas Once More! (16.2 (1865). Then the announcement was made that the crop had failed in Texas. Not a bushel of seed was expected to be offered to the prairie states (*Prairie Farmer.* 16.17: (1865).

Seed Vending Companies

Overmann, Mann & Company, with offices in Normal and Bloomington, Illinois, matched the prices of their competitors with the guarantee of Texas seed from the 1865 crop. A. H. Hovey of Chicago mentioned only sales at $2 a pound. Plant and Brother of St. Louis promised the lowest market prices. Musgove, Pence, and Barnes at the Young America Nursery in Warren County, Illinois, was the only vendor advertising Osage hedge plants in small or large quantities. (*Prairie Farmer.* 17 (1866).

Hedge Trimmers

Osage orange nurseries and seed vendors were not the only enterprises profiting from the living hedges. In 1866 *The Prairie Farmer* reported that the J. P. Frost Company of Galesburg, Illinois, had a remarkable piece of equipment on sale: "Oliver's Patent Hedge Trimmer. Can trim hedge at any height and shape on level ground on a hill side at the rate of several miles per day. For a light hedge requires two horse—for a heavy hedge four, and one man" (18.5 (1866).

Another hedge trimmer was advertised in *The Prairie Farmer* on January 5, 1867. The farm equipment with two wheels was offered with the claim that it would trim ten miles of the sides and top of hedges in a single day. For smaller hedges two horses would do the job. Despite the invention of hedge trimmers, the row of Osage orange living fences contained to draw criticism for their neglect by farmers who did not maintain them properly.

Turner and Wright: Divided Loyalty

Once Osage orange was established as the premier tree for prairie hedges, farmers began to ask who deserved the title of "father of the Osage orange hedge." Was it Jonathan B. Turner, or was it John S. Wright? Or was it a group? As editor of *The Prairie Farmer,* Ambrose J. Wight in June 1855 declared, "It is perfectly ridiculous to assert, as many are in the habit of doing, that this or that man introduced the Osage orange as a hedge plant." From the files of *The Prairie Farmer,* Wight found evidence that Wright had begun the agitation for the Osage orange and had discussed it before Professor Turner made his appearance in print. Wight recommended recognition for the influence of Alexander J. Downing, who drew national attention to the Osage orange in his Eastern publication, *The Horticulturist,* during February 1847. Downing had recommended the Osage orange along with the buckthorn as a hedge plant.

Wight recognized that *The Prairie Farmer* had paid this tribute to Turner: "Professor Turner did do two things necessary at the right time: he experimented with a shrub already widely and well known to cultivators, and made his experiments public (*Prairie Farmer.* 15 (June 1855):170-71). Turner was also given credit for saving an enormous amount of money in Illinois by his introduction of Osage orange hedges. One tribute to Turner concluded, "Many a farmer has read more, studied more, lived better and longer for himself and his family because Professor Turner saved him work and time" (Illinois College. *The Rambler* (29 June 29, 1899): 1).

Turner's legacy has been memorialized in a play about his introduction of Osage orange hedges to the Midwest. The original play was written by Bob Merris and a later version was written by Ken Grabury in 1996

("Jonathan Turner Focal Point of New Play"). It has been performed in Jacksonville and other towns in Illinois. Audiences have seen the play staged in a particularly historic setting, the old Springfield capitol building, where Abraham Lincoln once made renowned orations (Merris papers).

Wight also recommended recognition for William Neff, a wealthy Ohio horticultural zealot, who had made the first "extended and accurate" experiments with the Osage orange hedge. Professor Turner, Wight admitted, had "undoubtedly done more than any other man to get Osage orange before the farmers of Illinois, due principally to his articles "which were put forth in the columns of this paper [*The Prairie Farmer*]" (Lewis, Lloyd).

The controversy following Wight's promotion of Wright and demotion of Turner produced vigorous debates, but Wright and Turner made no public statements. Some of the reader response in support of Turner was the statistical claim that the professor was one of the major reasons Illinois increased its population more than 100 percent in the decade of the 1840s, elevating Illinois from the eleventh place among states in 1850 to third in 1860 (Lewis, Lloyd).

By 1857 a book from a New York publisher declared, "That the Osage Orange is THE HEDGE PLANT for the United States may now be fearlessly asserted." An Englishman wrote in the same publication, "Objections have been made to the Osage Orange, I maintain that it is the only good thing known, and fit for hedges in this country. Any other plants offered as a substitute, I consider worse than Useless" (Warder 35).

In the same manual on hedges and evergreens, Turner was given recognition for his promotion of Osage orange hedges as "not only the first man in Illinois but the first in the civilized world, so far as I have any knowledge, who boldly advocated, in the public journals and in private correspondence, as well as circulars the extensive claims of public journals and in private correspondence, as well as circulars, the extensive claims of this plant as the only practical hedge-plant for the farmers of the West" (Warder 198).

Still another nomination had been advanced by *The Ohio Cultivator* for the honor of being father of the Osage orange. Citing Osage orange trees "of great age" found in several parts of Ohio, the publication gave credit to the French or Indians as the Fathers of the Hedge (Warder 199).

Era of Osage Orange Supremacy

Osage orange was soon credited with making settlement of the prairies possible by providing hedges with "speedy, cheap, and lasting protection" (Droze, "Changing the Plains" 8). As Osage orange hedges became more indispensable, states began to pass legislation affecting the living fences. The legal height for hedges ranged from two feet in Kentucky and Virginia to six feet in Alabama, Florida, and Georgia. The required height in Texas was five feet. Willful burning of fences in Texas and several other states was punishable by fine and imprisonment (Warder chapter 10).

By 1850 Osage orange fences had begun to replace sod fences and ditches. Smooth wire was being tested on the Illinois prairies, but their acceptance would not come until barbed wire was perfected (Hewes and Jung 1983).

In the mid-1850s, interest in planting Osage orange hedges had accelerated to the point that the Patent Office's Division of Agriculture was disseminating explicit instructions for cultivating living fences (Droze, *Trees, Prairies, and People* 7).

In 1854, another factor in the growing number of Osage orange hedges in Illinois was the contracting with a firm for the hedging of the Illinois Central Railroad right-of-way from Chicago to Cairo. Twenty miles were to be planted each year (Danhof 182). An 1854 Illinois law required railroads to fence their right of way against livestock (*"Horse-High, Bull-Strong, and Pig*-Tight: 221-22*)*.

The expansion of railroads brought pine lumber from the forests of Minnesota, Wisconsin, and Michigan. Three-rail and three-board fences were made legal in most counties, and fencing remained the greatest expense and most burdensome burden on farmers of modest means, who made up the majority of the settlers. Smooth wire was tried for fences with little success (Gue 3:102).

Osage orange was touted by land speculators to improve the marketability of their lands, claiming that hedges increased the rate at which prairie land was evaluated by the government. Nine thousand miles of Osage orange hedges had been reported to have been set in the spring of 1855 (Danhof, "Fencing Problems").

By 1860 the population of Illinois had moved from eleventh place among the states to third in 1860. The legislature of 1871 extended the bounty of Osage orange, hawthorn, and stone fences (Richards, W. M.). Osage orange fences were credited as one of the major reasons for the increasing population of Illinois (Lewis, Lloyd 163).

In 1867 prize-winning hedges were characterized as thick and at least twelve feet high. They should also be dense, the result of close setting and wise trimming (Hewes 506). Praise for Osage orange hedges filled the pages of the report of the Commissioner of Agriculture for 1868. "For farm hedges there are only two plants which can be considered being perfectly satisfactory," the paean began. "These are the Osage orange and the black locust. The Osage orange is perhaps to be preferred in localities where it is sufficiently hardy. It is cheaply produced, of rapid growth, thickens its branches freely when pruned, has formidable thorns, is not liable to insect injuries, not eaten by cattle, and will grow in any soil of ordinary fertility" (Commissioner of Agriculture 1868, 194)

In 1867 the Kansas legislature voted to give financially stressed farmers $2 for every forty rods of hedge as an incentive for producing living fences. Shawnee County reported more than 300,000 rods of hedge fences in use in 1882, the equivalent of more than nine hundred miles (Rutter). By the 1870s, Kansans were planting miles of "fence" without the expense of posts or wire (Federal Writers' Project, *Kansas,* 500).

Predictions were made in 1868 by the Wisconsin State Agricultural Society of the many plants proposed for fences: "Osage orange will undoubtedly be found the best should it prove to be hardy, as far north as Wisconsin, of which many doubts are entertained" (195).

The Pennsylvania legislature authorized a bounty of $2 per year for each forty rods of hedge grown along a fence line which would successfully resist stock. Later it was discovered that these hedges prevent the proper maintenance of a road by causing snow to drift and by preventing the drying of the road. In modern highway building, all hedge which grows within the limits of construction is pulled at an average cost of ten centers per lineal foot. State laws provide for trimming of all other hedge fences to a height of not over four feet (Connelley 972).

As the size and importance of the Osage orange hedge industry grew, fifty nurserymen met in Bloomington on June 25, 1868, to organize a permanent Hedgegrower's Association, whose official name was the Northwestern Hedge plant Growers' Association. Capt. W. H. Mann of Gilman, Illinois, became the first president and emphasized that the hedge-growing interests of the Northwest involved millions of dollars of capital (Rice 38-39). Dayton, Ohio, for decades was headquarters for a patented method of planting settings and training them into barrier hedges (Werthner, 189).

In 1869 New Castle County, Delaware, reported that more than a thousand miles of Osage orange hedge grew in the county of 424 square miles (Commissioner of Agriculture 1868, 436).

Impetus for hedge growing followed the release in 1871 of a report on fencing by the U.S. Commissioner of Agriculture as the result of a questionnaire distributed the previous year. Returns from 846 counties showed that fencing costs in the United States were close to the national debt and about the same as the estimated cost of American farm animals (Rice 40-41). The report stimulated a frenzy of activity involving living fences.

The Kansas herd law of 1872 applied to the entire state, but individual counties had the option of adopting it. The law remained in effect in most of the central Kansas counties until it was no longer needed in the 1880s. The herd law restrained livestock owners from permitting their animals to run at large, and a lien on the animals damaging crops remained until damages were paid. County assessors had authority to judge the merits of each fence (Swineford and Swineford).

After the high costs of wooden fences had slowed the westward movement considerably, the rise of Osage orange hedges increased population on the prairies and lowered fencing costs. In 1871, the U.S. Department of Agriculture determined that "the combined total cost of fences in the country equaled the national debt, and the annual repair bill for their maintenance exceeded the sum of all federal, state, and local taxes. Because of a desperate need for reasonably priced alternative fences, several new types were tried" (Basalla 51).

Excuses for flaws in Osage orange hedge appeared in the 1872 report of the commissioner of agriculture. M. W. Robinson gave his reasons for preferring the Osage orange. The large majority of the failures with this fence are blamed on a lack of knowledge and the inexperience in its cultivation (Commissioner of Agriculture 1872, 478).

Statistics on the growing use of Osage orange hedges were dramatic between 1850 and 1880. Fencing statistics on U.S. agriculture did not record any data for hedge fences until 1860, when three million rods were reported on farms. In 1870, the number of rods had increased to four million, and in 1880 the report was for four million. In 1890 and later, no information was given for hedge fencing. Labor maintenance demands for hedges given by seven contemporary estimates were fifty rods per day for trimming (Primack 288, 290). Osage orange hedging not only required trimming but also dwarfing of the trees. The Osage orange trees could not serve hedges as tall trees but as altered dwarfs in dense shrubbery.

Hedgerows were one of the most successful alternatives, and Osage orange seemed to be the best plant for fencing purposes (Basalla 51). The triumph of the Osage orange would continue until the mid-1870s. Between 1850 and 1880 in Pennsylvania, Osage orange fences were highly endorsed, especially by nurserymen, as the "best defensive hedge plant; it is also highly ornamental" (Fletcher 70).

Not everyone deserted Osage orange hedge as barbed wire gained recognition. A testimony supporting hedges appeared in *The New Country Life* 1918: "I wish to defend the use of Osage, first, as hedge, second, as a source of revenue for the farm. The hedge in question is part of one planted by my father, nearly fifty years ago, around his farm. Though the farm is near a large and growing city, and though forty acres of it were planted in fruit, the hedge has proved an effective barrier to trespassers. And if it were to do over again, in the age of woven and barbed wire, I would follow my father's example and plant osage" (Osborne).

Only the stone wall of New England is thought to have equaled the hedge of the Middle Western prairie as such a prominent and distinctive man-made necessity that created a distinctive landscape (Hewes 525).

Ecological Value of Hedges

Hedgerows were praised for their ecological importance. They provided food and shelter to many forms of life: birds, insects, plants, and mammals. They were ideal for snakes, hedgehogs, and rabbits, providing not only food and shelter but a place to breed and hibernate (Patterson). At the same time, they sheltered weeds, vermin, and insects (Basalla 52).

Challenge to Osage Orange Name

As the Osage orange became a popular name on the lips of Midwesterners, occasional recommendations were made for a shorter name that was less ambiguous because of confusion recreated by *orange*.

By 1850, as the Osage orange was becoming established on the prairies, Wright himself proposed a name change to the Prairie Hedge Plant since "It is our plant—God made it for us, and we will call it by the name of our 'green ocean home'" (Lewis, Lloyd 161).

Around 1871, a letter writer to the *Republican Daily Journal* in Lawrence, Kansas recommended a change to *Maclura* in honor of William McClure, for whom the scientific name was given (Elliott, R. S. 20). Another proposed name change came from a correspondent to *The Horticulturist*. The cultivator of extensive living fences of Osage orange wrote, "Osage orange is beautiful, romantic, graceful, appropriate, all but universal. . . . Why don't they call the Hickory the Axe-Halve Tree? If one has a foolish whim that a horse ought to be called a saddle, let him do so himself quietly, but not disturb conventional Anglo-Saxondom, by printing silly arguments of this whim." The writer proposed that the new name for Osage orange be "the Prairie Hedge plant." The editor's response was, "We apprehend there is no great danger of his name succeeding" ("Editor's Table." *Horticulturist.* 11:33).

Thorny Wire vs. Thorny Tree

Osage orange was clearly the accepted champion of all hedge plants by 1850, and its reign continued until 1878, when the growing use of barbed wire and complaints about the laborious maintenance of hedges ended its supremacy as preferred fencing.

By 1876, barbed wire was consuming more space than the Osage orange in the columns of *The Prairie Farmer* and elsewhere. Articles and letters about Osage orange concentrated on maintaining hedges instead of planting new ones. Casting undesirable shade, hedges of Osage orange required several years of growth before effective hedges were formed, and the established hedge defied relocation (Van Der Linder and Farrar). Farmers were investing money and energy in pulling down hedges and stringing barbed wire.

Hedges Decline; Barbed Wire Rises

The decline of the planting and maintaining of Osage orange hedges has been attributed to three major factors: care needed to control the growth of hedges, large amount of land used by hedges, and extensive winter-killing. The rise of the Osage orange and the end of its popularity are clearly shown in statistics for fencing from 1850 until 1910. Hedge planting, with numbers indicating the millions of yards planted each year, were as follows: 0 in 1850, 23 in 1860; 54 in 1870; 84 in 1880, 0 in 1890, 0 in 1900, and 0 in 1910 (Primack 287-89).

As the appeal of Osage orange lost its luster, many of its features heralded previously as advantages had degenerated into liabilities. In the days the tree was promoted as the ideal hedge plant, its resistance to insects and other threats to wood were emphasized. Gradually, the list of threats to Osage orange began to grow. In 1929, the Department of Agriculture enumerated diseases of Osage orange as rust in Georgia, Louisiana, and South Carolina; cottony leaf-spot in Louisiana and Texas; mistletoe in Indiana and Texas; one type of leaf-spot in New Jersey; and another type of leaf-spot in Missouri (Anderson, Muenscher, Weld, Wood, and Martin 61).

After 1873, barbed wire also diminished the enterprise of growing Osage orange seed for hedgerows. Immediately after the close of the Civil War, increasing numbers of farmers in the Middle West began to use Osage orange hedges in lieu of rail fences. The seed had commanded a good price and could best grow on Texas blackland, primarily northeast of Dallas.

Central Texas farmers were just beginning to use hedges and to grow bois d'arc seed about the time barbed wire came into use. Some of the Central Texas hedges could be seen a hundred years later, but the demand for seed stopped as rapidly as it had developed (Poage 115).

In Texas when bois d'arc living fences were planted following the vogue in the Midwest, farmers objected to the trees' draining so much moisture and fertility from the soil. Their children and farm hands resented trimming the hedges while "resting" from field work on a rainy day.

When modern highways were planned, laws in states such as Kansas required that all hedge growing within the limits of construction be removed. Pulling of the hedges added ten cents per lineal foot to construction costs. Hedges were blamed for preventing proper maintenance by causing snow to drift and by preventing the road to dry. Additionally, state laws mandated that all other hedge fences be trimmed to a height of no more than four feet (Connelley 970).

Jonathan Turner's Legacy

Upon Turner's death in Jacksonville at age ninety-three on January 1, 1899, the faculty of Illinois College voiced "high appreciation" for his character and labors that were not confined to the college. The faculty resolution states, "The great need of society in that day was to preserve the distinction between mine and theirs. His neighbors' land-marks needed development and the Maclura aurantiaca lent itself to his purposes. Nor was this, great as it was, the most important of his works. A race was enslaved in our country. With voice, and pen and purse, Professor Turner labored for freedom and enfranchisement. In progress of time he saw these efforts successful; and then, to his fertile mind, one work remained. Labor, the best and most important gift of God, must be systematized and utilized. The Illinois Industrial University was the result of his thought and efforts to this direction" (Turner papers).

The final tribute in the faculty resolution acknowledged Turner's campaign for national legislation to establish land grant colleges. Elitism in education troubled the classics professor at Illinois College, and as early as 1850, he proposed a plan for the land grant state university. with funding provided from the federal government sale of public lands. Turner wrote, "I have been bothered that higher education was elitist. While there neither was nor is a royal class in America, only those financially capable of attaining a classic and professional education could rise." Noting the lack of education available to the farmer and the workman, he advanced the idea of diversity in education in Griggsville in May 1850 (Merris papers).

The Illinois General Assembly in 1853 petitioned the national congress to take the action that Turner advocated. Not until 1862 during Lincoln's presidency did a bill including Turner's ideas become law. The Civil War delayed immediate action on the legislattion in Illinois (*History of Morgan County* in Turner papers).

As a friend of both Lincoln and Douglas, Turner had helped organize the Republican Party in Illinois.

Turner is credited with initiating the idea for a state hospital for the insane, the state fair, and tenure of college and university professors.

After his teaching at Illinois College ended, he continued to experiment with living fences and growing Osage orange in Illinois for seed, cuttings, and saplings. He also developed the Turner raspberry, the most popular variety of the fruit (Lewis, Lloyd; Merris papers).

For several years Turner had engaged a man to acquire Osage orange fruit in the South and to prepare its seed for planting in Illinois. As the Civil War got underway in 1861, the law-abiding Turner wrote to officials in Washington, D.C., to ask if he could continue his business activities in the South without being considered disloyal. The response was affirmative, but there would be no government responsibility for losses.

During the war demand for hedges accelerated, and plants were selling for ten dollars a thousand. Eventually, the Southern agent wrote to tell Turner that he could not remain in Arkansas because his life was endangered because of his dealings with Northerners. The agent escaped to Jacksonville, and Turner directed his attention toward making Osage orange seed a locally grown product. As a result of Osage orange seed shortages in the prairie states, Turner encouraged the use of local trees to produce Osage orange seed and saplings, abruptly curtailing the importatation of propagation from Texas, Oklahoma, Missouri, and Arkansas (Carriel 62).

Barbed Competition for Fences

A prophetic threat to the dominance of Osage orange hedges was introduced by an 1858 article in *The Horticulturist.* The editor, commenting on neglected hedges, declared, "Bad hedges are a nuisance to the eye, to the pocket, and to any farmer's crop. The sooner we make up our minds to be thorough enough to secure a good hedge whether of Osage orange or not the better." Agreeing with that opinion, the editor of the *Northwestern Farmer* in Dubuque, Iowa, pointed out that the Osage orange would not answer the challenges of the northwestern region, where the temperatures are too cold for it. He proposed adoption of a new plant, the New Hampshire thorn, with formidable strong thorns. The recommended wood was extremely tough and hard, and easily bent. Its proponents also cited its hardy thorns of up to two inches in length, its shrubby nature improved easily by cutting, its size appropriate for fencing livestock, and its containment of man or beast if property planted (*Horticulturist.* (13 Jan. 1858): 5).

A Waco, Texas, historian traced the collapse of new Osage orange industries in his region. In 1873 barbed wire had begun to eliminate enthusiasm for growing Osage orange seed for hedges. The seed commanding attractive prices could best be grown on Texas blackland. Most of the seed was produced northeast of Dallas, but farmers in the Waco region were just beginning to use hedges and to produce seed when barbed wire came to their attention (Poage 115).

When factory-made barbed wire arrived in Iowa and other states, it revolutionized fencing. First mention of barbed wire in Iowa appeared in county agricultural society notes published in the state agricultural report of 1875, Barbed wire was being used in widely scattered counties: Harrison, Iowa, Jasper, Keokuk, Mitchell, and Story. By 1885, barbed wire fences led other types of barriers in most of Iowa (Hewes and Jung 199-200).

Triumph of Osage Orange Posts

Ironic in the loss of respect for Osage orange for hedges, wood of the tree was recognized as the best material to support barbed wire. The posts were produced by cutting mature trees, growing the posts from seed, or growing fence posts in place. None of these methods was a new idea. Years before, thrifty German-American farmers in southern Illinois had transplanted young cedars from pastures and woodlots in their fence rows. With proper spacing for supporting wires, the tree became permanent posts (Steavenson et al. 200).

Osage orange hedges declined, but they did not disappear. Hedgerows still define the landscapes in parts of Kansas, Illinois, Nebraska, and other midwestern states. In 1976, more than 6,000 miles of single row hedge, mostly thirty to sixty years old, defined the landscape in Kansas according to unpublished local estimates. Lumber production data for Osage orange in 1909 indicated that 340,000 board feet were manufactured, increasing in 1911 to 1,210,000, and to 3,000,000 board feet in 1945, of which two million consisted of fence posts (Burton, 5).

One problem in retrieving Osage orange posts from thorny thickets was penetrating the barrier. Expressing the sentiment of those who retired from hedge-post cutting, a Missouri lad who had envisioned enormous profits from cutting posts expressed his frustration: "To saw a post out of a hedge requires that first you get to the tree's trunk. To the beginner, this is a very educational experience" (Grace 52).

Aging gracefully, after about two years, the posts let their peeling bark drop to the ground. A few years later the light outer layer of wood, the sapwood, decays and softens. Then all that remains is the heartwood. If the post does not fall soon, an oldtimer comments ". . . [the] post was just cut under the wrong sign of the moon" (Grace 76).

In many of the central and western Kansas counties, barbed wire was attached to limestone posts rather than to Osage orange posts. The postrock limestone was soft enough to be quarried by hand, and it could be cut with an ordinary saw. These posts remained durable when the limestone was exposed to air (Richmond 142-43; Rafferty, "Limestone Fenceposts" 41-43).

Despite ominous predictions that Osage orange was not secure as the favored fence, from 1850 until 1875 the thorny plant had no serious competitors, and the majority of farmers believed that "God designed Osage orange especially for the purpose of fencing the prairies" (Steavenson et al.)

Before Osage orange surrendered its dominance in hedgerows, an estimated 96,000 miles had been lined with plantings of the tree, nearly enough to encircle the earth four times with droppings of the unique fruit of the female tree (Lembke 198).

In 1985 a writer for *Mother Earth News* observed, "Those who agree with Robert Frost that 'good fences make good neighbors' are likely to think of the Osage orange as both a good fence and a good neighbor and beast alike" (Wyman 121). The thought chain linking Frost to fence to Osage orange affirms the indelible association of Osage orange with its heyday as a living fence.

Thankless Pursuit of Science

An article in *Meehans' Monthly* more than a century ago reminds the reader of the twisting path of utility that the Osage orange has followed since its introduction to cultures beyond Native Americans in 1804.

The botanical journal generated ideas that clarify the unknown but changing roles of scientific discoveries: The article stated, "The question is often asked: what is the practical use of abstract science? . . . We have to wait and see whether the new fact or the new babe is of any practical use in the world. A good illustration of this is connected with the history of the Osage Orange. . . . Osage Orange trees were simply looked upon as curiosities and probably, if seeds could have been sold at that time, a few cents a package would have been considered their full value. But it came about the Osage Orange proved to be one of the best hedge plants that had ever been introduced. When we remember how little was known of the value of this tree when Lewis and Clark first gave McMahon a few seed who would ever have supposed that they would reach such value that a nurseryman eagerly would pay as much as this a bushel for them? And so it is. Science must go on pursuing in thankless course. It is only after it has gained the facts that we can possibly tell of what value they were to mankind" ("Osage Orange—Value of Scientific Facts," 79).

At the turn of the nineteenth century, Osage orange was unknown outside Native American communities, but farmers were already imagining the boon of a thorny plant with a potential for creating living fences. By mid-century Osage orange had been declared the ideal hedge plant, and prairie farmers were beginning to benefit from the tree's protection of their crops and livestock. As rivalry between Osage orange and wire fences developed, farmers found that the pre-Bessemer wire was adversely affected by heat and cold. First reports of barbed wire frightened livestock owners who feared that the sharp prongs would injure their animals. After 1878, anxieties subsided, and barbed wire became standard fencing. The golden age of Osage orange hedges vanished quickly. In the infancy of the twentieth century, artifacts from the decades dominated by hedges were monumental rows of Osage orange trees surviving in rows across the Midwest.

The attentive documentation of prairie farming by nineteenth century agricultural publications became quaint archives. But on the horizon were more adaptations awaiting the thorny, durable stamina of the Osage orange tree.

TEXAS
Osage Orange Seed Company

E. DEUPREE, } Jefferson,   C. D. RUSHMORE,
D. B. DEUPREE, }   Texas,   Mendota, Ill.

E. L. POMEROY, General Agent for the Northwest, 86 LaSalle street, Chicago.

Seed sold by this Company, has been gathered and prepared for market by members of the Company residing in Texas, and will be warranted prime and reliable in every particular. Full directions for sprouting will accompany each lot of seed. Seed now on hand to fill orders without delay. Prices $2 ⅟ lb. for less than 1 bushel.
$50 ⅟ bushel for 1 to 5 bushels.
 45 "   "   " 5 to 10 do.
 40 "   "   " 10 or over.
v17n4 14t.

New Osage Orange Seed.

OUR Brother, A. R. JONES, has been in Texas for the last three months, gathering Osage Orange Seed, and also having an uncle and a number of cousins residing there who have been assisting him, he has procured a quantity of fresh seed, well cleaned through the windmill. We expect the seed here in the month of February, and all wishing seed, either in large or small quantities, should send us their orders immediately, accompanied with the cash. All such orders are filed and will be filled in the order of their reception.

Our prices are as follows: Any quantity less than one bushel $2 per pound. From one to five bushels, $50 per bushel. From five to ten bushels, $45 per bushel, and for all quantities over ten bushels $40 per bushel. One bushel of seed weighs thirty-three pounds. Currency may be sent by express or drafts by mail.

Give full direction for the shipment of seed. We have already sold about one-fourth of our seed, and are receiving orders daily, and there appears to be an unlimited demand. Address

Our Osage Seed has arrived, and we are now ready to fill all orders promptly and with a good article that was not boiled.

C. & F. M. JONES, Towanda, McLean Co., Ill.
February 6th, 1866.   v16n6

HEDGE TRIMMER.

Prairie Farmer, 1867

5
Ascent of Barbed Wire

Smooth wire for fences was used four decades before barbed wire came upon the scene. No longer were farmers looking for a plant that could become a barrier hedge, but plain wire did not succeed until the thorns of the Osage orange inspired the invention of barbed wire. After pronged wire fences replaced Osage orange hedges, the tree still maintained a role in fencing by providing durable posts to support the strands of barbed wire.

When Samuel Freeman, a blacksmith and farmer in Scott County, Iowa, built a wire fence on his farm near Hickory Grove in 1859, he was agitated by cattle getting between the wires. Two years later, his son, Pembroke E. Freeman, fashioned a barb which he applied to the wire. Escape by cattle through the wires was prevented in what has been claimed as the first application of barbed wire to fences. Even though the fence was well known among his neighbors and other farmers in the county, Freeman did not exert efforts to apply for a patent for his invention. In

1867, a Mr. Hunt devised a spur wheel to be attached to wire, acting as a barb to prevent cattle from escaping the fence. Although he secured a patent for his device, it was never put into use (Gue 3:2).

Wire Mimicking Nature

George Basalla's *The Evolution of Technology* used barbed wire as an example of technology imitating nature to perform the same function. Basalla wrote, "It [barbed wire] originated as a deliberate attempt to copy an organic form that functioned effectively as a deterrent to livestock." Then he observed, "The steel barb is nothing more than a thorn, a spur the animal instantly retreats from, and thereafter carefully avoids." By mimicking nature, the barbed wire becomes what Basalla calls a *naturfact* (Basalla 55; Regis 28), Basalla concluded, "Barbed wire was not created by men who happened to twist and cut wire in a peculiar fashion. The inventors would then take a leaf from nature's scrapbook to produce thorn wire (Everett, Dick 297).

Léonce Eugêne Grassin Baledans has been identified as the first to make the thorn an appropriate metaphor for barbed wire. In his patent submitted in France on July 7, 1860, for a "Grating of wire-work for fences and other purposes," Baledans had in mind a "system of twisted iron" that could be applied to "everything that ought to be enclosed or fenced." Baledans has been largely ignored as the first to propose, among other features, the use of twisted wire with sharp projections" (Krell 13-14).

There was an obvious transfer from thorns to metal barbs in the patent filed in France on August 27, 1867, by Gilbert Gavillard, one of three granted in France during the 1860s. Gavillard's invention describes a fence composed of *ronces artificielles* [artificial thorns] caught between three strands of intertwined wire. In an accompanying sketch signed by the inventor, instead of the usual technical illustration, Gavillard presented a rural setting with an ox admiring fruit on an apple tree but separated from the delicacies which hang just beyond a fence with three strands of barbed wire (Krell 13).

During the transition from living hedges to thorned wire fences, the supplanted Osage orange got a nod of remembrance in the name of an early company manufacturing barbed wire as the Thorn Wire Hedge Company (McCallum and McCallum 55).

Early Potential of Wire Fences

Before the advent of barbed wire, other types of wire fences appeared on the market. Fencing with iron wire had been introduced in Pennsylvania as early as 1810 (Danhof 184). Plain galvanized wire was used for an estimated 350,000 miles of fence between 1850 and 1870. Cheap, easily transported, and handily erected, wire fence was welcomed by farmers in areas where timber was in short supply. Farmers were never happy with plain wire fences, which snapped in cold temperatures and sagged in heat. In 1854, Henry Bessemer in England improved the plain wire with his steel conversion process, but it did not become available in the United States until 1870 (McClure 3). *The Southern Cultivator* took note of what was a new style of wire netting for fences as well as other developments in wire fencing that were reported regularly (16 (1858):142).

Then, all at the same time, the idea of putting steel thorns on wire popped into the heads of several individuals. They began to work simultaneously in different locales, but the cluster of inventors in DeKalb, Illinois, won national interest. A barbed wire fence had many advantages over living hedges: it took less space than a hedge, it allowed crops closer to the fence line, it did not exhaust the soil, it did not shade the land, it did not demand trimming, it did not require years before it became functional. Furthermore, three men could build half a mile of the barbed wire fence in a day (McClure 3-4; Thorne 62).

Barbed wire has been recognized as the fourth invention that hastened settlement of the West. The fences with strands of barbed wire were considered an influence equal to the revolver, the repeating rifle, and the windmill (Clifton 3).

First Registered Patents

Early attempts to devise an effective wire fence started even before Jonathan Baldwin Turner found the Osage orange and advocated its use as a living fence. Patents in the United States and in several European countries preceded Turner's hedge experiments, which began in Illinois in the 1840s. In 1833, S. F. Dexter of Auburn, New York, patented a wire fence, but it was deemed of no use for farmers. The brittle wire slackened or broke with temperature changes. The wire snapped when cattle or horses came in contact with it (Wendt 29).

On November 8, 1853, William H. Meriwether of New Braunfels, Texas, filed a patent for "Black Iron with Faster Curl," a wavy strand of wire with no barbs. It would not break when the wire contracted and expanded in hot and cold temperatures (Glover fig. 389). On that same day, Meriwether applied for a second patent, "Improved Fence" (Early Varied Smooth Wire)." This early smooth-wire-and-board fencing incorporated several essential metal points, sometimes of cast-iron. Patent specifications provided for four strands of wire with "one rail of wood about three or four feet from the ground next below the top wire." The sharp points of metal pointing downward below the board were expected to keep small cattle from going under and large cattle from going over the fence. Meriwether's design foreshadowed at this early date a number of features incorporated into wire twenty-five years later (McCallum and McCallum 241-42).

By 1865, William D. Hunt of Scott County, New York, having taken note of the effectiveness of thorn hedges, used army fence wire armed with star-shaped metal spurs. The results were ineffective when the spurs failed to stay in place, but many farmers tried variations of Scott's basic idea (McCallum and McCallum 53).

Three Inventors from DeKalb

Another decade passed before three men in DeKalb, Illinois, found inspiration at a county fair near their home. The location of DeKalb at the edge of the prairie was a likely place to find men interested in designing new fences. Three local men saw the William Rose exhibit, a sixteen-foot strip of wood with steel barbs in it (McClure 16). Advertised as a "sure thing to keep your cows in," the board caught the special interest of these three spectators: Joseph F. Glidden, a farmer; Jacob Haish, a DeKalb resident who hoped to grow thorn hedges; and Col. Isaac Ellwood, a former auctioneer who arrived in DeKalb in 1855 to open a hardware store after a fruitless attempt to find gold in California (Wendt and Hogan 29-33).

Joseph L. Glidden

At about the same time Joseph Glidden had received his first revelation for inventing barbed wire from viewing the Henry Rose exhibit, so did Jacob Haish and Isaac l. Ellwood find their incentive to create a better barbed wire than any designed up to that time (McClure 30).

Many varied and conflicting accounts attempt to describe the milestones in the development of early barbed wire. The following story is told about Glidden and how he was inspired by Osage orange thorns to file his patent for barbed wire. In 1935, C. L. Douglas, a Texas newspaper reporter, recreated Glidden's defining moment of inspiration:

"Mr. Glidden was troubled. Here he was repairing fence behind a destructive herd of milk cows when he should be in his DeKalb workshop making eaves troughs. The cows smashed into the smooth wire strands and tore them from the posts as fast of Mr. Glidden could drive in new staples, and he had just about concluded that the successful business man . . . especially an eaves-trough maker . . . might do well to forego his pleasure of gentleman farmer.

"And then, even as he poised the hammer to drive a staple back into place, he saw it—the thing which was to doom the open range in the cattle country of the West.

"The staple was hanging loose on the smooth wire, its points directed toward the eaves-trough maker of DeKalb. His hand, already raised to strike the blow, fell. Here was an idea. If all this smooth wire could be strung with sharp barbs at regular intervals . . . ."

The next morning, so the story continues, "Glidden was in his tin shop early, fastening one of the smooth wires to a grinder and cutting a series of two-point barbs. With a crude wrench, he began twisting the barbs on the wire."

Later when a friend questioned him about the effectiveness of the barbed wire on cattle, Glidden responded, "Isn't it logical that cattle, once they have come in contact with the wire, won't go up against it again. Does a burned child return to the fire?"

An oral version of a popular anecdote heard in DeKalb was that Glidden scratched his arm on the Osage hedge while pulling a chicken out of its thorny branches after the fowl had tried to escape the living barrier around the barnyard. "Why can't we attach those thorns to wire?" he asked himself.

Another story accounting for Glidden's interest in the need for fences claimed that about 1872 Mrs. Glidden had a small flower bed, and neighboring dogs often trespassed. After her husband strung plain wire around her floral garden, she found it ineffective. She then had pieces of wire twisted around the plain wire, and she had no more problems with the dogs after the barbs were added (McClure 16; Webb, *Great Plains* 299).

How Glidden learned to twist two wires is explained in this account: "One day some wires became entangled, and in picking them up, he conceived the idea that two wires could be twisted together so as to hold the barbs in place and keep them from rotating. He was thinking about a method of doing this when his eye lighted on the grindstone, and he formed the idea of twisting the wire by means of a small crank on the grindstone. He asked his wife to turn the grindstone, which she did" (McClure 16). According to this version of the story, a common grindstone was the first machine to be used in twisting wire. Other tellers of the story say that Glidden first used in his wife's coffee mill to twist the wire (McClure 65).

Glidden, a native of Charleston, Cheshire County, New Hampshire, fashioned his first barbed wire in 1873 and made his first sale the following year. Glidden's application for a patent for his barbed wire was approved on November 24, 1874. His innovations had commercial attractiveness as well as sufficient novelty to withstand litigation (McClure 19).

Jacob Haish

Recollections of Jacob Haish have also been published about his innovations with Osage orange hedges and his patent for a barbed wire fence. The German lumber dealer in DeKalb sold Osage orange seed and experimented with Osage orange plants for hedge fences. He stated in his "Reminiscent Chapter" from the *Unwritten History of Barbed Wire* that at the time he was attempting to discover a good substitute for fence material, he often had Osage orange in his thoughts. He wrote, "It was in my mind [at one time] to plant Osage orange seed and when of suitable growth cut and wrest it into plain wire and board fences, using the thorns as a safeguard against the encroachment of stock" (McCallum and McCallum 31). At first he toyed with the idea of growing the thorny Osage orange plants and of weaving their thorny branches into a smooth wire fence when they had matured (McClure 31).

Haish experimented with link wire, four-pointed sheet metal barbs, and both wire and barbed band-iron, finally settling on the "S" barbed wire, which he patented on August 31, 1875. The barb was double-pointed, made from a single piece of wire bent at its center laterally so that all parts were in the same place to form the letter "S," creating two loops fashioned to clasp both of the strand wires. Thus Haish had advanced through three phases characterizing nineteenth century fence construction: first, Osage orange; second, attachments of metal to wood; and third, wire married to wire (McCallum and McCallum 41).

I. L. Ellwood

In his history of DeKalb County, I. L. Ellwood wrote, "In 1873, we had a little county fair down here about where the Normal School now stands, and a man by the name of [Henry] Rose, that lives in Clinton, exhibited at the fair a strip of wood about an inch square and about sixteen feet long and drove into this wood some sharp brads, leaving the points sticking out, for the purpose of hanging it on a smooth wire, which was the principal fencing material at that time.

"This sprig of wood, so armed to hang on the wire, was to stop the cattle from crawling through. Mr. Glidden, Mr. Haish and myself, all later looking at this invention of Mr. Rose's, and I think that each one of us at that hour conceived the idea that barbs would be placed on wire in some way instead of being driven into the strip of wood" (McCallum and McCallum 29-31). A fragment of the type of barbed board designed by Henry Rose was found on an old fence in Limestone County, Texas, and a photograph of the artifact has been printed in *The Devil's Rope* (Krell 22).

Henry Rose and Michael Kelly

Rose called his invention the "Wooden Strip with Metallic Points," and he was granted patent number 138763 on May 13, 1873. The creation had evolved from an experience with a "breachy" cow. His invention was not actually a fence but instead an attachment. At first he intended to hang the board around a cow's neck, but he decided that it was not prudent to inflict the animal with such a clumsy yoke. Instead, he hung the board with its barbs on the wire fence itself. (McClure 16; McCallum and McCallum 29).

In the marriage of wire to wire, twisting proved the crucial development, but Michael Kelly's patent 74379 in November 1868 in New York failed to stress one great advantage that it offered, namely a technique for twisting barbs in place between two wires, to keep them from sliding along the wire (Evans 75). The "thorny fence," as Kelly called his patent was recognized for its commercial possibilities. For a time twisted barbs seemed to be the greatest obstacle for Joseph Glidden's efforts to secure a patent on his "improved fence wire." Kelly's failure to specify that he had invented a way of locking the barb in place, and Glidden's patent with that specification clearly stated, won support from the court (McCallum and McCallum 55-59). "My invention," Kelly wrote, "[imparts] to fences of wire a character approximating that of a thorn-hedge. I prefer to designate the fence so produced as a thorny fence" (quoted in Basalla 53).

Patent Competition

Rivalry soon developed between Haish and Glidden. On June 25, 1874, Haish filed papers at the Patent Office in Washington, D.C. Haish attempted to delay the issuing of a patent on Glidden's original application, which was still pending, by filing a grievance. Glidden had applied for an application on October 27, 1873; Haish on Dec. 22, 1873, and Ellwood on January 7, 1874; but Haish was the first to be granted a patent (McCallum and McCallum 41).

On November 24, 1874, Glidden received his patent grant for fencing material with barbs wrapped around a single strand of wire and held in place by twisting the strand around a second one. He had chosen the nickname of *barbed wire* for his invention (Winer 10). He called his version of barbed wire "Winner," and it was the most commercially successful of the hundreds of subsequent barbed wire designs. Haish, who had filed for a patent on a similar "S barb" design, launched a legal battle that was unsuccessful in halting sale of the Glidden design.

When the principal manufacturer of smooth wire, Washburn and Moen Company of Massachusetts, began to note the high volume of wire orders going to Glidden's and Haish's companies in DeKalb, a representative was sent to make inquiries. When mergers were offered, Glidden aligned his interests with the Eastern firm, but Haish declined the offer Washburn and Moen made to him (McCallum and McCallum*).*

Forming a partnership with Ellwood, Glidden sold his interests, which included other barbed wire patents, to Washburn and Moen in May 1876. As an active partner in the new organization, Ellwood became sole agent and distributor for the South and West. By 1876, Washburn and Moen had acquired all major barbed wire patents, except those retained by Haish. The company, later absorbed by United States Steel Corporation, had thus succeeded in holding a near-monopoly on barbed wire (McCallum and McCallum 42-60; McClure 24-25).

Barbed Wire Triumph in San Antonio

As representative of Glidden and Ellwood's Barbed Fence Company, Henry Bradley Sanborn went to Texas in

1875 to promote the successor to Osage orange hedges. He made the first sales of barbed wire in the state, but he failed to convince the large market awaiting the new barrier that it was vital to Texas farmers and ranchers. In 1878, John Warne "Bet-a-Million" Gates staged a renowned carnival-like demonstration on Military Plaza. The event was in downtown San Antonio between San Fernando Cathedral and the old Spanish Governor's Palace (McClure 69). A fence made of Glidden's "Winner" wire corralled a herd of cattle. The longhorns charged time and time again, but the wire held. Before nightfall Gates had sold hundreds of miles of the wire at the prevailing price of eighteen cents per pound (McClure 72; Wendt and Kogan 44-51). Word circulated that Gates claimed his barbed wire was "light as air, stronger than whiskey, and cheap as dirt." As sales mounted, Texas saw barbed wire reshape forever land uses and land values ("Barbed Wire," *The New Handbook of Texas* 1:377). The end of Osage orange and briar living fences in Texas began to draw to a close in 1876 with the appearance of "The Winner" design of barbed wire (Greene,"Bois d'Arc Fences Reigned").

Cattlemen had resisted the use of barbed wire for several reasons, the most prominent being their assumption that livestock would be injured by the sharp prongs. Early patents had attached not only barbs but also wooden blocks along the wire to prevent animals from sustaining injury from the sharp points of the barbs (Richards, W. M. 18).

In 1872, a negative report from *The Nebraska Farmer* had pointed out that plain wire fences were "continually being broken down" and that "barbed wire injured stock." The article advocated increased use of Osage orange hedge (Hewes 514). Gates' success in San Antonio was proof that the beasts would not stampede into the dangerous barrier. If an animal felt the pain of a barb once, the creature avoided the inflictor of discomfort in the future.

By the end of the 1870s, barbed wire had become common in Kansas and Nebraska. Under the ownership of large manufacturing companies, barbed wire rapidly declined in price, placing it within the range of the homesteader (Everett, Dick 298). In 1874, barbed wire was priced at $20 per hundred pounds, in 1880 at $10, in 1885 at $4.10, in 1890 at $3.45, in 1897 at $1.80 (Webb, *Great Plains* 309).

In 1874, the fledgling barbed-wire industry produced 10,000 pounds of thorny wire for new fencing. Within a few years, orders for barbed wire were filling railroad cars with 600,000 pounds in 1875; 12,863,000 pounds in 1877, and 80,500,000 pounds in 1880 (Basalla 53; Webb, *Great Plains* 309).

Early Impact of Barbed Wire

The introduction of the Bessemer process of steel production from England in 1870 made a metal available that was cheap and strong, placing on the market a wire that was of sufficient strength and quality as well as cheap and efficient (Danhof). The advent of affordable, rust-resistant wire also stimulated the sale of barbed wire (Primack 287).

Between 1801 and 1881, the United States Patent Office had issued 1,229 wire patents. More than half of them had come from states west of the Mississippi. Litigation among inventors and manufacturers, especially over some of the earlier patents, were numerous and aggressive, not resolved until a final court decree in 1892. The decision of the U.S. Supreme Court was to sustain the rights of Glidden's "Winner Patent" and make Glidden the principal player in the barbed war patent drama (McClure 107). The intrigue of barbed war rivalries is chronicled in detail by McClure's *History of the Manufacture of Barbed Wire*, by McCallum and McCallum's *The Wire That Fenced the West*, and by Webb's *The Great Plains*.

The impact of barbed wire fences on the plains was summarized by one historian with this explanation:

"Barbed wire greatly hastened the agrarian conquest of the plains and sharpened the conflict between the herder and the agrarian, finally wreaking the rancher's doom" (Everett, Dick 297-99). As barbed wire triumphed, most of the Osage orange hedges were no longer trimmed. Neglected trees grew high above the once shapely contours of the hedge and soon regained spreading crowns (Burton and Barnett 5).

Texas historian Walter Prescott Webb credited the invention of barbed wire with revolutionizing land values and opening the fertile prairie plains to homesteaders.. (*Great Plains* 317-18).

Ironic Comeback of Osage Orange

In a paradoxical situation, the pronged metal barriers that ended the supremacy of Osage orange as hedges created a new market for the tree's fence posts. For durability and dependability as a fence post, no timber equals Osage orange. As hedges disappeared, plantations of Osage orange grown for posts provided a money crop. In 1905, posts were bringing ten to twenty cents each in local markets. A rod (16½ feet or 5½ yards) of old hedgerow could produce twenty-five fence posts, and new trees were being grown especially for that purpose (Rogers, *Tree Book* 242). The thorny tree that inspired the invention of barbed wire now supported multiple strands of barbed wire stretched tightly between its posts.

The contact of the post with the ground, a few inches above and below, was recognized as the Achilles heel of most timber being considered to support barbed wire stapled into its heartwood. Once the fence post is set in the earth, at that point oxygen and moisture combine to make ideal conditions for the fungi that consume wood. Osage orange is at the top of the list for longevity with a life expectancy of up to thirty years and beyond after being positioned in the ground. A Kansas historian, W. M. Richards, testified that some Osage orange posts had been in use for over half a century and were still rendering good service. Some farmers who had received a bounty for planting Osage orange fences received an income from the sale of posts cut from the hedges and still had their fences (18).

A charming story was related to Ron Hardcastle at his Osage orange archery display in 1984 at the Texas Folklife Festival in San Antonio. An elderly man visiting with Hardcastle recalled, "We always said when you cut a bois d'arc fence post, you put it in the ground, wait until it rots, turn it over and stick in the other end and then let it rot at that end." Hardcastle concluded, "That's how long the posts last. They're almost impervious to weathering and rot (Lowman).

When farmers stapled wire to the Osage posts while the wood was still green, there was no problem. Green wood held the staples firmly. But driving staples into dried wood was a formidable task. Sometimes barbed wire had to be attached to hardened, impenetrable posts with hay-baling wire (Lawrence, *Encylopedia* 182).

Results of a state-wide service test of fence posts begun in 1962 by the Texas Forest Service were reported in 1973. After ten years of service, 23.1 percent of all the treated posts and 16.4 percent of all the untreated posts had failed. Of the posts remaining in service, 58 percent of all the treated posts and 79 percent of all the untreated posts showed some indication of decay and/or insect attack, and 32 percent of all the treated posts showed some indication of decay and/or insect attack. Osage orange had the best record of resistance to decay, with 0% of the round posts and 5.6% of the split posts failing to decay (Westbrook 5-9).

In 1983, Osage orange led other trees with a probable life expectancy for untreated wooden posts of mostly heartwood. The life expectancy of Osage orange was 25-30 years, followed by red cedar and black locust with 15-25 years (Hansen 103)

In the 1970s, approximately three million posts were being cut and retailed annually in Kansas. At least one charcoal kiln in McPherson County, Kansas, operated for several years, burning only Osage orange wood from hedgerow removal (Burton, 5).

Lumber production data for Osage orange increased from 340,000 board feet in 1909 to 1,210,000 in 1911. In 1945, the lumber yield had jumped to three million board feet, of which two million consisted of fence posts (Burton, 5).

In a 2003 solicitation notice for government purchase of fencing materials, the U.S. Department of the Interior specified that Osage orange was the only one of the three species acceptable without treatment of the butt for a minimum depth in the ground (U.S. Department of the Interior. "Fencing Materials").

Barbed Wire Rivalries

Barbed wire quickly outgrew its original purpose of enclosing crops and livestock, taking on the now familiar roles in warfare and prisons. Barbs have been reshaped as razor-sharp blades to deter entrance into areas where valuable or hazardous property is kept. Glidden's design remains as the most common barbed wire for the familiar boundaries on farms and ranches.

Barbed wire has spawned organizations for collectors of the hundreds of styles of barbs, prongs, points, prickers, and stickers affixed to wire. Collections are mounted creatively on boards or used in other imaginative displays, such as stars, artistic silhouettes, or outlines of states. Jack Glover's *"Bobbed" Wire Bible* provides graphic sketches of 371 types of barbed wire, often with names of the wire, names of inventors, and dates of patents (Glover).

Competition among barbed wire interests is sometimes fierce. Challenge to the title of "Barbed Wire Capital of the World" sent La Cross, Kansas, residents in 1990 into action when residents of McLean, Texas, announced plans to convert a former bra factory into a barbed wire museum. Just in case the Texans posed a threat to their title, the western Kansas community began to plan an expansion of their museum. Delbert Threw, president of the Texas Barbed Wire Collectors Association, assured the Kansans that McLean's museum was not intended to strip away La Cross's title (Berry 22A).

Barbed wire had its genesis in "a calculated attempt to copy an organic form [Osage orange] that functioned effectively as a deterrent to livestock (Basalla 55). The new thorn-like metallic wonder soon became the ideal and affordable barrier with low maintenance. After being supplanted by barbed wire fences, Osage orange remains vital to fences because its posts were rated as the best material upon which to stretch the barbed wire.

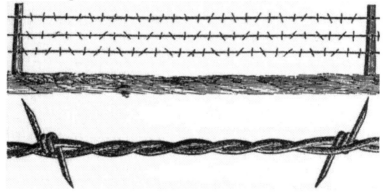

J. F. Glidden's Patent for Barbed Wire Fence
Prairie Farmer, 1870s

6
Windbreaks and Shelterbelts

While barbed wire became the most visible guardian of crops and livestock throughout the United States, Osage orange was chosen for new roles, including those of windbreaks and shelterbelts. With support from the federal government, Osage orange remained on the national landscape in a modified form.

When the success of hedges first became apparent, government agents recommended Osage orange trees for holding the soil against the rage of drying winds in shelterbreaks and windbreaks throughout the Midwest (Lawrence, Eleanor, *Book of Trees* 125).

Long before the dust storms of the 1930s, farmers on the Kansas prairies relied on Osage orange to provide windbreaks as well as hedges. President Franklin Roosevelt proposed the Great Plains Shelterbelt program to curb soil erosion and to stimulate the economy during the Great Depression. Because these hedges resisted insects and diseases better than any other shelterbelt plantings, Osage orange outperformed other trees. Prominent in the shelterbelts, Osage orange suffered from winter-kill north of the Platte River but was otherwise successful (Burton and Barnett 5).

Note was taken that in the drought areas of the Midwest, where Osage orange had been used with success as a screen and windbreak, the tree thrived under the most trying conditions (Wyman 171).

Windbreaks currently receive support from several agricultural agencies to protect soil erosion, offer refuge for wildlife and insects, and reduce the soil depletion by hedgerows. A special initiative was sponsored by the Forest Service in 1934 as the Shelter Belt program or Prairie States Forestry Project. With emergency funding from the president of the United States, the program continued for seven years. During that time 18,600 miles of forest windbreaks were created. In a worldwide search for the hardiest trees and shrubs, Osage orange was one of the trees selected to replenish rows between fallen native trees (Greeley 142-43).

A bonus from the use of Osage orange in windbreaks is that it produces posts for added income, and it grows in very dry situations (Bates, Carlos 14). In South Texas, windbreaks protected citrus groves and diversified farm crops. The windswept plains in the Texas Panhandle also benefited from windbreaks (Foster and Krausz 11).

In addition to cutting fence posts from Osage orange hedgerows after the widespread introduction of barbed wire fences, windbreaks became another successful type of living barriers. In 1982 the Great Plains Agricultural Council endorsed techniques for increasing crop yields adjacent to Osage orange hedgerows while allowing the hedges to remain on the land as wind barriers and game habitats (Gard "Before Barbed Wire";. Great Plains Agricultural Council 106).

A study showed remarkable success in the growth of adjacent field crops when root pruning of mature hedgerows was completed. Pruning the roots reduced their moisture competition with the crops. The Osage orange trees withstood the treatment without any side effects other than a slightly earlier leaf drop. After posts were cut from the hedgerow, new sprouts produced a replacement of fifteen feet in height within five years (Naughton and Capels 120).

Following the Dust Bowl era, Osage orange trees were endorsed as part of the shelterbelt program (Williams, John). In promoting windbreaks, the U.S. Department of Agriculture declared, "Osage orange hedge cannot be excelled." Furthermore, the government agency estimated that on the best soils the Osage orange might return as much as $12.51 per acre. On second class soils, from $3.94 to $11.85 was the estimate per acre. Osage orange was also commended for producing durable posts and growing in very dry situations (Bates, Carlos 16).

A 1943 report found that fields with hedges may support 60 percent more pheasants than those fields without hedges. Fields bordered by brush or shrubs have larger song-bird populations than those where clear fence lines prevail. An added advantage of hedgerows was that insect population, particularly grasshoppers and chinchbugs, appeared to be smaller in areas containing field borders (Steaveson et al. 257-61).

The *Yearbook of Agriculture 1949* indicated that records through January 1, 1948 attested that some 123,191 miles of windbreaks and shelterbelts had been planted since the middle of the nineteenth century. Osage orange hedges planted between 1865 and 1939 by farmers of Kansas accounted for 39,400 miles encouraged by a state bounty (192).

Promoters of windbreaks recalled the glory days of Osage orange hedgerows when shelter was given to millions of pheasant chicks and crows, birds, rabbits, and other animals. Animals were finding refuge in the windbreaks as well (Associated Press, "Scarce in Illinois" Pt. 1, p. 1).

In 1987, Bill Ebert, district conservationist with the U.S. Soil and Water Conservation Service in Kankakee, Illinois, pointed out that an unplanned benefit of Osage orange hedges was soil conservation. "I believe that any standing row of any kind of trees has got to help—not only slow down the wind velocity and its corrosive forces but to slow the moisture loss in the fields as well," Ebert continued (Lyons). Although hedgerows contended with farm crops by shading nearby roots, they benefited wildlife by sheltering shade-tolerant shrubs and briars that serve as food source and cover," Ebert said.

Additional praise was given Osage orange shelters when W. P. Flint completed a four-year study in Illinois. His findings showed that insect damage was definitely reduced where shelters existed for songbirds and parasitic insects (Steaveson et al. 257).

The U.S. Department of Agriculture provided data to show that beneficial effects of tall-growing Osage orange as windbreaks would offset, in terms of crop yield, the more apparent sapping effect (Steaveson et al. 258).

Increasing land values were a deterrent to the campaign to create windbreaks. The warning was given that since the fences and windbreaks had been abandoned, the tree had escaped over a broad range, and "it is a wonder that it has not become an obnoxious wood tree" (Deam, Charles C. *Flora of Indiana* 395.

In 1948, the Osage orange was recognized as a valuable tree used for shelterbelt planting on the Great Plains. The conception of President Roosevelt to plant a wall of millions of trees down the center of the country had been applauded as a noble idea. The project would extend windbreaks 1,000 miles from the Canadian border down to the Panhandle of Texas (Baker 66).

Trees were the backbone of the windbreaks, performing a check on the winds that annually carried away the soil and ensnared moisture. Some authoritative voices predicted failure, but windbreaks flourished and attracted helpful birds as an added function (Baker 64-66).

As Osage orange windbreaks became targets of total bulldozing, Kansas State University botanists began studies of root-pruning. The object was to allow single row Osage orange hedgerows to remain on the land as viable upland game habitat and windbarriers. The hedges with shallow, wide-spreading root systems were consuming large amounts of soil moisture and reducing crop yields in adjacent fields for approximately one and one-half times the tree height. Results showed that increasing crop yields exceeded the cost of the root-pruning (Naughton and Capels 233).

Trees have undertaken a new role as reclamation plantings on land disrupted by strip mining. Farmers on the Great Plains still depend upon the Osage orange as single-row windbreaks (Burton and Barnett 7). Thus, Osage orange trees survive on the plains as important components of windbreaks and shelterbreaks.

Paling Fence, Hunt County, Texas, 1980s
Photograph by James Conrad

7
Favored Wood of Archery

Modern archers are rediscovering the qualities of Osage orange that were appreciated by American Indians centuries ago. For these contemporary bowyers, new-fangled compound bows have lost their appeal, and they now see a bow in every eight-year-old fence post or gnarled Osage orange tree. Mike Rhoades and Mike Bare of Gretna, Nebraska, had made about eighty bows each in 1996 and were eager to try different types of wood. A favorite of both was Osage orange, known as hedge apple in their region (Porter, Larry C3).

"This wood [Osage orange] is considered by modern bowyers as one of the first bow woods available." *The Encyclopedia of Archery* reported. "It has been and still is the first choice for a fine hunting bow," the endorsement continued (Hougham 106).

Three generations ago Robert P. Elmer, a leading American archer in the 1920s, valued Osage orange next to yew as material for bows. He wrote, "Everyone knows the tree, with its great, round, sweet-smelling but utterly useless fruit. One of the best bows I own is of Osage orange. The bow has no sapwood . . . " (*Archery* 243).

The power and elasticity of Osage orange wood is impressive. When the crushing power of certain bow wood was tested in 1966, black locust came in first with 10,800 pounds per square inch, and Osage orange was runnerup with 9,800 pounds per square inch (Hamilton 60).

High-Priced Bow Wood

By monetary investment, Osage orange is one of the two highest-priced woods in the world sought for making bows. The other wood is yew. In terms of the three best woods on the planet valued by archers, Osage orange ranks with yew and tropical lemonwood, the latter wood with no relation to the lemon tree. But unfortunately, a bowyer observed, farmers are cutting Osage orange and grubbing it out by the roots. In Indiana, farmers burn enough prime bow wood over a two-year period to arm a thousand archers. In Illinois, where Osage orange keeps the wind from disturbing the naked soil while enclosing the cattle and crops, thousands of staves could be harvested (Andrews 46).

The international acceptance of Osage orange for modern bows was evidenced in 2003 by book sales climbing to 15,000 in Germany for an English language book on bow making including Osage orange as one of the woods.. A German language version soon followed (Bennish B7).

Modern Archers and Bowyers

In 1927, Fred Bear, then twenty-five, saw a movie in Detroit entitled "Alaskan Adventures," starring Art Young, a bowmaker and namesake of half of the Pope and Young Club, keeper of archery records. Inspired by that movie, Bear joined other Michigan hunters in 1937 for the state's first deer bow-ting season. Bear got a small buck with his own bow made of Osage orange wood and using birch arrows (Porch 11F).

A Dakota Sioux, Jim Welch, considered the loss of traditionally made bows as a missing segment of his past. In 1991, he responded to his sense of loss by starting to make Toh-Kah bows to order in Shakopee, Minnesota. Later he quit his fulltime job to devote himself to his newfound passion. His basic Osage orange bow is 60 to 68 inches in length, drawing 50 to 65 pounds at a maximum draw length of 28 inches. Welch enjoys telling his fellow archers about the virtues of Osage orange. His research revealed that Blackfoot Indians had Osage bows, and they lived 1,000 miles from the nearest Osage orange tree (Atwill, "Gift of a Bow," 66).

The strength of Osage orange amazes archers as material for bows. A few woods have greater compressive and tensile lab-tested strengths, but few, if any, have the rate-of-recovery or snap that Osage orange possesses. One of the secrets in success with Osage orange bows lies in the seasoning of the wood. Walking Elk, an Oklahoma bowmaker, recommends that the wood be seasoned at least a year, preferably two years. "I find that bows will continue to increase in strength up to two years sometimes," Walking Elk contends. Welch gives this testimonial: "I've shot an Osage bow made in 1927. It pulled 50 pounds when new. After three generations of shooters, it has lost only 5 pounds of draw weight" (Atwill, "Gift of the Bow" 66).

Another person who could not resist the lure of bowmaking and of Osage orange was Dean Torges, a doctoral candidate in American literature at Ohio State University in the 1960s. Drawn to woodworking, especially to the 2,500-year history of crafting bows, but starting as a cabinetmaker, he gravitated toward the bowyer's art and soon concluded that Osage orange is the king of bow wood (Bennish 87).

Metaphysical Osage Orange

Among the best known archers and bowmakers in Texas is Ron Hardcastle of Austin. When he was a lad of eleven in Arkansas in 1951, he succumbed to the charisma of Howard Hill demonstrating his mastery of archery in a movie. Then he read in Robert P. Elmer's book written in 1946 about how he had established a flight record with a Texas Osage orange bow in 1928. Osage orange became Hardcastle's favorite bow (Lowman).

Aside from practical uses of Osage orange, Hardcastle finds something especially "poetic and sentimental" in the fact and archers are attracted to the tree. He says archers are of the earth, and so is wood. "Fiber is not of the earth," he emphasizes, referring to artificial material used for bows. "Fiber is of factory." The naturalized Texan sees "magic ingredients in Osage orange . . . a gift from the gods." A science teacher by profession, Hardcastle devotes twelve to thirty hours to making a good Osage orange bow (Lowman).

Hardcastle would like to be reincarnated as a piece of wood, not just any wood, but as an archer's bow made of Osage orange. He believes that inside every Osage orange tree is an unborn bow. Furthermore, once crafted and broken in, a bow gets used to an owner (Hansen 15, 19).

Heritage of Archery

When 10,000 history enthusiasts gathered in St. Charles, Missouri, for Lewis and Clark Heritage Days during a May weekend in 1996, a popular exhibitor was Paul Jarvis, a bow maker from Troy, Illinois. He showed replicas of a bow from Denmark dating back 8,000 years and a North American bow dating to 1660. He told how Indians from Missouri and Kansas had traveled to Oklahoma and Texas to bring back Osage orange tree seedlings to plant. "They [the Indians] knew that kind of wood would be the hardest and longest lasting, so they used it to make their bows and arrows," Jarvis said. (Wohler 1).

Popularity of Osage orange for both bows and arrows is growing among modern bowyers as they gain appreciation for the wood's qualities. Among Native Americans many are returning to their traditional heritage of Osage orange archery. Osage orange now ranks in the top tier of bow woods alongside yew and lemonwood.

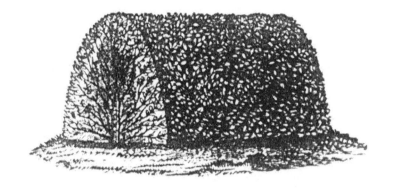

Trimmed Osage Orange Hedge
Horticulturist, 1862

8
Food for Silkworms

Around the world, mulberry leaves come to mind as the food that nurtures silkworms before they begin to incarcerate themselves inside cocoons that produce strands destined for valued fabrics. When Osage orange was introduced outside American Indian tribes and assigned to the Moraceae family, in which the mulberry tree is a prominent member, speculation began that Osage orange might be substituted for mulberry leaves in silkworms' diet since the two trees were of close kin.

Osage Orange Feeds Silkworms

As early as 1836, agricultural publications had foreseen the potential of Osage orange as food for silk worms. *The Farmers' Register* in 1836 had this report in an article on the substitution of Osage orange for mulberry: "The late frosts that unexpectedly destroy the young leaves of the mulberry, and would leave the silk grower without means of keeping alive his newly hatched worms are of rare occurrence; but whenever they do occur, without sufficient precautions, the worms must perish—and the whole business of that year be at an end. Hence the great value of any plant that even furnishes a cheap and sufficient substitute for the mulberry, during the short duration of such seasons of scarcity" ("Of the Leaves of the Maclure").

As the federal government began to promote American silk production, the use of Osage orange leaves as the diet staple of caterpillars took on new value in the economy. The number of silk mills operating in the United States was 1882 was 380. One testimonial came from Professor Riley, entomologist of the Department of Agriculture in Washington, D.C.: "Every year's experience with the Maclura confirms all that I have said of its value as silkworm food. Silk that I have had reeled from a race of worms fed on it now for eleven consecutive years is the very best quality while the tests made at the recent silk fair at Philadelphia showed that in some instances a less weight of cocoons spun by *Maclurafed* was required for a pound of reeled silk than of cocoons from mulberry-fed worms" (Davidson, Mary, *Bombyx Mori* 50).

In Dayton, Ohio, when feeding Osage orange leaves to silkworms came into vogue, families took up the culture during the early 1870s but soon recognized that the expense of labor made competition futile with the less expensive exports from the Old World (Werthner 192).

Domestic Silk Production

The author of a history of silk culture in 1885 warned that it would be unwise to pass over Osage orange, a food already grown in the Western states, and refuse to utilize it in the production of silk. The writer had observed that if care is taken in handling Osage orange leaves on thorny limbs, there would be no "insuperable objection" to the alternative to mulberry. She noted that the worms seem to learn the same caution by winding dexterously around the stem and avoiding the thorns. (Davidson; Mary, *Silk, Its History* 145).

As encouragement for domestic silk production, the government shipped eggs to any citizen making the request. These eggs would hatch into silkworms. Julia Rogers received a shipment about 1880, and twenty-five years later, she wrote an account of her experiences in *The Tree Book*. Julia and a girl friend fed lettuce and mulberry leaves to the little caterpillars, but later nothing but Osage orange leaves were available in a quantity great enough to appease the worms' enormous appetites. The girls risked injury from the thorns as they cut leafy twigs. As the worms began to spin, the twigs were soon adorned with fat cocoons. When the cocoons hatched, Julia Rogers wrote, "The dead twigs blossomed with white moths whose beauty and tremulous motion passed description" (Lembke 196-97).

In recording her memories with Osage orange and the silk industry, Julia Rogers wrote, "I had a personal experience with the Osage orange. The leaves are food for silkworms, so the nurseryman told us, and we could have silkworms' eggs from Washington for the asking. . . . Silkworms and Osage orange offered a combination and suggested possibilities which set our imaginations on fire. Lettuce leaves suffice for the young caterpillars—then the little mulberry hues, but the lusty white worms so ghastly naked and dreadful to see, and so ravenous, we fed with Osage orange leaves, cut at the risk of much damage from ugly thorns and with much weariness. But what were present discomforts compared with the excellency of the hope set before us! Not Solomon in all his glory was arrayed as we expected to be. And the worms—while we loathed them, we counted them and ministered to their needs.

"At last our labours ended. They began to spin, and soon the denuded twigs were thickly studded with the yellow excrements of the translated larvae, to the relief and wonder of all concerned. But ever as we wondered, the dread twigs blossomed with white moths whose beauty and tremulous motion passed description. We were filled into a state by the spectacle.

"'Whom the gods would destroy they first make mad.' A hard-hearted but well-informed neighbour told us that the broken cocoons were worthless for silk. 'You'd ought to have scalded 'em as soon as they spun up.' Clouds and thick darkness shut out the day. We refused to be comforted.

"This explains why the mere mention of the Osage orange tree, or the sight of a hedge, however thrifty, brings to my mind a haunting suggestion of 'old unhappy far-off things'" (Rogers, Julia, *Tree Book* 243-44).

Rogers concluded, "Experiments of feeding Osage orange leaves to silk worms have been successfully made at different times, but nowhere in America has silk culture succeeded. Since the white mulberry is a hardy tree and its foliage is the basis of the silk-growing industry in the Old World, it is futile to look for substitutes in the Osage orange" (Rogers, Julia, *Trees Worth Knowing* 100).

Mary Matilda Davidson, another silk culturalist, warned in using Osage orange leaves for silkworm fodder, "the . . . milky and succulent terminal leaves should be thrown aside and not used, as they are apt to induce flaccidity and disease" (*Bombyx Mori* 3).

Another Failed Venture

Once again Osage orange was at the center of a failed venture, just as it had been with living hedges. Despite the abundance of Osage orange leaves and federal support, caterpillar culture in the United States never triumphed, and Americans today still rely upon silk imported from other countries.

9
Famous Osage Orange Trees

Wherever Osage orange trees thrive, there is likely to be a single tree that, through its location, appearance, or brush with history, has garnered some measure of fame in the region. State champion trees and other famous trees are likely to be found in towns, on campuses, and around farmsteads where people take notice of them, making these the easiest to locate and measure. Furthermore, the really big trees simply do not stand out in a forest background (Winingham). Some of the champions are identified in the alphabetical listing of states in Chapter 12. The following vignettes tell the story of various Osage orange trees that have somehow escaped obscurity.

Many other Osage orange trees enjoy fame in their neighborhoods. Their size or their historical associations usually determine their celebrity. Perhaps this list will grow as Americans become more aware of their regional Osage orange trees.

Patrick Henry Tree

The tree at Patrick Henry's estate in Brookneal, Virginia, became the national champion Osage Orange in 1972, with measurements of 24'6" circumference, 51' height, and 92' spread (Godfrey, Robert 482).

Freedman's Bois d'Arc in Texas

On June 20, 1865, masters and slaves from fourteen plantations in western Brazoria County assembled in the shade of two bois d'arc trees to receive news that would forever change their relationships. They would hear the announcement from the Bureau of Freedman informing slaves that they were free men and women and advising them of their rights and responsibilities. When nearby Galveston surrendered the day before, Union officers brought tidings that President Lincoln's Emancipation Proclamation had freed slaves in January 1863.

The announcement on Brazoria Plantation was made by a spokesman for the Bureau of Freedman, who climbed up one of the two bois d'arc trees growing in front of the John B. Sweeny, Jr. plantation house a mile west of Old Ocean. Today only one of the bois d'arc trees still stands, serving as a monument to the historic event occurring here. The surviving bois d'arc tree is listed by the Texas Forestry Service as one of the famous trees of Texas (Texas Forest Service *Famous Trees*).

Starhill Forest, Illinois

An Osage orange tree named Cannonball for its supersize fruits attracts attention at the Starhill Forest Arboretum in Menard County, Illinois. Guy and Edie Sternberg bought twenty acres and started their private arboretum here. Tours linger at the Osage orange tree in the Sternbergs' front yard, where Guy enjoys telling stories about the tree being driven south by the advance of glaciers, becoming isolated while most of the other plants reclaimed their former ranges. When asked if there is any truth in the old wives' tale that pungent Osage orange fruit will ward off insects, Sternberg offers his opinion with a smile, "They work best when you drop them directly on the bug" (Young 21).

McCree's Little Panhandle Tree

Famous in the Texas Panhandle, McCree's tree symbolizes the tenacity of residents in that region. On the treeless windswept High Plains, pioneers lived in dugouts or in covered wagons. No landmarks interrupted the horizon from the edge of the caprock to the Canadian River breaks. Thomas McCree claimed a section of land west of Panhandle, Texas, in 1881 and brought his new wife to their home there. According to tradition, Mrs. McCree told her husband she could tolerate the loneliness, but a thing of beauty would be essential in their new environment (Carson County Historical Committee, letter and marker application to Texas Historical Commission 27 March 1963).

Hearing of McCree's determination to plant a tree, neighbors scoffed, "Surely the high winds of the plains would have blown in a seed decades earlier, and if trees could grow here, one would have taken root long ago" (*Amarillo Daily News*. 28 May 1970).

Despite the negative attitudes, McCree travelled thirty-five miles to Turkey Track Range and brought home in his wagon a small, scraggly Osage orange. He planted the tree at the north edge of a buffalo wallow known as Creek Lake. Although the tree lived, proving the naysayers wrong, its stature was not as mature as most Osage oranges, but green leaves sprouted each spring. In 1963, Texas Governor John Connally dedicated a historical marker recognizing the tree (Carson County Historical Committee, letter to Texas Historical Survey Committee, 7 March 1963).

In the 1970s a negligent airborne cropduster released poison on McCree's tree, and it soon died. A new tree, offspirng of the original plant, grew just outside the fenced area. Replanted at the site of the parent tree, it also died (Porter, Jack. "Famed Area Tree Feared Near Death." *Amarillo Daily News*. n.d.). In 1990, Moggie R. McCray, chair of the Carson County Historical Commission, found a replacement for McCree's tree, and on March 19, 1990, the Texas Historical Commission approved a supplemental plate attached to the original marker post and later dedicated (McCray, Moggie R. Letter to Fred Tarpley, 14 July 1990).

Today ranchers who once got their bearings from McCree's tenacious tree now enjoy shade trees surrounding their farm and ranch homes, but McCree's Osage orange remains the symbol of pioneer determination in the Panhandle (Carson County Historical Commission).

Log in New York Museum

In the late nineteen hundreds, visitors to the Museum of Natural History in New York were taking note of an Osage orange specimen in the Jessup Collection of North American Woods. The log, grown in southern Arkansas, was twenty-four and one-half inches in diameter and displaying 134 layers of annual growth.

Big Max the Bois d'Arc

In the early days of the Bois d'Arc Bash celebration in Commerce, a search was conducted for the largest bois d'arc tree within the city limits. The champion was found in a fence row in a residential section. Called Max or Big Max by local citizens as a shortening of *Maclura,* the scientific nomenclature, the tree has been registered as a famous and historic tree by American Forests..The tree is recognized as the second largest Osage orange in Texas.

Tree Trunk in Commerce, Texas

Jerry Lytle was on a daily jog approaching South Sulphur River two miles from Commerce when he spied the massive trunk of an Osage orange. It had been removed by the highway department from the course of the river after falling into the watercourse somewhere upstream. Chainsaw marks on the tree indicated that someone attempted to cut the trunk into smaller pieces until he or she had discovered the saw blade was no match for the tough wood. The futile task was abandoned. Lytle called Fred Tarpley, then director of the annual Commerce Bois d'Arc Bash, to recommend that the remains of an immense Osage orange tree be taken to the city park in Commerce. With the cooperation of Randy Manning and the Pine Company in providing transportation and of Bill Funderburk of the city staff for determining the park location of the trophy tree, it was installed as a new attraction in the Commerce City Park.

The park was soon full of local children who took a balanced walk down the length of the trunk, crawled through a tunnel in the lower end of the hollow trunk, and examined the hard, gnarled wood while their parents admired the enormous specimen of Osage orange (*Commerce Journal.* 4 Sept. 1988, p. 5A).

L. Q. C. Lamar Home

The massive Osage orange tree growing at the former home of L. Q. C. Lamar, one of Mississippi's most renowned statesmen, is believed to have been planted about the time the house was built in 1857. Lamar served in all three branches of the federal government: as congressman, secretary of the interior, and as a Supreme Court justice (Farish).

New York's Great Trees

Among the Osage orange trees listed ac the great trees of New York City are those in Knolls Crescent, Souyhen Duyull, in the Bronx; those linked to notable people in an Osage orange grove on Staten Island; others at a historic landmark in Crecheron Park, Bayside, Queens; and a stand of trees near Lemon Creek on Staten Island, reportedly planned by Frederick Law Olmsted, designer of Central Park (Carmody 27).

Hampden-Sydney's Romantic Tree

In the back yard of Gen. Sam Wilson's home on the campus of Hampden-Sydney College in southern Virginia, an Osage orange tree has witnessed many a romantic wedding. One of them was an afterword to the Vietnam era novel *We Were Soldiers Once and Young,* which became a popular film. A young Army captain, Thomas C. Metsker, died after he gave his place in a helicopter to a more severely wounded officer. Twenty-five years later, the author of the novel wrote a story for *U.S. News & World Report* on Metsker's heroic death, and Metsker's daughter called the author, telling him she would be at a reunion of her father's military company on Veterans Day weekend 1990. There the writer met the beautiful daughter of the war hero. The writer's wife later died of cancer, and on Oct. 24, he and Metsker's daughter were married under the spreading arms of the ancient Osage orange tree at Hampden-Sydney (Galloway G2). The legacy of the tree is well known to students and their friends.

Edmond, Oklahoma

The most famous Osage tree in Edmond, Oklahoma, was planted in 1906 at the original site of Mitch Park. So special is the tree that the Oklahoma Forestry Service checks its well being annually. The female tree resides at the northwest corner of North Boulevard and Campbell on the original site of Edmond High School (www.waymarking.com/waymarks/WM92GT)Bois'darc) tree) Edmond_OK) Retrieved 21 June 2010.

Kewanee, Illinois

In 1976, an Osage orange tree was recognized as probably the oldest tree in Kewanee, Illinois. With a circumference of fifteen feet and a height of fifty feet, the tree was once part of a hedge. The tree stood in front of the

General Telephone Company's high tower (Randall and Clepper 80).

Texas Prize Logs

Like prize-winning cattle that have taken blue ribbons and top bids at livestock exhibitions, the Texas prize logs are no longer around to bask in their glory. Although the Texas prize logs were not alive even when they attained fame in newspaper headlines, the logs deserve notice as Osage orange specimens that enjoyed brief acclaim.

In 1903 when E. H. R. Green, president of the Texas Midland Railroad, offered a prize for the longest piece of Osage orange piling, P. S. Williams of Howland, Lamar County, claimed the award. Mr. Williams delivered to the railroad an Osage orange piling timber that measured fifty-six feet after it was trimmed. With a diameter of two feet at the butt and ten inches of thickness at the opposite end, the timber was so straight that a tapeline stretched from the butt to the little end touched the body of the log at every point ("Prize for Bois d'Arc." *Dallas Morning News.* 22 Dec. 1903). The durability of Osage orange in earth and water made its logs ideal for bridge pilings.

Another recognized Osage orange log from the early twentieth century was on display by Bounds and McGraw from McFadden, four miles north of Nevada, Texas, in Collin County. Estimated to be about 150 years old, it measured four feet at the base and was twelve feet long The log, valued at $150 in 1912, was called the largest ever seen in this region, and it was to be cut into wagon falloes, a popular use of Osage orange wood at the time ("150-Year-Old Bois d'Arc Log).

Washington, D.C.

A frequently visited tree in the national capital is the ancient Osage orange at the Soldiers' and Airmen's Home in northwest Washington. Considered one of the oldest and most beautiful trees on the grounds, it grows at the Lincoln cottage (Choukas-Bradley 48-49).

Osage Orange Grave Marker
Ingram Hart Cemetery in Delta County, Texas
Photograph by: Fred Tarpley

10
Celebrating the Osage Orange

Annual festivities focusing on the Osage orange tree occur annually throughout areas where the tree is prominent on the landscape. Osage Orange Day has been a renowned spring event at Illinois College since 1882. Other events have recent origins, and one plantation in Georgia suspended its festival after unsuspecting celebrants were struck on the head by falling horse apples. It is wise to go online for details of individual events before making travel plans to attend the Osage orange celebrations.

Osage Orange Day at Illinois College

The nation's oldest continuous celebration of Osage orange takes place each May at Illinois College, the institution that lured Jonathan Baldwin Turner from New England to the prairies, where he experimented with Osage orange living fences. The Osage orange-themed campus event began in the spring of 1882.

The tree and its trimmed hedges were prominent in the campus landscape. With the passing of years, the aging hedges lost their handsome appearance as the campus boundary, and the administration decided that they needed to be removed by grubbings. Those familiar with the arduous labor involved in attempting to remove the tenacious hedges decided that student manpower was needed. The fact that Professor Turner attended the grubbing, although he was no longer on the faculty, indicates his approval of the event (Frank 85).

The college president offered a college holiday if students would participate in the grubbing assignment. Professor Turner arrived, telling the boys that it would be a cool day for labor and advising them to procure their axes and spades. The boys worked from morning until four in the afternoon until all of the stubborn Osage orange trees had been grubbed. (Rammelkamp 301). After the college community enjoyed a day of camaraderie and pleasure, students issued a general demand for the observance of Osage Orange day the following year (Frank 56). The celebration quickly became a tradition for students, faculty, and community.

In 1891, despite student protests, Osage Orange Day was rescheduled on commencement weekend (Rammelkamp 308), and it continues on that date. President Edward Allan Tanner and the faculty responded wholeheartedly, and the Osage orange celebration is now a time-honored event. At the inception of the special day, Illinois schools and colleges did not have sports teams, and the Osage orange event began to focus on athletic contests. Oratory was also an emphasis of the annual program.

After a century and two score years, Osage orange day at Illinois College is the oldest celebration in the country inspired by the Osage tree. The annual event still draws the college community, the town of Jacksonville, and visitors to Illinois College each spring (Carriel 86).

Bulloch Hall, Roswell, Georgia

An annual Osage Orange Festival is held, usually in September at historic Bulloch Hall, an antebellum Greek Revival mansion, in Roswell, Georgia (Campos, Carlos H1).

Signs warn visitors to be on the lookout for falling apples from twenty-one Osage orange trees surrounding Bulloch Hall in Roswell, Georgia. They usually start dropping between August and October (Campos, Carlos). Local lore explains that the trees were originally planted to protect the mansion from insects (Stepp H3).

Several years ago a visitor from Florida was hit on the head by a falling fruit. Pam Billingsley, director of the property, recalls the incident. The Floridian was knocked to the ground, thinking that somebody had thrown a ball at her. When paramedics arrived at the scene, the woman declined to be taken to the hospital.

Barbara Gross, former director of Bulloch Hall, said that an Osage orange once came crashing through the back window of her parked Mercedes. Though officials said the action had nothing to do with failing fruit, Bulloch Hall decided not to host the Osage Orange Festival in 1995 while they tried out a variety of new events (Campos, Carlos H1).

Atlanta Arbor Day

On Atlanta's first Arbor Day in 1933, Miss Hattie Rainwater, a local teacher, organized the first celebration that led to the creation of Atlanta Memorial Park on Northside Drive. Sketchy reports of the inaugural events claim that Eleanor Roosevelt donated the first Arbor Day tree, a stately Osage orange tree growing in the park today (Park Pride Atlanta and Susan Newell, Atlanta city arborist).

From a one-day celebration Arbor, Day has mushroomed into a full week of activities. The Osage orange tree still stands in a changing Atlanta (Crenshaw D11).

Bois d'Arc Bash

The twenty-fifth annual Bois d'Arc Bash will be celebrated in Commerce, Texas, on September 24-26, 2010. In her designation signed on July 27, 1994, Texas Governor Ann Richards "proclaim[ed] Commerce, Texas, as the Bois d'Arc Capital of Texas and charge[d] the citizenry of Commerce, Texas, herewith all Bois d'Arc Ambassadors at large with the responsibility of sharing bois d'arc lore, information, and general Texana wherever they go."

Earlier in her proclamation, the governor had stated, "The bois d'arc tree is indigenous to a total of 10,000 square miles in a narrow boot-shaped area of rich bottom lands in Northeast Texas, Southeast Oklahoma, and Southwestern Arkansas or roughly the Red River Valley."

She continued, "Commerce, Texas, has, since 1986, celebrated the colorful history of the bois d'arc tree, as well as the town's rich heritage associated with it, every September in a commemoration called the Bois d'Arc Bash" (Richards, Ann).

After a successful centennial celebration of the incorporation of Commerce in 1985, the city and chamber of commerce wanted to continue the festivities on the third weekend in September of each year to coincide with the date of incorporation. A theme was sought, but towns in East Texas had already claimed the most obvious motifs: roses in Tyler, cotton in Greenville, yams in Gilmer, and even the fire ant in Marshall.

A proposal was submitted to celebrate the bois d'arc tree, whose prominent ripened fruit was beginning to fall each September by the third weekend. "The very foundation of Commerce, Texas, rests on bois d'arc," one supporter of that theme pointed out, alluding to the fact that the oldest local buildings rested on bois d'arc blocks until cinder blocks began to replace them. When researchers found that Commerce lay smack in the middle of the only area in the world that is the tree's native habitat, there was no question that the festival would honor bois d'arc. Dr. Jack Bell, head of the local university journalism department, applied his love of alliteration in coining Bois d'Arc Bash.

Each September the celebration enlivens the town with a parade, vendors lining the downtown streets, barbecues, automobile shows, a 5K run, a wine tasting, entertainment stages, a dance on the square, and many contests and displays featuring the bois d'arc tree. For three consecutive years, Bud Hanzlick, the nation's leading crafter of bois d'arc furniture, came from Kansas to sell his unique furniture that remains in homes throughout the area. Texas bowyer Ron Hardcastle of Austin came to display his bois d'arc bows and to demonstrate his skill in shooting a bois d'arc arrow into a bull's eye.

Students competed for prizes by coming forward with the largest and smallest horse apples. Art classes decorated horse apples in stylish themes. Visitors competed in bowling with bois d'arc apples or attempting to drive nails into seasoned bois d'arc logs.

Local craftsmen offered their writing pens lathed from bois d'arc wood, their bois d'arc walking canes, their home-baked flowers made from slices of horse apples, their Texas-shaped bois d'arc clocks, and horse apples guaranteed to rid homes of cock roaches and other unwanted pests. New items crafted from bois d'arc trees appeared each year.

Historians James Conrad and Janet Peek conducted tours along Bois d'Arc Street to point out heritage sites including two rows of bois d'arc trees planted by an early land developer. Conrad wrote an informative book on the bois d'arc tree released at an early bash and still available, and Fred Tarpley, founder of the bash, plans to release

148 Fred Tarpley

Wood Eternal. The Story of Osage Orange, Bois d'Arc, etc., a comprehensive 350-page book based on thirty years of research, at the 2010 bash.

Osage Orange Day Program
Illinois College, Jacksonville, 1891

11
Famous Folk and Osage Orange

The ties of Thomas Jefferson; Lewis and Clark and other nineteenth century explorers; Thomas Nuttall and other early botanists; Jonathan Baldwin Turner and John S. Wright; and other Americans associated with Osage orange are part of national history. Encounters with Osage orange by other personalities also deserve mention.

Without doubt, some of these famous folk enjoy their acclaim only in their provincial circles. Nevertheless, wherever the Osage orange is found, there are likely to be individuals who have achieved some degree of celebrity because of their involvement with the Osage orange tree.

Noah of Ark Fame

The biblical patriarch who survived the world's greatest flood would be astonished to find himself so firmly linked to the Osage tree through folk etymology. When Americans heard the pronunciation of bois d'arc as "board ark," they found meaning in an association with boards and a nautical ark rather than the French word *arc* referring to the bows Indians created from the wood of a particular tree..

Therefore, the only meaningful reference, as every biblical scholar should know, would be to Noah's ark. The strength and durability of Osage orange reinforced the idea that its wood was used to withstand the flood, providing a reliable floating refuge for Noah's family and the pairs of animals he had taken aboard.

Newspaper and magazine articles have long reported this misconception, and a new professor of English at Southern Methodist University in Dallas soon discovered that many locals firmly believed that ancestors of rows of bois d'arc lining Lovers Lane near the campus had made an ancient sacrifice to provide wood for Noah's ark (Spiegelman 365).

Patrick Henry

The story told at Patrick Henry's home in Virginia during tours and in publications is that the champion Osage orange growing in the yard was one of the early saplings sent to the East by Meriwether Lewis in 1805 after the first shipment of 1804 had failed to survive plantings. Henry died at the home in 1799; therefore, a mathematical puzzle has developed with the claim made about the tree's age in relationship to Lewis' discovery of Osage orange, Henry's death, and other aspects of the story.

The story is also told that after Henry died in 1799 and was buried at the base of the tree, his physician went to his patient's grave in deep sorrow and with agonized breast beating. The physician had been unable to save Patrick Henry's life (Thomas). There is little argument that the tree is a magnificent specimen of Osage orange in Virginia, but much of the story generates doubt.

A Virginia newspaper report claimed that the Patrick Henry Osage orange tree was more than 400 years old in 1996 (Williams, Jerry G 10). That calculation today would make it 200 years older than the Lewis and Clark Expedition, which first introduced the tree to areas beyond the Midwestern Indian tribes five years after Patrick Henry died in 1799. No one questions the massive size of the Osage orange tree at Red Hill and its qualification as a national big tree, but whether it dates to the time of Patrick Henry and beyond is troubling (Springfield E-1).

The Osage orange tree in the yard of the Patrick Henry home at Brookneal, Virginia, is in the American Forest Association's Social Register of Big Trees (Butler 28).

Queen Victoria

Thomas Meehans, an early Philadelphia botanist and editor of *Meehans' Monthly*, in 1893 wrote about an experience with Queen Victoria when he was an apprentice in Kew Gardens in London. He recalls the event in these words: "The writer of this paragraph once saw Queen Victoria biting at an Osage ball, under an assurance from Sir William Hooker [director of Kew Gardens], who was evidently in earnest, that they 'were eaten by the natives.'" Meehans was opening a barrel of Osage orange fruits from America when the perfume of their fruits wafted to the royal nostrils of Queen Victoria, who was touring the gardens with the director. Meehans saw the queen throw the fruit to the ground after she bit into it, the white juice dripping onto her royal dress. He heard Hooker remark, "I understand they are a delicacy in America. We must not know their proper recipe for preparing them" ("The Osage Orange. Value of Scientific Facts" 77).

Meehans added that at the conclusion of the Civil War ". . . on the opening up of communication with the Southern States, the answer to an application for seed brought the reply that 'it was too late, the balls have been all eaten by the negroes.' This is all that *Meehans' Monthly* can tell 'an inquirer' about the Osage Orange as an edible fruit. There ought to be more to be told, and the information would be welcome" (*Meehans' Monthly* 5 (1895):17; "Fruits and Vegetables," *Meehans' Monthly.* 10 (October 1900): 5

Davy Crockett

In December 1835, Davy Crockett's wagon train from Tennessee arrived in Clarksville, Texas. He enjoyed a few days of hunting bears in Fannin County in a grove of trees laden with honey, an area later becoming the town of Honey Grove. Then he made his way southward to meet his fate at the Alamo.

En route to San Antonio, he stopped in San Augustine and wrote a letter dated January 9, 1836, to his daughter Margaret and to her husband, Wiley Flowers. The connection of the coonskin hero to the Osage orange lies in the following sentence: "I expect in all probability to settle on the Bodark or Choctaw Bayou of the Red River. That I have no doubt is the richest country in the world good Land and plenty of timber and the best springs and good mill streams good range clear water every appearance of good health and game plenty" (McLean 8:Item 618).

If Crockett had survived the Alamo, he might have settled, as the letter indicates, in Fannin County at the center of the native habitat for Osage orange.

Charles Goodnight, Cattle King

In addition to establishing the first cattle outfit in the Texas Panhandle at Palo Duro Canyon in 1876 and being the namesake of the Goodnight-Loving Trail, Charles Goodnight (1836-1929) also became a legendary figure for his association with the world's first chuck wagon. He invented the first chuck wagon and became eternally linked to Osage orange by restyling an Army surplus wagon with Osage orange lumber that could absorb bumpy rides across the prairie. He added the distinctive sloping chuck box at the rear of the wagon (*New Handbook of Texas* 3:242). The original chuck box may be viewed in the Panhandle-Plains Museum in Canyon (Davis, Walt).

In 1866 Goodnight and his partner, Oliver Loving had organized a cattle drive over a route that became the Goodnight-Loving Trail. The route ran from Young County, Texas, southwest to the Horsehead Crossing on the Pecos River, to Fort Sumner, New Mexico, and on northward to Colorado. It was later one of the most heavily used cattle trails in the Southwest (*New Handbook of Texas* 241, 244).

T. E. Ball, Bois d'Arc King

"The Bois d'Arc King of America." That is what local newspapers called T. E. Ball of Farmersville, Texas, when he died in 1931. In an interview with his son, W. B. Jack Ball, at the Texas Institute of Cultures in San Antonio on March 11, 1983, more than enough details were related to confirm that title (MacMillan).

The elder Ball, born in Kentucky on the Cumberland River, came to Texas with his wife, Mary Philpot, in 1881. They moved to Farmerville, about forty miles north of Dallas, in 1885. T. E. lived comfortably with profits from his farm implement business until he was burned out twice. Forsaking machinery sales, he began to look for other enterprises which would restore his livelihood.

Six miles west of Farmersville in Pilot Grove, T. E. became interested in a creek bottom about two miles wide and twelve miles long. There stood an astounding number of native bois d'arc trees.

T. E. found similar growths of the tree eastward near Bonham, near Ladonia, and all the way to Idabel, Oklahoma, across the Red River. He recognized the demand for fence posts, house blocks, bridge pilings, and other necessities by a growing population in his region. He decided that harvesting bois d'arc would be a good business to enter.

The first railroads built had no law requiring fences along their rights-of-way. After livestock owners protested that trains were killing their animals, legislation in the 1880s began to require fences. T. E. provided bois d'arc fence posts for "practically all of West Texas and Western Oklahoma." In one order he sold the Missouri Pacific a shipment of 100,000 fence posts for its right-of-way through Arkansas.

T. E. sold bois d'arc posts and foundation blocks in rail carload lots only. And he supplied gigantic Texas lumber yards like William Cameron and Lyon-Gray. T. E. made a fortune from the tree, but he lost it in the panic of 1914 and again in the panic of 1921 when income from cotton collapsed after he had invested heavily in high-priced land at a time cotton was selling high during World War I.

Then concrete started replacing wooden house blocks. Furthermore, the large stands of bois d'arc were just about exhausted by entrepreneurs by the time of T. E.'s death, his son explained (MacMillan).

John Nance Garner

The story about the Lone Star State exporting Osage orange all over the country was a Texas brag John Nance Garner enjoyed extolling as vice president of the United States in the 1930s. Garner was a native of Red River County, Texas, located near the center of the native range of Osage orange. Until 1872, steamboats came up the Mississippi River, continued northwestward on the Red River, entered Caddo Lake a few miles above Shreveport, Louisiana, and exited the lake to reach the last port of call, Jefferson, Texas, on Big Cypress River. Removal of a log jam from Red River and competition from railroads ended the steamboat traffic.

Garner enjoyed spinning tales he had heard about farmers hauling their cotton to the Jefferson wharf, where bales were loaded onto boats for destinations afar, to textile mills in the northeast, and to cities like St. Louis and New Orleans on the Mississippi River. When farmers learned of the demand for the heavy, seed-filled fruit of the Osage orange, they loaded into their wagons not only with bales of ginned cotton but also with baseball-size Osage oranges. Landowners on the Midwest prairies were eager to obtain the seeds for planting living hedges .

On the Jefferson docks, carts were filled with horse apples, as the fruit of the Osage orange was called locally. Shippers were partial to this freight because the Osage orange balls added ballast for the steamboats. The ballast was unloaded and sold at ports along the waterways, where heavy machinery replaced the fruit with bales of cotton (Lawrence, C. Walker). Colleagues of Garner reported that the vice president never tired of telling the story of Texas bois d'arc seed.

Grandfather of Meriwether Lewis

The grandfather of Meriwether Lewis of Lewis and Clark fame was granted a 6,000 acre parcel of land in Albemarle, Virginia, in 1740. At the site of the original structure at Locust Hill, an Osage orange tree, called "magnificent" by the locals, spread its branches beyond the roof of the house. The Lewis home remained in the hands of his family for 250 years until it was purchased by Dolly Boswell. Inside the home is an Indian bow made of wood from the Osage orange (Walsh 4-5).

John Adams of Franklin, Tennessee

In Franklin, Tennessee, a local exhibit honors John Adams, a graduate of West Point and once a rising star in the U.S. Army. He died in the Battle of Franklin in 1864. His military advance near the Carter House was thwarted by a thorny barricade of Osage orange shrubs. After guiding some of his command around the formidable obstacle, Adams led a charge against a portion of the Union line held by the 65th infantry. ("Losz Exhibit Spotlights

Adams' Life"). Adams' heroic charge, not even thwarted by the stubborn barrier of Osage orange, lingers today as an indelible memory of a courageous leader in the Battle of Franklin.

Col. Bob Lee

Soon after the Civil War, a deadly feud developed between the Lee and Peacock families in a Northeast Texas area known as the Four Corners. The name came from the convergence of the tips of four counties: Grayson, Fannin, Collin, and Hunt. Bob Lee, a former Confederate officer fell out with Union Reconstruction authorities in 1867, and bloodshed resulted, stirring animosity between the Lee and the Peacock clans as well as involving other families in the region.

When Bob Lee was waylaid and shot on May 24, 1869, and Lewis Peacock was killed on June 13, 1871, the feud came to an end. The Lee family placed a six-foot Osage orange tree trunk at the head of Lee's grave. Years later, the Osage orange monument was replaced by a stone memorial (Hodge), but to this day Colonel Lee of the Lee-Peacock Feud is still associated with the massive Osage orange trunk that marked his grave and attracted attention for many years.

Recent historians have reinterpreted the events as having been a series of incidents representing more lawlessness than feud at the Four Corners (Smallwood, Crouch, & Peacock).

Bois d'Arc Doerle

The first man to manufacture bois d'arc wagons in Dallas was Bois d'Arc Doerle, a blacksmith who earned his nickname because of his involvement with the stalwart tree and wagon manufacturing in Dallas.

Doerle arrived in Dallas the same year as the city welcomed its first railroad, 1872, and established his shop where the new Dallas County courts building now stands.

His wagons, crafted with reliable, sturdy wood, repeatedly won blue ribbons at county fairs, and their maker's name was recognized as a household name far and wide (Acheson).

Hattie Rainwater

A school teacher, Miss Hattie Rainwater, gained a place in Atlanta, Georgia, history when she planted an Osage orange at the first observance of Arbor Day in that city in 1913 in Atlanta Memorial Park near Northside Drive (Crenshaw E11). Hattie and her tree are remembered at annual Arbor Day observances.

James A. Michener

As the Texas Sesquicentennial approached in 1986, Gov. William P. Clements invited James A. Michener to come to the state as a writer in residence to complete a novel titled *Texas*. With careful research, Michener used a fictional framework of determining the essence of Texas as a fictional sesquicentennial committee reviewed the history and visited every significant locale in the state.

The research files for the novel are now part of the Center for American History at the University of Texas at Austin. It is possible to witness Michener's attraction to Osage orange in the *Texas* papers and his meticulous measures taken to achieve accuracy.

Michener's draft contains this paragraph: "The first amazement was a tree that the locals called bodark, a wonderful, thorny thing which produced enormous green apple-like fruit of thick skin and absolutely no use to men or their cattle. The proper name, of course, was bois-d'arc, later to be known as Osage orange, and what made this particular tree memorable was that on its branches devoid of leaves clustered no less than forty huge round balls of green plant life with no detectable means of sustenance. 'Mistletoe,' Jubal said, and Mattie was pleased when her son climbed the bodark to detach a cluster for her study."

Attached research notes from Michener's assistants offered three comments. For the bodark tree, the comment was "The tree in question here, *Maclura pomifera*, is dioecious, which simply means they are either male or female. Both flower, but only the females bear fruit. Thus in a natural stand you should only expect about half of the specimens to have these horse apples, as they are commonly called in Texas."

For mistletoe, the comment was "This description does not fit mistletoe; it fits *Tilandaia recurysta*, which is an epiphytic plant in the Bromeliad (or pineapple family). Everybody calls it ball moss." In the manuscript *mistletoe* was replaced by *ball moss."*

The third comment, also referring to mistletoe, reported, "I checked the dictionary for this, and since the Spanish moss does not grow out of the ground and does not have a stem, perhaps it should not be called a vine. It, too, is epiphytic, which simply means that it grows on something else, but is not parasitic like mistletoe.

One other change was made in the draft of the paragraph: "enormous green apple-like fruit" was revised as "horse apples, enormous green fruit" ("Michener Papers" Center for American History). Michener was determined to get Texas botany right.

T. E. Crowley, the Bois d'Arc Man

T. E. Crowley, who lived on Highway 24 about five miles south of Paris, Texas, caught the attention of motorists who spotted his massive gate west of the thoroughfare. Atop two massive Osage orange tree trunks standing as sentinels beside the fence opening was another handsome specimen of the distinctive wood spanning the space between the pair that supported it.

As if the gate were not enough to give the landowner the name of "the Bois d'Arc Man," anyone who went inside his impressive ranch style home and admired his bois d'arc flooring or read *Dallas Morning News* columns about him in "Tolbert's Texas" was provided convincing information that Mr. Crowley deserved the title.

Writing to Walworth Harrison, Hunt County historian, Crowley stated, "If you are interested in 'bodark,' if you ever come to Paris, I wish you could go and look at the home I built. . . . I put two bodark floors [living room and hall] in it and one pecan. I also have a bell post there that is shaped like a bell, and I have a large bell hanging in the fork of it. As you go toward town, I have two large bodark bows over two of my gates. You can find nearly any shape of bodark that you want to if you look long enough. It took us nearly two years to find my bell post, and then I found it right close to me" (Waldrop Harrison Papers).

Crowley continued, "I guess I am a Bois d'Arc man. If you don't believe me, then step up and look at some of the things I have made with it. I have worked with it all my life, and like I stated in the article that you referred to, it is about the only wood that will be here when you leave and be here when you come back" (Waldrop Harrison papers). To illustrate his point, Crowley said he had a bois'arc fence which has been in the ground since 1868. "This I know about because my father told me. There may be others that have been in the ground longer," Crowley added. "I planted some seeds in 1941 or 1942, and they've grown, and now you could take five or six posts from each of these trees," the Bois d'Arc Man continued (Tolbert, "About Mr. Crowley, Bois d'Arc Man").

Martha Stewart

The TV maven of gracious living and household ingenuity is likely to be more closely associated with her cooking and home decoration or with her fashionable sojourn in prison than with the Osage orange tree. However, her spotlight on Osage orange during her TV appearances qualifies her as a celebrity ally of the tree.

The following TV exchange demonstrates her enthusiasm for Osage orange:

McEWEN: You know, fall is the time when nature just explodes with color. Now you can bring some of that beauty into your home using nature itself to supply the color. The September issue of *Martha Stewart Living* has some bright ideas. And Martha's here to tell us all about natural dyes. Hello, Martha.

MARTHA STEWART: and this is an Osage orange, which turns everything a bright yellow.

McEWEN: Pretty color.

MARTHA STEWART: Yes, these are great, great colors. So that's all the natural kinds of dyes. Now to get to the dyeing after it's soaked in the mordant (CBS "This Morning").

Doris Taylor, Plant Doctor

At the Morton Arboretum Plant Clinic in Lisle, Illinois, Doris Taylor enjoys celebrity status at her clinic where she attracts people eager to receive the diagnosis she will give them about their ailing plants. When Rosemary Macko Wisnosky showed the botanical physician a branch with glossy green leaves, she asked, "Can you tell me what this is? "It flowers in the spring but there's no fruit." Taylor announced the good news that Wisnosky owned an Osage orange. The bad news was that she would have to choose between the Osage orange and the young butternut tree nearby. "Both could not thrive in such close proximity," Doris explained (Pyke F1, F2).

Bois d'Arc Beame

Bois d'Arc Beame was famous in Oklahoma, not only because of his nickname, but also because he was an outstanding coach and sportsman. As far as can be determined, the popular Choctaw coach at Murray State University in Tishomingo, Oklahoma, was a respected educator, whose character resembled that of the rugged, stalwart tree. He died in 1987. (Online information from the Choctaw Nation). One of Coach Beame's grandsons revealed in a telephone conversation that he had known several Indian lads in Oklahoma who had been given the nickname of "Bois d'Arc").

Jack Bell, Joann Parkhouse, Fred Tarpley

Small town celebrity came to the trio of civic leaders who launched the annual Bois d'Arc Bash in 1986. Jack Bell was head of the Department of Journalism at East Texas State University (now Texas A&M University-Commerce), as well as the Commerce mayor. Joann Parkhouse was president of the Commerce Chamber of Commerce. Fred Tarpley was an ETSU professor of English who conceived the plan for an annual celebration of the Osage orange and who served as director of the festival for its first five years. The celebration spotlighted the role of bois d'arc in Commerce history and the town's location in the heart of the tree's native habitat. The festival is held on the third weekend of September when the horse apples are ripe and just beginning to fall.

Earliest Bash Logo
Designed by Gordon Thomas

Bois d'Arc Bash Program
Commerce, Texas, 1993

Big Max, Second Largest Bois d'Arc in Texas
Courtesy of Commerce Chamber of Commerce

12
Uses of Osage Orange

Osage orange is recognized most often for its roles as a hedge, a durable fence post, a favored bow wood, and a dye source, but many other practical and sometimes dubious applications have been made. Presented below in alphabetical order are various uses of material products from the surprising tree or manifestations inspired and influenced by the Osage orange.

Ammunition for Youth

A newspaper columnist for the *Washington Post* recalled his childhood defense of a miniature fort as an ample supply of Osage oranges to throw at the invaders.

Antioxidants

Researchers at the Texas Research Foundation near Dallas in 1967 found isoflavones, osajin, and pomiferin from the Osage orange to be "remarkably effective in delaying the onset of oxidative rancidity in large and other oleaginous substances." The Osage orange antioxidant increases the stability of hydrogenated soybean oil two and one-half times and that of hydrogenated lard about four times. Use of the antioxidants was predicted for such materials as oil-soluble vitamin concentrates, cosmetics, pharmaceuticals, lubricating greases, and many other substances subject to oxidative deterioration. (Lundell).

Arrows

In the past Osage orange was used far more frequently as wood for bows by Native American tribes than for arrows. Modern archers favoring Osage orange bows are likely to use arrows crafted from other woods. Arrows, long ago and currently, are often made of cane. Osage orange arrows have not become obsolete, however. Ron Hardcastle, an internationally recognized Texas bowyer, crafted Osage orange bows and arrows for the CBS miniseries *Lonesome Dove,* based on the novel by Larry McMurtry. It was Hardcastle's Osage orange arrow that killed the Robert Duvall character in the miniseries (*The Traditional Bowyer's Bible* 1:2). The lethal bow, of course, was of the same wood.

Art

Osage orange provides the subject matter and building material for several art installations across the United States. A landscape piece titled "Bodark Arc" (1982) was built into the prairie of the Nathan Manilow Sculpture Park at Governors State University just south of Chicago. Large geometrics are marked by sunken granite walkways cutting through the yellowed grass. An Indian bow has a long, straight string in an ancient stand of twisted Osage orange growing here for years before Martin Puryear chose the site. Puryear's "Bodark Arc" covers three and three-fourths acres. Viewed from a rooftop, the work resembles a bow and arrow (Kirshman 58).

At the Lincoln Memorial Garden in Springfield, Illinois, Lynn Hull fashioned a raft made of crisscrossed boards and curls of Osage orange branches. The creation is drydocked in front of a cattle pond in a thirty-acre parcel of land acquired by the garden. Its real function will be to attract painted turtles, slider turtles, snapping turtles, and perhaps a few sun-loving birds and frogs. The festoon of Osage branches atop the raft was selected for their resistance to insect infestation and creation of visual interest. (Bettendorf).

Peter Rockwell, the son of artist Norman Rockwell, graduated from Haverford College in Pennsylvania as an English major in 1958. The college placed three tons of stone in the center of the campus for his sculpture, and in 1990, he fulfilled his longtime vision of a work of art based loosely on the "climbing tree," an Osage orange located alongside Haverford's library. As a student and a young father, Peter Rockwell often brought his son to play among the twisted roots that crept along the ground. His "climbing sculpture" is a squarish piece of Indiana granite embellished with faces and limbs ("Rockwell's Son"; Mundell).

An Osage orange in bronze is a prominent part of a statue honoring Thomas Jefferson as a naturalist at the Missouri River Basin Lewis and Clark Interpretive Center. The statue by C. A. Grenda, a Montana sculptor, stands ten and one-half feet tall, holding a fruit from the Osage orange, the tree popular among many American Indian for making bows and arrows and for trading the valuable wood with other tribes.

The sculpture will depict a contemplative Jefferson standing amid a crate of artifacts and specimens of Great Plains flora and fauna that the commissioned explorers shipped to the president in 1805. Also appearing are a caged magpie; elk antlers; a peace pipe decorated with eagle feathers, horse hair, and porcupine quills and ribbon; and a prairie dog captured in what is now northeast Nebraska (Hendee 18).

Artificial Limbs

The strength and elasticity of Osage orange made it useful in the creation of artificial limbs (http.//www.Windsorplywood.com.worldofwoods/northamerican/Osage Orange).

Awls

For crafting awls, a small, pointed tool for making holes in wood and leather, the tough, hard Osage orange wood qualifies as a popular material (Thomas).

Barrel Staves

In the construction of barrels, strong and flexible wood provides the thin, shaped strips of wood that are placed edge to edge on the top of the barrel structure. These staves are often shaped from Osage orange wood.

Barriers

Intruders will be thwarted by the vicious thorns and dense growths of Osage orange enclosing property. The tree's irritant causes scratches to itch and smart for hours, if not days. The diaries of many nineteenth century horsemen attempting to ford streams report that they were often stopped by thick growths of Osage orange in bottomlands (Totemeier).

Baseballs

For a game of catch or batting practice, horse apples can replace sports store baseballs. A bat turned from Osage orange would rival a Louisville Slugger. Wearing gloves will protect skin from dermatitis caused by sap from the horse apples.

Bird House Refuge

After Jerry Hutton of Commerce trimmed low-hanging limbs of several bois d'arc trees, he placed houses for bluebirds in the upper branches and on trunks about five feet from the ground. He reports that the birds enjoyed their refuge in the accommodating trees. He followed advice given by a bird book to mount the houses so that they faced east (Hutton).

Bird Prey Sanctuaries

An Ohio newspaper reporter observed a loggerhead shrike (butcher bird) impaling prey on thorns within an Osage orange hedge in Licking County, returning later to the larder to feast upon it. The local name came from the way the butcher bird would hang its meat on a thorn in the manner a butcher hangs a side of beef on a hook. The birds enjoyed mice, small birds, grasshoppers, crickets, and other large insects. With the disappearance of Osage orange hedges in Ohio, the birds' population declined (Switzer 16D).

Bows

Ron Hardcastle of Austin and Jim Hamm of Azle are partial to Osage orange for fashioning bows and arrows with techniques used by American Indians thousands of years ago. Both Texans participate in bow camps to pass their skills on to other bowmakers (Associated Press. "Bowmakers Still Make Them Like They Used To").

Bowling Balls

Premium size horse apples, a smooth surface (perhaps a sidewalk), and ten pins can substitute for a bowling alley. Gloves are recommended for bowlers who may be allergic to the sap of the fruits, which can cause dermatitis.

Bowls

Osage orange is a favorite wood for craftsmen who turn objects on a lathe. The grain of wood is a handsome display, and the surface takes a high polish (Marsh B2, 14).

Boxes

Osage orange is a wood of choice for wooden boxes sold by Appalachiana in Bethesda, Maryland. The craft shop claims the boxes are ideal for a dresser top because they will increase chances of getting the dresser dusted more often.

Bridge Floors

Many of the floors of old-fashioned bridges in Texas were made of Osage orange (Johnson, Mildred)

Bridge Pilings

Osage orange wood was "much used as piling for bridges" ("Bois d'Arc," *Texas Almanac 125*). See Texas prize logs in Chapter 12.

Building Pegs

When John F. Daugherty interviewed Andrew J. Carnes, in Caddo, Oklahoma, on April 26, 1937, he was told that Carnes had been born near Caddo in a log cabin built in 1855 and still standing in 1937. The three-room home was built of logs mortised together, but there were no nails in the structure. Instead, pins made from bois d'arc trees were holding the logs securely in place (www.choctawnation.com/history/people/original-enrollees/carnes-ansrew-j/). Retrieved 20 June 2010. Other records indicate that bois d'arc pegs or pins performed the role of nails for many early buildings.

Business Names

Various common names of the Maclura have provided appealing names for businesses. Bed and breakfast establishments called Hedgeapple Acres Bed & Breakfast near Moran, Kansas, and Bois d'Arc Bed & Breakfast in Commerce, Texas, capitalized on the reputation of local trees. Bois d'Arc Energy and Bois d'Arc Real Estate have also been named for the tree.

Cancer Treatment

Osage orange has been reported as a traditional cure for cancer used by Native Americans and folk herbalists. Dr. Les Moore introduces himself as a pioneer and leader in Integrative Medicine. He has published two books on healing and currently serves as director of a clinic in Clinton Springs, New York, where he specializes in the medical use of Osage orange.

According to online information from Dr. Moore, for several decades modern science has isolated a new class of lectins from the Osage orange and suggested its potential as a treatment for cancer. *Lectins* comes from a Latin word meaning "bind" or "pick and choose." They form "an irreversible covalent bond in a manner similar to antibodies." Dr. Moore is a doctor of naturopathic medicine and director of integrative medicine at Clifton Springs Hospital in Clinton Springs, New York. (http://www.classicalformulas.com/osageorange.html).

Chemical researches and pharmaceutical scientists issue periodic reports on the potential of Osage lectins in medicine.

Children's Activity

Properly dried, the fruit of the Osage orange can be decorated with cloves by children to produce a natural pomander. Parents are warned that if improperly dried, the fruit will rot and become a maternity ward for small flies.

Christmas Switches

Steve Killam of Lufkin, Texas, enjoys recalling this childhood memory: "On Christmas morning, as my brother and I looked at our stockings, we saw something long and thin sticking out of the tops. 'Oh boy—walkie talkies,' squealed my brother Bill. They weren't walkie talkies; they were just long thin limbs from a bois d'arc tree. When we officially woke up, after daylight, we went hack to the living room to find toys. The only things we found were those pieces of wood. (I broke mine up and put them in the fire.) My father informed us that Santa had left us switches because we had not been nice to each other." . . . Dad had a good laugh. Mom was not as amused. She brought out the real gift and gave Dad the remaining switches for his Christmas" (Killam).

Chuck Wagons

Hungry cowboys have Charles Goodnight (1836-1929) to thank for providing hot meals on the range. In 1866, when Goodnight and his partner, Oliver Loving, prepared to drive 2,000 longhorn cattle from near Fort Belknap in northern Texas to Denver, Goodnight purchased an army surplus Studebaker wagon from the government and had it completely rebuilt to his specifications. He chose bois d'arc, the toughest wood available for the project so that the wagon could withstand the bumps while being pulled across rough terrain (Eads, Google chuckwagon).

What distinguished the chuck wagon was a sloping box on the rear with a hinged cover that could be lowered to become a culinary worktable for cooks. The name of chuck box was soon applied to the chuck wagon. *Chuck* was cowboy slang for food, derived from the meat business reference to the lower priced part of the beef carcass as the "chuck," The word began to appear in print in England in 1723 (*Merriam-Webster's Collegiate Dictionary*, 11th ed.) American cattle drives began in the 1790s, but chuck wagons with their portable kitchens did not appear on the trails until after the Civil War (About.com, Inventors).

Goodnight, a Texas Ranger, is credited with inventing the American ranching industry. In 1876 he organized the first cattle outfit in the Texas Panhandle and later helped create the famous Goodnight-Loving cattle trail from Texas into New Mexico and Colorado (*New Handbook of Texas;* About.com, Inventors).

When Charles Goodnight, the famed Texas traildriver, designed the world's first chuck wagon for providing meals along the cattle drive, he sought wood that could withstand the hills, fords across streams, and rough prairies. He did not want a chuck wagon that would need constant repair. He avoided these problems using the wood from the rugged Osage orange tree.

Clue to Tracking Deer

Archers in the big woods can pick up the trail of deer that have browsed on Osage orange fruit by looking for fresh droppings and indications of deer feeding. Bucks will be feeding near thickets where they bed (Pearce 82).

Coffins

Responding to a newspaper article on Osage orange inviting reader encounters with the tree, Pat Logan of Tyler, Texas, recalled that her mother, born in 1906 in Farmersville, Collin County, Texas, would recite doggerel learned in her childhood about "Handy Dan, the bois d'arc man." "He sold coffins made of this wood, which indeed might outlast some of the much-touted metal kinds," Logan added (Baggett 46A).

Community Names

Bois d'arc, Missouri; Bois d'Arc, Texas; Orange Mound, Tennessee; Orangeville, Texas. These are a few of the community names derived from *Maclura pomifera*. Bois d'Arc was the original name of Bonham, Texas, given for nearby Bois d'Arc Creek. Bois d'Arc Creek is now considered the first creek to bear that name. The stream flowing northeasterly across Fannin County to its mouth on the Red River has been identified as the center of the native habitat of the Osage orange tree in Northeast Texas.

Costumes

Halloween characters at a spooky event at the Hawk Mountain Sanctuary near Kempton, Pennsylvania, included Poison Ivy, Witch Hazel, and Miss Osage Orange. No details were given about the costume designs ("Hawk Mountain to Teach Owl Spotting" B5).

Upstaging the Pennsylvania children, Jim Conrad appears at the Bois d'Arc Bash in Commerce, Texas, and at other events dressed as an Osage orange tree, wearing a costume created by Evonne Richardson.

Crime Detection

The clue that solved a murder in Hunt County, Texas, in 1897 was a piece of a bois d'arc fence picket used to splice the broken shaft of a wagon. The body of a young farm hand, Ben Stonecypher, was found at a burned house on the J. J. Roach farm near Celeste. When Sheriff Max Patton discovered wheel tracks in the seldom-used road near the burned house, he observed that the top of one of the pickets on a bois d'arc fence was broken off close to the top wire and that a strand of wire had been twisted off. He found evidence that a horse and buggy had stood near the fence. He began a search for the buggy and the person who had driven it.

In nearby Wolfe City, he vistited a buggy repair shop that had replaced the broken shaft, which remained in the livery barn. The owner was identified as Charlie Little, a farm laborer. Little was arrested and then tried at the spring term of court in 1898. After a jury verdict of murder in the first degree, Little was hanged in the Hunt County jail.

A few days before the execution, Little wrote a letter explaining that he and Stonecypher had returned to the vacant house to continue drinking and to play cards. Suspecting Sonecypher of cheating, Little reached for the poker pot, and Stonecypher grabbed a shotgun that Little kept in his buggy. When Little refused to relinquish the poker pot, Stonecypher hit him on the head with the gun. Little grabbed an old cultivator near the porch, struck Stonecypher dead, and fled after mending the break in the buggy shaft. He avowed that he did not set the fire, claiming that it must have caught from the candle they were using for light while playing cards.

Thus, the broken bois d'arc picket began the chain of evidence that put the rope around Little's neck (Neville. *The Red River Valley Then and Now*).

Crutches

Individuals needing assistance in walking found excellent support from crutches made of Osage orange, The strong, long-lasting wood supported their weight and was a reliable material that would neither break nor decay. The crutches were long-lasting and dependable.

Debris Catchers

Landfills have tried different solutions to prevent paper and light-weight garbage from flying in the wind from the spot where trucks are unloading. Airborne litter clutters the countryside. The usual solution is to build high fences with small net wire to capture the debris.

At the Duncan Republic Services landfill near Commerce, the Bois d'Arc Capital of Texas, Lanny Caffey took note that a fencerow of bois d'arc trees not far from the base of the rising elevation of the landfill. In appreciation of the Osage outfielders snaring the flyaway refuse, when he replaced the barbed wire fence in front of fencerow, he moved it away from the line of trees to give them plenty of breathing space. The elevation at the landfill, known as Mount Maloy because a school community of that name was once located nearby, now stands at 615 feet above sea level (Caffey).

Decay Resistance

Osage orange and black locust were listed as the most effective methanol extracts from durable woods for their toxic effects on wood-destroying organisms such as brown rot and white rot (Kamden 30-32).

A doctoral dissertation at Michigan State University investigated heartwood extractives of Osage orange and their role in decay resistance. The study identified the compound as having the greatest inhibitory effect on wood decay fungi (Wang 1-2).

Decorated Mottles

The mottled patterns or coloring of wood obtained from selected Osage orange logs have been artistically incorporated into a wide variety of American crafts (Constantine).

Decorations

The fruit of the Osage orange, gilded or silvered or embedded with cloves, decorates homes in imaginative ways, especially at Christmas time. Arrangements of the fruit become centerpieces on festive tables. At Belle Grove in the Shenandoah Valley, a fan-shaped window over the front door, sports an arrangement made from Osage oranges gathered on the property (Rogers, Patricia Dane). Sage Cottage in Franklin, Tennessee, offered a class on how to make herbal ornaments, including Osage orange medallions (Burch).

Duck/Turkey Calls

Osage orange is one of the dense woods used by Paul England in Minnesota for making single-reed duck and goose calls. He turns out a wooden call in a couple of hours while a plastic call requires at least three hours (Smith, Doug 10C).

Bill Decker is one of dozens of Oklahomans now making and selling their own turkey calls. Brass gets slick and must be kept "scuffed up" to test the desired sounds, but brass calls in Osage orange wood avoid these problems and are Decker's best sellers (Godfrey, Ed).

Durable Wood

When wood was required to be strong, durable, dense, elastic, decay-resistant, and heavy, Osage orange passed all tests. Consequently, Osage orange was popular for wagons, crutches, wheel spokes, fence posts, and a number of other uses.

Dyes

Indian tribes and pioneer Americans relied on Osage orange for yellow dyes long before the nation developed an appreciation for dye from the tree as early as early as 1916, when the onset of World War I interrupted the importation of fustic, the source of khaki dye for military uniforms (Jacobson). By 1914 more than 25,000 tons of Osage orange wood waste material were being used each year for dye extraction (Harrar *Hough's Encyclopedia*, 80).

In 1916, a Dallas newspaper reporter addressing the opportunity the plentiful supply of Osage orange in Texas had to supply fustic as a source of dye wrote, "The grade [of dye] upon which American users depend is imported from Germany, and America must produce dyestuff or we won't have any color dye." In meeting the demand for the dye, economic opportunities were foreseen for Texas and Oklahoma in supplying Osage orange for its pigments. ("Osage Orange Wood May Have Good Use. New Industry Possible of Development in Southwest as a Result of War").

Rafinesque in 1819 appears to have been the first botanist to point out that Osage orange contains a yellow dyeing element essentially similar in all important respects to that obtained from the wood of the tropical fustic tree ("A Brief History of the Wood of the Osage Orange Tree." *Textile Colorist*).

Maclura xanthorne, the main pigment of Osage orange, is a photo reactive compound. The roots, the leaves, and the bark all yield yellow dye. Commercial Osage orange dye is often sold as sawdust, chipped wood, or as shredded heartwood. The wooden extract is also sold in liquid, powdered, or granular form. Colors obtained from the tree range from true yellows to yellow greens

(Bliss). One half ounce of extract with a chrome mordant yields a gold color. With an alum mordant, a soft yellow appears. This color may be saddened and changed to gold by an afterbath of chrome and acetic acid (Davidson).

During World War II, the accelerating need for olive drab dye for soldiers' uniforms gave farmers in Red River County, Texas, a new source of income. They began to sell Osage orange wood to the American Dyewood Company of New York City. The sale included barking and sapping the wood in Clarksville, requiring that the bark be trimmed and the sap of the outer growth cut off until only the heart remains. At the processing plant in Chester, Pennsylvania, the wood was pulverized to extract the dye contents. The residue pulp was used in manufacturing explosives and airplane plastics. Thus an Air Corps pilot from Texas might be wearing, shooting, and riding on the Osage orange tree that once grew in Texas. The Clarksville vendors received $6.50 per 2,400-pound ton for peeled wood and $4.50 for rough wood ("Texas-Grown Bois d'Arc Supplies Army with Dye for U.S. Soldiers' Suits").

In 1945 a textile publication claimed that fabric dyes with Osage orange were mildew resistant after six weeks of weathering (Huang 1).

In handmade Navajo blankets, Osage yellow is a traditional color. Commercial use of Osage orange has been extended beyond cotton and wool to leather goods.

Martha Stewart called hues of Osage orange "great, great colors" on her "This Morning Show" (CBS "This Morning." "Tips on Using Natural Dyes to Dye Your Fabrics Successfully").

The hue of Osage orange enjoyed a short period of popularity in 2004, when fashionable ladies began to shun basic black for bright colors. One store painted the walls in women's clothing with Osage orange green, and the sales zoomed upward (Renwald G6).

Instructions for attaining different hues from Osage orange and applying the dye to various materials and surfaces are detailed in many volumes devoted to the use of nature's colors (Grae).

The voice of opportunity extolling the potential income from Osage orange dye remains unheeded today: In 1934, an article in *Nature Magazine* stated, "Perhaps the greatest value of this tree lies in its use as a source of dye. Thousands of tons of bois d'arc annually go to waste which might be used to produce dye. Altogether about 40,000 to 50,000 tons of waste are available yearly in Texas and Oklahoma alone. This tree is another of Nature's gifts to the people of America" (Hutchins. Ross E. 39).

Since the advent of synthetic dyes, Osage orange is seldom used and only locally (Panshin and Zeeuw 581).

Fabric Design

Images of Osage orange have not been confined to landscapes, artistic renderings, and photographs. A sketch of Osage orange trees started in 1933 by John Steuart Curry later evolved into an acclaimed fabric design in the 1940s. The artist began with a sketch of the Osage orange in Kansas during the summer of 1933. He completed an oil and tempera painting of the same subject in Connecticut in 1934.

So far as is known, Curry was the first important artist to use the Osage orange tree as the subject of a painting. It proved to be the most romantic and stimulating of all the Southwest flora and fauna Curry painted (Schmeckebier 146-48). Between 1936 and 1941, he used the Osage orange image in three other paintings.

The motif appeared in a mural for the Kansas state capitol in 1940, the same year Curry created the fabric design. Leaf and branch motifs were recurring subjects for textile designs in the late 1930s, and when Curry was given a commission for the fabric, he became one of the first American fine artists to design a textile. The success of his

Osage orange fabric attracted many well-known artists to follow him into textile designs (Corpier 62-64; Schmeckebier 148).

Falloes

The rim of a wooden spoked wheel is made of many segments called falloes, felloes, or felly. When a survey was made in 1941 by the U.S. Department of Agriculture Forest Service, ten to twelve thousand wagons with Osage orange wheel rims were being manufactured annually in the United States (Burton and Barnes).

Fedges

A resident of rural Kentucky, Deborah B. Hill was familiar with fedges, the name given to the combination of fence and a hedge. a standard fence with a living one. Here was a way standard fences could be used with living fences in a person's yard. The result was an attractive setting for the home landscape (Hill).

Fence Posts

Osage orange is at the top of the list for durability with its resistance to insects, rot, and decay in earth and water. Longevity tests report the lifespan of Osage orange posts to be up to thirty years. One appraisal commented, "Fence posts of either wood [Osage orange or black locusts] may safely be regarded as permanent (Vera 74). Not always straight but usually full of knots, Osage orange has another disadvantage of being difficult for driving staples into its wood to attach wire.

Ironically, when barbed wire began replacing Osage orange hedges on the prairies, interest in the tree was revived when it was determined that its posts were the most reliable ones for holding the barbed wire securely.

Firewood

According to the University of Kentucky College of Agriculture extension service, the Osage orange as a heat-generator is "top of the line" ("Firewood Facts Keep You from Getting Burned" 10). Research at Iowa State University found that burning Osage orange wood produces twice as much heat as basswood (Associated Press. Ames, IA).

Warnings given for Osage orange mention that the wood spits, putting out sparks that could be hazardous in a home (Soltes, Fiona 3). Nevertheless, Osage orange appeared in the top nine hardwoods for fireplaces (Carey and Carey).

Gregory Stephens, a forester with Louisville's Natural Resources Conservation Service, calls Osage orange "the best firewood you can get." He adds, "But Osage orange is seldom for sale, even though it's plentiful on the landscape. [The] wood is so hard it breaks chains on woodcutters' saws. They just won't fool with it" (Farmer). The mixed feelings about heating with Osage orange were expressed in these words: "It is an excellent firewood despite its tendency to snap, crackle, and pop in the fireplace" (Michaelson).

Flights of Fancy

Sometimes the Osage orange sends writers into flights of fancy, as in the case of Barry Fugatt, who applied his creativity to an interpretation of the book of Genesis. Fugatt wrote, "Therefore knowing that God is love. I'm certain that God strategically placed comfortable benches in the garden for Adam to periodically rest his weary bones during their walks.

"I'm less certain, however, of the type of material God used to construct the benches. If He wanted the benches to have a fancy look, He probably used teak or mahogany. If He wanted to save a few bucks (not at all like God), He may have used common redwood. But if He wanted the benches to last as long as Adam (930 years), He surely used the unusually and ageless Oklahoma native wood of Bois d'Arc (say BO-dark), also known as Osage orange" (Fugatt D1).

Flooring

T. E. Crowley, known as the "Bois d'Arc Man" who lived south of Paris, Texas, used different woods for flooring in his showplace home. One wood was Osage orange, usually called bois d'arc throughout Texas. He also used massive bois d'arc tree trunks to design entrance gates to the pastures on either side of his home (Tolbert "About Mr. Crowley").

Charles J. Barr, a Liberty, Nebraska, farmer responding to a newspaper article about Osage orange, commented that one of his neighbors had a floor made of polished hedgewood (Baggett 46A).

Flowers

A favorite adaptation of Osage orange fruit is the fashioning of flowers from thin slices of the globular material. Slices of no more than one-fourth inch thickness are placed in an oven at low heat until the edges have curled upward, and the color becomes a tarnished golden hue. Then the cupped rounds are removed from the oven, and a sprig of a wild plant is inserted in the center. Next, the decorated slice is attached to florist wire. A short length of wire will produce a boutonniere, and a long length will make a long-stemmed Osage orange flower suitable for bouquet arrangements in a vase.

Folk Remedies and Superstitions

Warts. Anoint wart three times with the milk from a Hedge ball and then bury the ball (White, Newman 328)

Warts. Apply milk taken from an Osage orange and apply it three times to your wart. You must afterwards bury the Osage orange from which you took the milk.

Warts. Punch a hole into an Osage orange about the size of your wart, and having twisted the substance from the hole over the wart three times in a circle, throw the

Osage orange over your left shoulder without looking back. This will cure the wart (Hyatt, 52).

Wounds. Osage orange can be soaked in alcohol or whiskey to make a liniment to apply over the affected area, according to A.H., an eighty-one-year-old female farmwife living in Brunswick (*Popular Beliefs and Superstitions*).

Use by Noah. Noah used this hard wood to build his flood-withstanding boat (Spiegelman 2). Such is the folk etymology derived from bois d'arc.

Dark of the Moon. Almost everything—Osage orange, especially, brush shrubbery, sprouts, and timber—will die when cut in the dark of the moon during August (Hyatt 52).

Food

Although chemists and botanists have declared the fruit of the Osage orange tree to be a nutrient high in starches and other food element, the tree figures only marginally in the diets of a few wild animals. Human consumption has not been reported, except for the seeds. When coated with cinnamon sugar and baked slowly, the seeds are touted as snacks as tasty as sunflower seeds.

In 1961, L. B. Jensen reported in *Chemical Abstracts* that a heat-stable nontoxic antibiotic useful as a food preservative was obtained from the heartwood and root of Osage orange (Huang 1-20).

Food Processing

Several chemists have predicted significant economic use of the proteolytic enzyme found in the fruits of Osage orange. Among these chemists are Ramsbottom and Paddock, 1948; Schwimmer, 1954; and Hokes, 1976. These enzymes break down proteins into peptides or amino acids. Potential uses are for making cheese, tenderizing meats, clearing and chill-proofing beer, bating of skin in the leather industry, and shrink-proofing wool (Smith, Jeffrey 15).

Forever Sticks

All of Jerry Lytle's grandchildren treasure their forever sticks, sometimes called everlasting sticks by the youngsters. These gifts were carefully selected and crafted by their grandfather, who lives near Commerce, Texas. Jerry pulls bois d'arc branches from streams where they love seasoning in the mud, he cuts them from his trees, or he chooses them from trees that neighbors have felled. He looks for the most interesting wood grain, the most distinctive shapes, and the most captivating colors in the six inch polished sticks he gives the grandchildren. He tells each of them, "Keep your forever stick in a safe place where you can always find it. Enjoy its strength and character. Think of your grandfather. The stick will last forever, just like your grandfather's love. You can pass it on to your grandchildren" (Lytle).

Foundation Blocks

House blocks, short posts set under the corners of buildings instead of masonry foundations) were an important product of Osage orange tree trunks (Burton). A slogan of the annual Bois d'Arc Bash in Commerce, Texas, has been "The very foundation of Commerce rests on bois d'arc," alluding to the use of sections of durable wood to support buildings in the community. So renown was the dependability of Osage orange wood that in some areas of Texas, house loans were rejected unless the structure rested on bois d"arc blocks or piers (Cox and Leslie)..

Several family fortunes in North Texas were made by cutting Osage orange tree trunks into foundation blocks. The thriving business wiped out vast stands of the tree growing along streams and rivers in Dallas, Collin, and Fannin counties.

Railroad stops were established as shipping points of the Osage blocks became the nuclei of new communities which survived the decline of the foundation blocks as the supply grew scarce and cement blocks became more popular. Prominent shipping points were created in Bonham and Randolph, Fannin County; and McKinney, Collin County.

Fragrances

Osage orange is a source of perfume fragrances ("Science Fare" 10D).

Fruit

A valuable source of edible oil, sugars, resin, and pigments has been found in the fruit of Osage orange trees. A palatable protein-rich food remains once these substances are removed. Researchers have announced that the oil should be acceptable to the edible oil trade. It may also be valuable in the field of drying oils, whether when blended with drying oils or when having its drying properties enhanced by various modification treatments already known. The resins offer uses in the paint and varnish trade as well as in protective-coating and adhesive industries.

Research reports also claim, "The Osage orange fruit contains 15 percent of water-soluble sugars which consist mainly of a mixture of glucose, atabinose, and an unidentified disaccharide. The sugars should be useful either collectively or individually in the food and fermentation industries." Potential value was seen for the pigments as vegetable dyes and as chemical raw materials for use in several compounds on a commercial basis (Clopton 470-78).

Furniture

When Osage orange hedges were bulldozed in the wake of urban development in southern Nebraska, and Bud Hanzlick, a Belleville, Kansas, railroad man, was laid off for a time by the Long Island Railroad, he started making rustic furniture. During his layoff his wife asked him to build some lawn furniture that would not blow away in the north Kansas winds. He chose Osage orange, called hedge in his locale, because it was famously heavy. Soon neighbors were buying his yard furniture, and he was creating other designs. Bud hit the big time when Robert Redford's *Sundance Magazine* featured his love seat on the cover of an issue. For three years Bud and Pat Hanzlick were featured guests at the Bois d'Arc Bash in Commerce, Texas.

Hanzlick,was one of the first craftsmen to recognize the beauty and versatility of Osage orange wood for the rustic furniture trade. He appreciated its natural color, a lovely burnished orange, which, if left outside, will acquire a silvery patina.

Hanzlick's tables, chairs, love seats, benches, tables, bowls, lamps, hall trees, plant stands, and other home furnishings have been sold all over the United States ("Home Furnishings Fit for a Museum" 9).

After a freak storm destroyed eight hundred trees and damaged another one thousand at Kew Gardens, Britain's prime botanical garden, some of the rare trees, including Osage orange, were offered to five furniture designers. When most of the fallen trees were burned, there was a public outcry, and Kew officials selected designers who worked imaginatively with wood and offered them the timber free if they would pay for it to be planked and kiln dried. Wood that might have cost thirty pounds (about $60 per cubic foot) cost the designers under ten pounds ($20). The completed furniture was exhibited in the gallery at the entrance to Kew Gardens and later sold at premium prices because it was Kew timber (McKee C5).

Throughout the United States, a few sawmills equipped with carbide-tipped saws have undertaken the cutting of Osage orange into commercial lumber. An example of a business man who saw the potential of Osage orange was George Lack. In 1983 he announced his intention to open an establishment for sawing bois d'arc, oak, and other hardwoods found north and south of Dallas in the Trinity River bottom in an inexhaustible quantity. "I will supply furniture factories and other factories with this wood in such dimensions and quantities as may be desired ("Metro Past." *Dallas Morning News.* March 15, 1983.

Since 1993, two University of Cincinnati professors, Sam Sherill and Michael Romanos have been rescuing fallen Osage trees and a few other species from a predestined future in a landfill or fireplace. They are determined to give the tree a new life as furniture (Haas).

Glue

In Pottawatomie County, Oklahoma, the Great Depression dragged on until World War II, and school children had to be resourceful in finding substitutes for costly supplies. At Johnson Elementary School, Larry Souders, now a reference librarian at Stillwater Public Library, used the milky, sticky sap from horse apples for school projects requiring glue. "It worked better than Elmer's," the librarian recalls.

Grave Markers

Wherever Osage orange grew, its wood was substituted for stone in fashioning grave markers. The wood similar in shape and size to the headstones found in U.S. national military cemeteries. Sometimes names and life dates would be carved into the wood. When placed in the ground and subjected to water, insects, or decay, the Osage orange was protected by its own chemical resistance. Rural cemeteries in Osage orange country still have graves marked by Osage orange from earlier generations. In Fannin County a bois d'arc tree trunk six feet tall once identified the grave of Bob Lee, a slain family leader in the Lee-Peacock Feud, until it was replaced by a stone monument (Hodge 13).

Mrs. and Mrs. William Jernigan, founders of Commerce, were buried in the Ingram Hart Cemetery in

Delta County near their earlier home of Cow Hill. Their graves are marked by Osage orange "headstones" (Tarpley, personal investigations).

Again, Osage orange grave markers began to disappear when marble and granite became more readily available, but the longlasting wood was adapted to another purpose to serve as reliable bases for stone monuments. A local historian wrote, "Inglish Cemetery in Bonham [Fannin County, Texas] has many Bois d'Arc bases as solid as the day they were placed there" (Hodge 13).

Hanging Limbs

Hanging trees were designated everywhere that justice was achieved with rope nooses looped over sturdy branches. Wherever available, a mature Osage orange tree often served as an execution site. The slant of the limbs and the strength of the wood were suitable for hangings. In Bonham, Fannin County, Texas, a dozen Osage orange trees in Simpson Park on North Center Street are too old for fruit bearing, but they are remembered as hanging limbs in the days when justice depended on a strong tree (Hodge 13).

Hats

Stylish green hats made of Osage orange leaves and joined together by the tree's thorns serving as pins were a favorite summertime craft for youngsters. Dorothy Tarpley Miville of Dallas recalls her childhood in Leonard, Texas, a community south of Bonham, and her creation of the botanical hats. She competed with friends for the most original design and enjoyed relief from the summer sun when she let the leafy chapeau lie cool and flat on her head.

A student report included the following statement about Osage orange hats: "Fun hats can be made for and by children. Using the largest leaves pinned together by the thorns from the tree, make a ring big enough for your head. Then fill it in with smaller rings to complete the hat. This was a fun way to spend some time under a shade tree in the hot summertime. The play while wearing the hat was limited only by the child's imagination (Fred Tarpley collection of student reports).

Hedges

The greatest use of Osage orange in the United States in the nineteenth century was as a rugged hedge plant (McDaniel 45). Remnants of an era of lengthy hedges traversing the farmlands survive throughout the Midwest.

Indian Clubs

Indian traders reported that Osage orange wood was valued by tribes for making bows, arrows, and clubs. The clubs, used in battle, were heavy and deadly. Blades similar to those of a knife and attached to the bottom of the club were reported in early descriptions of the weapon (Bradbury) Nightsticks currently used by policemen are said to be variations of the Indian clubs.

Insect Repellent

Since the early nineteenth century, the Osage orange tree has been reported to be an effective insect repellent, but many detractors scoff and demand evidence. On the Long expedition, Dr. James Long recorded that members of the party resorted to smearing themselves with the milky juice of the fruit as a protection against the torment of wood ticks (Saunders 221). In 1944 an American volume on plant geography stated, "A distillate once extracted from the fruit was used as an insect repellent" (Cain 88).

Gardening columnists are delighted in answering questions about the effectiveness of Osage orange fruit as insect repellents. A favorite put-down is to say that the massive orange-like globule will not repel unwanted varmints unless it is thrown to hit the pest between the eyes. In recent years, scientists have taken the repellent properties of the fruit more seriously, and chemical evidence supports the claim that the odor of the fruit is offensive to insects, skunks, armadillos, and other undesirable guests. Inebriated squirrels have been reported staggering away from a feast on fermented fruits (Cox and Leslie 149).

Cliff McInan of Kansas State University says, "We found that hedge apples repel crickets. But it kills cockroaches, though not right away" (Phillips, Richard). Kansas State University has been an important research center for Osage orange as insect repellents.

For insects, advocates of the fruit as a deterrent recommend that it be cubed and placed in women's hosiery to be hung from the ceiling of a closet or from the drain pipe under a sink. Precautions are given for not allowing the fruit to touch anything that could be discolored by contact with it.

Crushed fruits of the Osage orange were said to attract and kill cockroaches by a website listing repellent plants and pesticides (SBE's List of Natural Pesticide Plant Sees from Around the World). The crushed fruit is harmless to humans but lethal to cockroaches, a San Diego newspaper report assured readers ("Plants That Really Bug Garden Pests" H21).

Anne Raver, garden columnist for the *New York Times,* knows that Osage orange fruit is a time-honored organic cockroach repellent because she purchased a "few bumpy balls (for $1 each) . . . at the Union Square Greenmarket" in Manhattan, and they seemed to work under her bed, in a dark corner, and by the kitchen sink.

Anne Magruder of Nashville uses Osage orange fruit to control silverfish (Soltes 8D). A negative vote for Osage orange as an insect repellent was given by Chip Tynan in the *St. Louis Post-Dispatch,* writing, "But count me among the skeptics. Years ago, I used Osage orange fruits to try to repel moths and spiders from closets but found the fruits more likely to attract mice than to repel pests" (Tynan 32).

A bulletin from the Missouri Botanical Garden reports, "one green fruit placed in a room infested with roaches will drive them out in a few hours" ("Jelly, Cotton Gins Waste, Starting with Poultry, Osage Oranges and Armadillos 23).

For larger critters, such as skunks and armadillos, which may invade the underpinning of a building, the experts recommend that several fruits be thrown under the structure without being enclosed.

Knife Handles

Osage is sometimes used for the handles of pocket knives and hunting knives. *Dallas Morning News* columnist Dennis Baggett wrote, "The other day I invited my friend Greg Roberts of Richardson to hunt on our place in the country. Afterward, he gave me a gift--a hunting knife with a stainless steel blade and a beautiful polished bois d'arc handle." The friend told Baggett that the handle would probably outlast the blade.

Landmarks in Land Descriptions

The long life of Osage orange wood gave land surveyors the idea of using the living tree, a post, a stump, or a stake as a landmark in describing property for land abstracts. A land description from the Fannin County, Texas, Tax Appraisal District used a post in defining boundaries: "The tract or parcel of land situated in the Northwest part of Fannin County, Texas, being a part of the Joseph Jeffries Survey, Abstract No 567, more fully described as follows: BEGINNING at a Bois d'arc fence post standing at the southwest corner of a tract of land . . . " (572:37). Abstract offices throughout Texas and the domain of Osage orange attest to the fact that Osage orange has figured prominently in land descriptions.

A classic case of Osage orange determining property ownership occurred in Gilmer, Texas, in 2005. A lawyer took a judge and about forty courtroom observers back to 1838 when he described tree stumps and stakes in the ground that he said would prove that the 5,000-acre William King survey was really two miles west of its alleged location. G. W. Hooper had written his field notes eleven years before the Texas General Land Office had patented the king survey. Oil company and land office attorneys say the 1849 survey has been in the right place from the beginning. Lawyer Roger McDonald told Visiting Judge Paul Banner about the survey. The notes guided Gary Gilley, head of the forestry department at Stephen F. Austin State University to a large water oak, a red oak stump, a bois d'arc stake, and a cat-iron pipe buried in the ground (Evans 71).

Leather Tanning

Tannin from the Osage orange tree was an important element in tanning leather for its many uses during the nineteenth century. Experiments in Texas concluded that hides could be tanned more quickly with the rich tannin of Osage orange wood than with oak bark (U.S. Department of Agriculture 1891 466).

Literature

In literature Osage orange lurks unexpectedly in pages that mention the tree or involve historical characters. associated with its role in the story of America. Here is a brief sampling of literary uses of Osage orange.

Many poems have been written about Osage orange ,and works of fiction make passing references to the tree, but none has made its monumental mark in the literary world. Perhaps closest to being a literary landmark is a short story entitled "The Osage Orange" by William Stafford, a significant American poet who taught at Lewis and Clark College in Portland, Oregon.

This work has been anthologized in high school English textbooks and has gained critical acclaim and a significant number of readers. William Stafford, born in

1914 in Hutchinson, Kansas, gives the Osage orange a prominent role in the story. The narrator, a newspaper carrier, is attracted to a girl in high school. She tells him her father will subscribe to the newspaper, but their house is off his route, and she wants to meet him at the Osage orange tree to get the paper each afternoon. The boy and the girl develop a tender friendship. When Evangeline does not come to graduation, her brother, the janitor, tells the narrator that she could not come because "She stole the money from her bank—the money she was to use for her graduation dress." No one was at the tree that day, and the narrator went to her house. A woman came to the door and said, "Go 'way, go 'way! We don't want no papers!"

The story concludes, "I stopped at the bridge, halfway to the road. I looked toward town. Near me stood our ragged little tree—an Osage orange tree it was. It was feebly coming into leaf, green all over the branches, among the sharp thorns. I hadn't wondered before how it grew there, all alone, in the plains country, neglected. Over our pond some ducks came slicing in. Glancing round, I flipped that last newspaper under the bridge and then bent far over and looked where it had gone. There they were—
a pile of boxed newspapers, thrown in a heap, some new, some old, and weathered, by rain and snow (Stafford).

In 1949 Winnie Mims Dean, a Jefferson, Texas, resident, published *Diamond Bessie* a novel about a historical character whose life ended there in 1877. The two murder trials of Abe Rothschild, her accused assassin, have spawned many legends in Jefferson (Tarpley, *Jefferson Riverport)*

As local color, Dean injects references to Jefferson as the historic riverport that prospered by shipping cotton and Osage orange seed. Dean lets readers of her novel know that in 1872, 228 steamboats arrived at the port of Jefferson and that 9,721 bushels of bois d'arc seed were exported in that year (Dean, Willa Mims 191).

On page 115 Dean writes, "Josh, I want to thank you for handling the bois d'arc apples for us. Makes about fifteen wagon loads you've disposed of for Big Sam and me. We've got to thank you for that, for the lake is loaded with them, and you said those settlers out on the prairies are buying them for seeds to sow along the lines of their land to grow hedges and make fences, and they call them Osage oranges. They don't have wood out there to build rail fences like we do.

"That's right, they don't, and there's quite a demand for them now. Bring them down, and I can get you a good price for them, for there are boats that are taking as much as that up the Mississippi into Missouri, and some taking them to Galveston and the Brazos River country. Then, I sold some for you right on the wharf, bought by waggoners going back to the prairies (Dean, Willa Mims 115).

Janice Holt Giles' *Johnny Osage*, a novel published in 1960, combines fiction with the Osage-Cherokee wars in the Ozarks starting in 1821. Although the Osage orange tree plays no role in the story, readers interested in the tree will take note of several elements in the story that are related to the species. The endpages are based on the Thomas Nuttall maps of 1819, indicating the location of Pierre Chouteau's trading post near the Osage village where he obtained the tree introduced to Lewis Meriwether in Chouteau's St. Louis garden in 1804. Nuttall was the botanist who gave the tree its scientific name of Maclura pomifera in 1818, visited the locale of the novel, and made maps in 1819.

Chouteau's name is mentioned in Giles' novel on page 17 when Wolf, an Osage Indian leader, says, " . . . our friend Chouteau told us that the king was no longer our great father and that our father was now the Great White Father in Washington and that the French were not our brothers now, but that our brothers were the Americans. . . .

Our French brothers lived among us honoring our ways. Our French brothers did not want Osage land."

Later the Osage leader says, "Osages talked to their friend Chouteau and he said the land the President wanted was not worth much to Osages. . . . He said it would be a good thing if we gave this land to the President. He said if we gave this land to the President he would set up a place at Fire Prairie where Osages could take their furs and buy things they need. . . . He said the President would give Osages many presents if they did this thing" (Giles 18).

In the epilogue (287-88), Giles reports that in June 1825 the Osage Indians ceded to the government "all their lands to the state of Oklahoma. By 1836 they were all removed.

Mauls

Participants come to the Annual Page County Woodchoppers Ball & Virginia championship Rail Splitting Competition at Luray Fairground equipped with fine-honed axes, Osage orange beetles (mauls), dogwood gluts (wedges) among their instruments made of hard steel and hardwoods (*Washington Post*. N.d.).

Medicine

American Indians, especially the Comanche, were known to use Osage orange for a root tea recommended as an eye medicine or as an eyewash for sore eyes (Foster and Duke; Moerman; Lewis and Elvin-Lewis). A boiled root solution was reported to relieve irritation eyes. Additional drugs extracted from the fruits include a cardiac active chemical. In modern medicine, a drug extracted from the Osage orange fruit is a cardiac active chemical (Smith and Perino. 24-62; Lewis and Elvin-Lewis).

In 1953 a 20% ointment of the extract of Osage orange wood used in vanishing cream was reported to have marked antifungal activity by C. F. Peterson and E. W.

Brockemeyer in the *American Journal of Pharmacy* (Huang 2).

Memories

The sight of Osage orange often triggers memories, such as those reported below:

Memories of R. S. Power's childhood in Paris, Texas, stretched to 1917. He told the *Dallas Morning News* that when he was small boy in Paris an American general named Black Jack Pershing , in trying to cope with Pancho Villa on the Mexican border, summoned reinforcements from the North. Troop trains coming down through Oklahoma were held over in Paris until a Santa Fe crew arrived. While in Paris the troops were confined to their rail cars.

Powers and other young entrepreneurs appeared on the railroad platform with baskets of gloriously golden bois d'arc apples. For a dime a piece, they were offered to the troops. For skeptical buyers the price plummeted to a nickel. The boys departed happily with their cash, and the soldiers had their oranges. What the defenders of America felt later when they bit into the fruit was of no concern to the vendors. And besides, the customers were now many miles away (*Dallas Morning News* columnist 2 Nov. 1973).

Hunt County historian Waldrop Harrison preserved his family's account of their involvement with bois d'arc apples. In his papers at the Harrison Public Library in Greenville is this version of the family story: "My great uncle William Harrison wrote about the [bois d'arc] apples when he was a boy. His father lived in Gibson County, Tennessee, where David Crockett lived. His son William went to school in the little one-room building with David's children. He said they had never heard of bois d'arc over there, and when he started for Texas, two neighbors went along as far as Honey Grove, Texas, which is not far northeast of Greenville. The two neighbors turned back to

Tennessee at this point, and Crockett went on to his death in the Alamo sixty days later.

"These two men who returned to Tennessee stopped and had supper with my great grandfather, Gideon Harrison, who had planned to follow Crockett to Texas shortly. Uncle William, who was a little boy at the time, related that these men who ate supper at their house told of his ordering the bois d'arc apples. He was convulsed by their account of their unsuccessful attempt to eat the apples. They got the sticky pulp in their beards and had an awful time. They tried cooking the apples and finally had to give them up as hopeless. The one who did most of the talking finished with the statement, "God, they are no account" (Waldrop Harrison papers).

John Sillick wrote in the *Buffalo News*,"Under one of the big willows, which rule the hill, I found a small pile of scrubby, old, crooked posts, each about the thickness of a forearm. I picked one up and whacked it against the thick trunk of the willow, expecting the post to break. Instead it vibrated in that painful way a baseball bat does at spring practice when your hands are cold. There was only one kind of wood that could stubbornly defy time like that— Osage orange. I dropped the posts in holes nearby on the new fence line."

Byron Crawford wrote in the *Cincinnati Enquirer,* "In a faded red cardboard box, lost somewhere in the X-files of our house, is a treasured snapshot that I took years ago of a small thicket of Osage orange on a hillside, a quarter-mile behind the Kentucky home where I grew up."

Carol Bradford wrote in the *Syracuse Herald-American*, "Maclura pomifera (osage orange): One of those odd trees grew on the Arts Quad at Cornell when I was a student there. The tree is tough and extremely thorny. It tends to develop a messy twiggy crown of interlacing branches The next problem is the hard, green, inedible, softball-sized fruit produced by the female trees. Plant them only if you want to encourage target practice."

John Williams reminisced about Osage orange, writing, " Jesse, my Texas porch hound, knows all the important things in life. A bois d'arc ball is one of the most important. When the pressures of life get too heavy, a bois d'arc fruit is Jesse's way of putting my world in its proper perspective. What's more important: the state budget crisis or a game of fetch the bois d'arc ball?" (Williams, John 34).

Raymond Wiggers wrote in *The Plant Explorer's Guide to New England,* "This is the unique North American thicket tree, Osage orange. Native to a small area in the South Central states, it has often been used by Midwestern farmers as a windbreak planting. It has without a doubt one of the most bizarre-looking fruits imaginable. When ripe, it matches a handball in size and specific gravity. On top of that, it has an unsettling chartreuse color, and convoluteds that bear a striking resemblance to the naked human brain. I have seen youngsters in Brooklyn's Prospect Park use it to pelt passing police cars; personally, I'd rather be hit by a cruise missile" (173-74).

Growing up in Tyler, Texas, Walt Davis revealed his inclinations toward natural science as a first grader when he performed his first scientific experiment. He had heard the debates about whether or not the horse apples of the Osage orange tree were eaten by livestock. Recruiting another first grader as his research assistant, Walt gathered fourteen horse apples to heave across a fence near some cattle. Three days later he returned to the farmyard and counted fourteen intact fruits among the cattle. Conclusion: cows do not eat horse apples. He reported his scientific observation to his first grade class. Decades later, Walt learned that when the fruits are green and the cows are not hungry, they are not tempted to eat them. By then he was an accomplished water colorist, a celebrated Texas naturalist, and director of the Panhandle-Plains Museum in Canyon, Texas.

Mine Timbers

Osage orange beams fit the bill when underground mines require ceiling support from wood that is extraordinarily dense, strong, decay-resistant.

Mottled Decorations

Mottled wood from cross sections of Osage orange tree trunks have been heralded by decorators as an arresting and attractive object. The growth ring, blotches, streaks, and spots of different shades of yellow, orange, and brown combine to make popular décor. Annual growth rings attract attention because of alternating colors, made up of a comparatively dark, thin band of summerwood and a lighter one of colored, frequently narrower springwood (Betts; Smith). Selected logs provide decorative mottles (Constantine, 262).

Mouthwash

"Osage Orange: The Future of Development of Mouthwash" was the essay that made Jessica Johnson one of the nine national finalists in the 2004 Young Naturalist awards, sponsored by the American Museum of Natural History in New York. The high school student from Claremore, Oklahoma, had seen her first Osage orange tree a few months earlier at a nature preserve and was curious to determine if the fruit was toxic. Experimenting with a bacteria culture from her teeth, Jessica found that flesh from the fruit killed the bacteria. She talked with area dentists about the possibility of the fruit's being used as a toothpaste or mouthwash (Morgan, Rhett A18).

Musical Instruments

Guitar makers praise the acoustical qualities given by Osage orange used on the bottom and on the sizes of instruments they make. The wood is also popular as inlays in musical instruments.

The first piano to arrive in Fort Worth came by riverboat from New Orleans to the port of Jefferson, Texas, and then overland another 225 miles to the Texas town where the West begins. For several years, the piano was on exhibition in the Fort Worth Public Library, but it could not be located when a recent inquiry was made.

Names

By 1818, bois d'arc was being sold for landscapes around Philadelphia as the Osage orange, a name with a double meaning, the orange (dye) of the Osage Indians and the orange (-like fruit) of the Osage orange tree. One double name led to another, and some people began calling the bois d'arc a horse apple, a name they also applied to dried horse droppings. The names mock orange, naranjo chino, yellowwood, hedge apple, and hedge ball came later (Williams, John 35).

The use of any of the common references to Maclura wins notice and causes comment. Race horses have been named Bois d'Arc (United Press. Oklahoma. "Friday's Blue Ribbon Downs Entries").

Jim Hamm, a bowyer in Azle, Texas, who was partial to bois d'arc bows, owns the Bois d'Arc Press. The Osage Orange Press in Madison, Wisconsin, was the publisher of a book on poet John Donne in 1972.

Paul Johnson, a Commerce, Texas, psychologist and a native of Durant, Oklahoma, heard about a fellow Oklahoman named Bois d'Arc Beame and wondered how the name had affected its bearer.

In Memphis, Tennessee, the Osage Mound neighborhood developed in 1890, taking its name from a row of Osage orange shrubs on a plantation (Elliott-Tenort CC1).

In Dallas, the Bois d'Arc Patriots chose their name for old-fashioned steadfastness and survival. The East

Dallas organization resisted changes and disintegration in their section of the city. In 1977 the group threatened to release rates in the neighborhoods of city council members if the council passed an ordinance that would make it the tenants' responsibility to rid their apartments of mice and rats. The ordinance did not pass. (LaTour).

Bois d'Arc is the name of communities in Missouri and Texas as well as other small settlements not appearing on maps or in gazetteers. Osage orange is not found as a community name, perhaps because the two-word designation is rather clumsy. It may be that some settlements and streets known as Osage actually refer to the tree instead of two the Indian tribe or river.

One place name in Fannin County, Texas, is known to have originated as a reference to the tree. When visitors from New York who had never seen an Osage orange tree came to the Texas community which was known by another name at the time, they admired the trees ripe with their fruits in September or October. The trees were growing around the store owned by Mr. Parmelee, founder of Valley Creek a few miles away. When the visitors referred to the orange trees, the natives were amused that the large balls of the Osage orange had been mistaken for actual oranges. Locals decided to rename their settlement Orangeville, and that name remains on the map today (Tarpley, *1001 Place Names,* 154-55).

The municipal utilities company in Windom, Texas, is named Bois D Arc Municipal Utilities.

Neck Yokes

Along with singletrees, wagon staves, and felloes, neck yokes for animals were made from Osage orange (*Arkansas* 314).

Nightsticks

The policeman's nightstick is viewed by a tree expert as a modern version of the ancient Indian war club.

Martin L. Davey, Jr. claims, "Today's noggin-buster is often made of Osage orange," the preferred wood of Native Americans for their war clubs. The Osage orange wood is hard, heavy, flexible, and strong ("Origin of Nightstick").

Paving for Streets

In 1889 a *Dallas Morning News* thought the earlier selection of Osage orange blocks for street paving was cause for congratulation. The selection had been made from the various materials used for construction thoroughfares at that that time—wood, stone, asphalt and macadam. The newspaper article declared that the chosen wood was better than granite for city streets ("Bois d'Arc for Paving" 3).

Bois d'arc was assigned the task "of literally lifting Dallas out of the mud" by paving streets. During prolonged periods of wet spells, Dallas downtown streets became impassable. Paving was undertaken in earnest in the 1880s, and two men emerged as trailblazers in the process. William M. Johnson, credited with being the first person to pave streets with bois d'arc blocks in Dallas or anywhere else, patented a process for cutting and treating the blocks. Tom L. Marsalis, a wholesale grocer and the "father" of Dallas' Oak Cliff section, agreed to bear the cost of a strip of paving along a portion of Elm Street (Acheson).

In 1896, James Madison Cochran of Bonham, Texas, published *The Value of Bois d'Arc Timber*, in which he wrote convincing arguments for the use of the tree, which was plentiful in his region, as a source of paving bricks for the miles of roads needed as the nation grew and vehicles for transportation multiplied.

For the Osage orange timber, Dallas was depending upon the surrounding counties of Kaufman, Rockwall, and Collin, with the largest amount supplied from Collin. Wood was being cut into paving blocks at three sawmills in Dallas. Streets were excavated one foot below the original grade, a six-inch layer of gravel or sand was added, and stones were placed in position preparatory to receiving the blocks. Small pieces or wedges of the wood were driven down with a heavy handax between the blocks. Then joints were filled with fine sand. Finally a boiling mixture of coal tar was poured into the remaining inch of the joints to cement the whole surface together before about half an inch or more of coarse sand is spread on. Now the street is opened to travel ("Bois d'Arc for Paving" 3).

Other cities were choosing different paving materials: mesquite in San Antonio but cedar in some Texas towns. In St. Louis, Chicago, New Orleans, and other cities using granite, a horse was said to be good for only four years when walking on that surface ("Bois d'Arc for Paving" 3). From 1888 until 1930, resilient Osage orange blocks paved Beaton Street, the primary downtown thoroughfare in Corsicana, Texas. Then one of the Great Depression government agencies covered the surface with conventional brick (Compton).

In later excavations of Dallas streets paved with wooden blocks, a local reporter claimed that *bois d'arc* had become a generic name for any wood used to pave streets. He had discovered that brick-size blocks of wood had been examined when they were removed from a downtown street and that they were not bois d'arc. That may well have been the case of that street in Dallas, but there is unmistakable evidence that bois d'arc was used in street construction elsewhere. In 1893, *Garden and Forest* magazine wrote, "The town of Dallas has its principal streets paved with blocks of this wood [bois d'arc]". Readers had no reason to believe that it was not actually wood from the bois d'arc tree.

When a section of Washington Street in downtown Greenville, Texas was repaved in the 1970s, some of the bricks were examined and declared to be bois d'arc.

The Hunt County Historical Commission encased the bricks in individual plexiglass boxes, attached an explanatory label, and sold them as historic relics. A brick was presented to Bud Hanzlick during his first of three annual visits to the Commerce festival. He brought his famous bois d'arc furniture promoted by Robert Redford's *Sundance* magazine to sell at the Commerce Bois d'Arc Bash.

Paintings

The art world took note of the acclaimed John Steuart Curry 1934 painting of Osage orange as the first time the tree had been the subject in the hands of a major American artist (Schmeckebier 146-48). Botanical artists had been presenting graphic representations of the tree in publications since the very early 1800s. The Osage orange was one of tree included in *The Botanical Paintings of Esther Heins* in 1987 (Leet).

Pestle

On display in the Sheerar Museum in Stillwater, Oklahoma, are an Osage orange pestle and a pine mortar made by Osage Indians. The Native American apparatus for pulverizing food stuffs was originally in the museum at Oklahoma State University. The four-foot long pestle is attractively designed and used to pound vegetables, seeds, and other provisions placed in the hollowed pine trunk, which serves as the mortar.

Photographic Model

The photogenic Osage orange fascinates many photographers, and the tree is often the most photographed object at a tourist destination. Such is the case with the famous Osage orange at the farm home of patriot Patrick Henry in Virginia. The tree has character, history, and the designation of the nation's largest Osage orange tree.

Photographs are exhibited in Memphis, Tennessee, of a nearby bois d'arc tree that has posed for Pete Ceren in a Mississippi pasture for more than a quarter of a century.

"I knew that when the sun rose, the tree would light up like a glass sculpture. I just had to make pictures of it," Ceren, a local photographer, says fondly of the tree. Ceren and the tree met when a painter friend took him to the pasture. "It has become a place for me to go to connect the corners of my life. It's a stable point, like church; here I have been able to go, night and day, and chill out," Ceren said in an interview ("1 Tree = 7,000 Photos! Peter Ceren's Been Shooting His Orange Tree for 20 Years. But He Isn't Done Yet.")

Especially popular among photographers were Osage orange trees grown on farms as windbreaks. Strong winds in open country blew these trees out of shape to grow at a precarious angle. Even though their roots were firmly anchored in the ground, they seemed to be falling (Solota 62).

Pins

In Jean Holt Giles' *Johnny Osage*, a female character living in Osage country, uses a thorn to pin together a cloth garment. The author stops short of identifying the makeshift pin as coming from the thorny branches of the Osage orange. The reader familiar with the tree and its namesake Indian tribe will likely surmise that the thorn pin was indeed from the Osage orange tree. Even today some children attach the tree's shiny green leaves with two-inch thorns imitating the role of straight pins in making summer hats. Perhaps the thorns inspired metal straight pins in the same way that the thorns influenced the invention of barbed wire. If such is the case, then straight pins could be another example in which modern technology borrowed from models found in nature to develop a replacement for the natural object.

Plows

Before the invention of the steel plow, the tough, durable wood of Osage orange was used by farmers to open furrows in the earth and deposit seeds for their crops (Thone).

Policeman Clubs

Policeman clubs, or nightsticks, are discussed under the category of nightsticks.

Pomade Balls

"Many years ago, as impecunious newlyweds seeking inexpensive gifts in Ohio, we made pomander balls from the fragrant Osage orange-scented fruits and gave them to family and friends as presents during the Christmas season," recalled B. E. from Ballwin, Missouri (Abraham and and Abraham).

Potential Uses

The Texas Research Center at Renner in 1949 reported agricultural studies involving by its staff (Lundell 1967). One of the studies completed it the Renner staff was "Osage Orange, a Potential Source of Edible Oil and Other Industrial Raw Materials" (Clopton and Roberts 470-72). The authors were quoted in the Renner report as having reached the following conclusion: "The fruit of the Osage orange tree has been found to be a valuable source of edible oil, sugars, resins, and pigments. When these are removed, there is left a palatable protein rich food. From a commercial standpoint the Osage orange fruit provides a rich source of several valuable industrial raw materials. The oil . . . should be acceptable to the edible oil trade and may hold considerable promise in the field of drying oils, either when blended with drying oils or by having its drying properties enhanced by various modification treatments known to the trade. The resins should prove useful in the paint and varnish and other protective-coating and adhesive industries" (Lundell 42).

The research also isolated potential uses of the fruit's water-soluble sugars, its pigments, and its palatable and nutritious feed containing thirty to thirty-five percent protein

Projectiles

Always a child's favorite as projectiles for a toy catapult, Osage oranges were hurled into the air against imaginary foes. The use of the Osage orange fruits as projectiles became a subject of serious research at Virginia Military Institute in 1996. Rebuchets were the Big Berthas of medieval times, more powerful than catapults, and these machines represented the maximum firepower of the period. VMI freshmen in a mechanical engineers class made models of rebuchets in their design course, firing balls with their models. Osage balls were also hurled on the soccer field in Richmond as part of a physics class's studies of projectile motion. The Osage orange balls soared up to three hundred feet, the instructor said (Orndorff, Beverly. "The Trebuchet Changed Face of War Before Cannon, Gravity Device Wrecked Walls E-1).

Pulley Blocks.

Wood for pulley blocks had to satisfy the requirements of being strong, heavy, and tough enough to endure the heavy loads pulled by ropes or chains passing through the pulley. Such a timber was Osage orange, and it was used extensively (Collingwood, 267).

Railings for Stairs and Porches

For strength and rustic accents, railings for stairs and porches made from Osage orange are unrivaled. In Texas, Dan Phillips grew up attracted to landfills and building things. He started building eccentrically charming, low-cost houses in Huntsville. His raw materials had been scavenged from discards at construction sites, contributed by friends, and salvaged from contractors who had ordered too much wood or the wrong materials. Phoenix Commotion, alluding to the legendary bird that rises from its own ashes, is the name of his project.

Branches form bois d'arc trees are turned into hard as steel railings for stairs and porches or even a faucet for the bathtub (Johnson, Patricia).

Railroad Ties

Mechans' Monthly reported in 1894 that a correspondent had related in 1874 that a railroad crosstie from an Osage orange had been placed in the road bed of the New York division of the Pennsylvania Railroad. The tie was found to be sound after twenty-one years of service. Because of its strength and resistance to decay and insects, Osage orange ties served the railroads well (*Meehans' Monthly*. 4 (1894):123).

When railroads were required by state laws to fence their rights-of-way, so many Osage orange fence posts were cut that for a time the tree seemed to be in danger of extinction. An Osage orange tycoon in Farmersville, Texas, once filled a single order for 100,000 fence posts from a rail line needing to fence its route across the state of Arkansas. As the demand for hedges declined, prairie farmers rescued the tree by planting it as windbreaks (Wright 21).

Reservoir Names

In Texas the state senate approved Bill 1519, introduced on March 10, 2005, for construction of Lower Bois d'Arc Creek Reservoir north of Bonham in Fannin County (Texas Senate Bill 1519, 2006-2006. Introduced by Senator Duell, March 20, 2005). Construction will begin in 2013 or 2014). Botanists have recently identified Bois d'Arc Creek as most likely in the center of a twelve-county area defined as the only native habitant of the Osage orange. These researchers now view the wider area previously considered the native habitat to include places where the tree was planted.

Another stream impoundment has been given the name of Bois d'arc Reservoir. It is attracting fishing and outdoor enthusiasts to the bois d'arc wildlands near Hope in southwestern Arkansas,

Resistance to Decay

Methanol extracts from the heartwood of Osage orange and two other durable woods proved toxic to some wood-destroying organisms in aspen blocks. Osage orange was second to intsia bijung but ahead of black locust in effectiveness (Kamdem 30-32).

Rope

Indians made ropes from the inner bark of Osage Orange (Grace, 52).

Rubber and Latex

Considerable public interest was attracted about 1912 by reports from Kansas University that Osage orange was a source of Indian rubber. However, an investigation shows no significant amount of rubber present (Womack 138). At the beginning of World War II, on April 28, 1942, a *Dallas Morning News* editorial titled "Bois d'Arc Chemicals" listed the tree as a source of rubber and latex. Although attempts were made to extract rubber and latex from the tree, such efforts were soon abandoned.

Rustic Bentwood

Osage orange trees resist rot and insects. Combined with its flexibility, these qualities make Osage orange ideal for rustic bentwood projects. The presence of thorns on its branches can be removed easily with a pruner. Taking care to use the wood when it is green and before it has hardened, the crafter will find Osage orange wood ideal for making distinctive trellises and very sturdy bentwood furniture (http://www.ipm.lastate.Edu/ipm/hortnews/hnl19996/5-2441`995.bent).

Sayings

Bois d'arc has inspired folk sayings that flavor colloquial conversation. "He's about as dense as a bois d'arc stump" is a popular insult for a person whose lights do not burn brightly in the attic. "His head is as hard as a bois d'arc block" is equally derogatory.

Texas Sportsman's Association President Henry Beyer, concerned that the Texas Parks and Wildlife officials had not acknowledged concerns expressed about declines in deer numbers, said, "And it is our opinion this bureaucracy just flat has not listened to anyone. It has been said to get their attention, you need to hit them with a strong bois d'arc limb in the back of the head" (Pike).

"Bois d'arc's budding; winter's over." Other sayings emphasize the longevity of Osage orange: "Oak posts last a long time, mulberry lasts still longer, cedar lasts one hundred years, bois d'arc lasts forever (MacMillan).

My father and his friends localized the familiar saying, "See you next Sunday if the creek don't rise" by incorporating the name of a famous Fannin County creek. Their version was. "See you next Sunday if the Bois d'Arc don't' rise."

Sculpture

As a material for museum sculptures, Osage orange is found in several locales. Worthy of note in the Center for Contemporary Art on Staten Island is John Deane's "Monotaur" carving on Osage orange, a handsome rust-colored wood with a very dark grain. Depending on the viewpoint, the piece is said to suggest the upraised head of a Great Dane or a tree trunk metamorphosing into a human figure (Raynor 25).

Silkworm Food

From the time botanists first examined the leaves of the Osage orange tree, predictions were made that there was potential for substituting them for the leaves of the mulberry tree, the long-established source of food for silkworms.

When the federal government began to encourage silk culture to compete with imported silk, 380 silk mills were operating in the United States. The distasteful aspects of encouraging caterpillars to gorge on the leaves followed by the repulsive chore of scalding the worms inside their cocoons, combined with the cheaper production costs in Europe and Asia, led to the demise of American silk culture.

Throughout the years of feeding Osage orange leaves to silkworms, the tree proved itself equal to, if not superior to mulberry as the source of their diet that was vital to the production of silk.

Soap

Some annotators of Cabeza de Vaca's journals think that the explorer might have used Osage orange in 1533 to wash cotton shirts at San Miguel on the Pacific Coast (Pickering 869).

Souvenirs

Mementos fashioned from the Osage orange tree are offered as souvenirs of communities connecting with the tree. In Commerce, Texas, home of the annual Bois d'arc Bash, visitors had the opportunity to take home "horse apples," as the fruit of the Osage orange are known locally. These fruit are considered novelties by cityslickers who have never seen them up close. "Flowers" fashioned from the fruit of the Osage orange are also available. Local citizens slice the fruit into one-fourth inch circles, which were baked in an oven until the edges curled, resembling a cupped flower. Then dried bristles from a wild plant are pushed into the center of the Osage slice, which is attached to florists' wire as a stem. The bash is also experimenting with offering Osage fruit seeds, shown to be non-toxic and high in protein. The seeds that have been sprinkled with cinnamon sugar and baked are expected to be a tasty, high-energy treat.

In an effort to reinvent itself, Elk Falls, KS, population 121 near the Oklahoma border, greets motorists with "Welcome to Elk Falls, Gateway to the Kansas Ozarks. In a ploy to get business from tour bus passengers headed for Branson, Missouri, in the real Ozarks, a visitors office has opened. Among other novelties, the town sells souvenir packets of saw dust from the Osage orange Tree, almost the only tree that will grow on the prairie ("Elk Falls Reinvents Itself Via Some Clever Marketing" 2G).

Speed Bumps

On a rural road near Cash in Northeast Texas, young motorists once raced at night until residents lined up horse apples across the road as speed bumps. After whirling wheels splashed sticky sap on their cars, most of the drivers would slow down or stop to remove the grapefruit-size fruit from the pavement. Soon they were seeking a friendlier racetrack (LeBlanc).

Starch

As early as 1929, researchers such as Professor Norton had discovered at Shaw's Gardens in St. Louis that the fruit of the Osage orange had almost as much starch in its composition as the potato but that the abundant resin had no doubt prevented its utilization for food (Smith, J. Russell).

Street Names

In regions where Osage orange is a significant tree, communities frequently name their streets for the local name, thus placing Bois d'Arc Street or Hedge Street on the map. The use of the clumsy name, Osage Orange Street, is extremely rare, an exception being Osage Orange Road in Glenview, Illinois. It is suspected that some of the Osage Streets refer not to the Osage Indian tribe but to a shortening of Osage Orange. One such example is found in a small Shenandoah Valley town, where Osage Place was named for the "venerable, five-trunked trees with many branches hanging over the road" (Lembke 202).

Tree names are one of the four basic patterns of street names in the United States. Originating in Philadelphia, where streets given the names of trees ran east and west, and numbered streets ran north and south, this theme was repeated in many other communities. The tree motif is a dominant pattern in naming American streets.

Swing Limbs

When Sharon and Michael Johnson of Commerce, Texas, were selecting a tree on their horse farm for suspending a child's swing in preparation for visits by their granddaughter from Denver, they trusted nothing less than a bois d'arc tree near their barn. As savvy Northeast Texans, they knew the strength and dependability of the wood for holding a youngster's swing.

Tannin Wheel

Tannin in the ridged and scaly bark of the Osage orange is extracted to tan leather (Weed 166). In Delta County, Texas, a gigantic wheel made of Osage orange wood was once used by a leather tanner to squeeze the tannin from Osage orange trees (Albright).

Telephone Poles

Use of Osage orange for telephone poles was acknowledged in an American publication in 1905 (Rogers, Julia, *Tree Book*).

Tobacco Pipes

Although seldom used for tobacco pipes, Osage orange meets the basic requirements of density, resistance to heat, and durability.

Tours

Osage orange trees often turn eyes during nature tours in several states. At the Patrick Henry's River Farm near Alexandria, Virginia, the famous Osage orange tree, crowned national champion for size, is an important stop on tourx of the property. Guides tell stories about the tree's ties to American history (Van Mullekom).

On less formal tours, such as a trek during the Trinity River Fall Fling at the McCommas Bluff Nature Preserve in South Dallas, Osage orange is a featured point of interest. When Jim Flood led a group of hikers along the Trinity River, he pointed out an Osage orange, generally called a bois d'arc in Texas. Osage orange trees once grew so abundantly along one of the forks of the Trinity that it was known as the Bois d'Arc Fork.

At Arbor Day celebrations in Montgomery, Alabama, tours showcase trees that have withstood the test of time. In Montgomery Park is an Osage orange planted as the beginning of a hedge by farmers in the mid-nineteenth century. The farmers hoped it would grow into a hedge, and it did (Grey).

Guides through the undulating landscape for the Big Woods Hike point out curiosities such as fallen fruit of the Osage orange tree. They explain that the fruits are treats for the squirrels and foxes that thrive here, a contradiction to the statement often found in print that animals ignore the fruit of Osage orange.. The Big Woods Hike is in Massachusetts in the Ipswich River Wildlife Sanctuary, where the Masconomet tribe once hunted..

Guides at the Starhill Forest Arboretum in Menard County, Illinois, pause before an Osage orange tree named Canonball, renown for its extra large fruits. When asked if the pungent Osage orange will ward off insects, the Sternberg brothers, owners of the private arboretum, smile and offer the opinion, "They work best when you drop them directly on the bug."

In Atlanta, Arbor Day tours of the downtown park recognize the Osage orange tree planted there by the first Arbor Day president, Hattie Rainwater, at the city's initial celebration of Arbor Day in 1933 in Atlanta Memorial Park (Crenshaw E-11).

Travel Trees

Travel trees, also called Indian Trees, Marker Trees, and other names, were bent to the ground by Indians and pointed to a trail, a source of water, or some other useful landmark in the area. Several organizations have been recording locations of such trees, but no printed material or online source has listed an Osage tree among the identified markers. Because Osage orange possesses every qualification for being a reliable travel tree, it is expected that a member of the durable species will soon be found performing this function.

Treenails

Tree nails are pegs fashioned from trees to join timber in homes, fences, and other wooden structures (Van Der Linden and Farrar). See trunnels.

Trellises

An herb farmer in Arkansas, Jim Long, thinks landowners should hesitate before putting a fallen tree limb through the chipper. In his book, "How to Make Romantic Bentwood Garden Trellises," he says that bentwood garden accessories are a great way to recycle storm-downed limbs.

His book offers craft-like patterns for making trellises, fences, and rustic gates. The best trees recommended for bentwood, according to Long, include Osage orange, red cedar, and bald cypress (Cerny).

Trunnels

In February 1622, after five days of strenuous labor, men hammered the last wooden spike, or trunnel, into the protective fence around their village, now known as Plimoth Plantation. The spike-topped fence logs were hastily erected after the Massachusetts pilgrims had learned that Native Americans had massacred English settlers in

Virginia. The new palisade, made from oak logs harvested from groves around the state, was completed 374 years later at Plimoth plantation to replace a historically inaccurate fence.

Violating the plantation policy to use authentic material in most village structures, the final trunnel came from out of state. Michael Burey, a timber framer, said, "It's made out of Osage orange, a naturally yellow wood. It's the golden trunnel like the one completing the transcontinental railroad (Weston).

Wagon Axles

The strength and slight-swelling properties of Osage orange wood made it ideal for wagon axles (Grace 52).

Wagon Spokes

Spokes and hubs for wagon wheels, and sometimes the entire wagon, would be constructed of Osage orange. In North Texas newspaper archives are recods of advertisements from wagon and buggy factories using Osage orange wood (North Texas Bois d'Arc Is Unsurpassed Material for Wagon Spokes and Felloes").

Wagon Shafts

Wagons need tough, strong wood for shafts attached for horses that pull vehicles on wheels. The pressure of horses on the poles when the wagon is propelled requires material that can withstand the stress of the acceleration, as well as the bumps along the route.

Wagon Tongues

The flexibility, durability, and strength of the Osage orange perfectly describes a wood suitable for the workload expected of a wagon tongue (Grace 51-52)

Wagons

For fifty years W. A. Ewing owned a prosperous wagon shop in Bonham, Texas, on the east side of the sqauare. He used Osage orange as material for wagon beds, tongues, shaves, spokes, and wheel rims (Hodge 13).

Walking Sticks and Canes

Like crutches, walking sticks and canes need a certain type of dependable wood that would provide the necessary aid to walking. Limb contours growing at right angles and creating a natural handle at the top of the canes are often chosen. Other shapes are slected for walking sticks. Knobs, gnarls, and wood grain add to the character of Osage orange canes. Again Maclura is a favored wood for fashioning walking sticks.

War Clubs

The wood of the Osage orange was the favorite substance for war clubs of the Osage Indians (Weed). Sharp metal resembling knife blades were often attached to the bottom of the weapons.

War Paint

Before going into battle, American Indians smeared their spears with the juice of the Osage Orange (*Meehans' Monthly.* 10 (1900): 155).

Washington's Wooden Dentures

In American folklore, myths abound about George Washington's false teeth made of wood, which "still rank as the most famous set of dentures in history" ("Man or Myths? The Real Truth About George Washington"). A 1975 brochure by scholars at Washington's Mount Vernon on the Potomac informs visitors of myths involving the first U.S. president.

The myth about his wooden teeth is listed right after the fabrication about chopping down the cherry tree with his little hatchet. The tree-whacking legend grew from the fertile memory of Mason Weems, an early biographer of Washington.

The brochure verifies that Washington wore false teeth. But they were constructed from ivory, metal, and human teeth, not wood. When the story about the wooden teeth reached residents of the Osage orange domain, locals decided that he must have chosen the strongest wood available—Osage orange, no doubt.

The original lower denture for Washington was made in 1789 by John Greenwood of hippopotamus ivory, first containing eight human teeth retained in place with gold screw rivets. A hole was bored into the base to permit Washington's one remaining tooth to slip through. Further evidence that the Osage orange could not have been used is the documentation that the tree had not been introduced beyond Native Americans until 1804 and that the Osage orange was not part of the tree inventory during Washington's time at Mount Vernon (Mount Vernon Ladies Association of the Union, letter to Fred Tarpley, June 12, 1990).

In Gilbert Stuart's famous "Athenaeum" portrait, the peculiar tight-lipped expression of the president no doubt encouraged interest in his dental problems. Washington later let his dentist know that he was uncomfortable with the ill-fitting dentures when he posed for the portrait ("Man or Myth? The Real Truth about George Washington").

Whip Handles

In Port Acres, Texas, near Beaumont, Preston Murphy recalls how he was taught to make Western whips by his father, who in turn had been taught by his father. For his handles, he uses only the extremely hard wood of the Osage orange. "This wood is so hard people can't cut into it," he says. As a child, Murphy would skin the hide off his father's cows, salt it down, and dry it out. He would turn the leather into the loudest whip a cow could hope to hear (Rust 28A).

Wind Shelters, Windbreaks

Windbreaks and wind shelters survived the decline of Osage orange as the favored plant for living fences. A need continued for barriers that would prevent soil erosion and provide shelter for wildlife. These hedges were not expected to meet the criteria of the hedge fences: horse high, bull strong, and pig tight. Although the two words are often used interchangeably, a windbreak, first appearing in English print in 1861 is defined as "a growth of trees or shrubs serving to break the force of the wind; *broadly*: a shelter (as a fence) from the wind (*Merriam-Webster New Collegiate Dicitonary*, 11th ed.).

Wood Carvings

As his grocery stock began to disappear, Alhert Reazu Crowley would fill the shelves with his wood carvings of West Texas windmills, covered wagons, and outhouses. He made the transition from carving meat to carving wood at age fifty-nine. He especially enjoys carving faces of those he has encountered growing up in Snyder or in associations with Eskimos during World War II. His choices of logs for carving are bois d'arc, mesquite, and mimosa (Spurlock 15).

Woodcrafts

Many types of carved, turned, or inlaid woodcrafts are fashioned from Osage orange. Howard Stephens, a woodcraft artist in Tyler, Texas, praises the versatility of Osage orange, telling admirers of his creations that the wood is the hardest, heaviest, and toughest produced by native trees. He uses well seasoned dead trees and salvaged wood for creating many unique items. (Stephens, Howard).

Because of its hardness, seasoned Osage orange is difficult to work with. It dulls saw blades and defies nails although it holds glue and screws well (Stephens, Howard)

When the wood is green before it hardens, it provides no problems.

Writing Pens

Crafters of ballpoint pens and mechanical pens include Osage orange among the woods they place on their lathes and turn into attractive writing implements. The hard wood, its bright yellow color, interesting grain, and ability to take a high polish are advantages of Osage orange. Every time Dr. Gary McBryde, an Oklahoma physician, writes a prescription, opens a letter, or tells time, he is using one of his own creations from Osage orange. Pen Prescriptions is his hobby and parttime business. He acknowledges that Osage orange and other woods used in his pen, clock, and letter opener sets are the real selling point (Watkins 1).

Bois d'Arc Love Seat
Furniture by Bud Hanzlick

13
Global Range of Osage Orange

United States and Possessions

An alphabetical listing of the fifty American states, as well as two of the United States possessions, presents information about the Osage orange, whether a native or an introduced tree. Significant reports about favored habitats, historic roles, personalities, and events associated with the tree are included.

The U.S. Forest Service, in producing the Forest Inventory and Analysis Database, has plotted on a map the locations of the Osage orange as surveyed between 2000 and 2008. The data were collected by the Forest Service only on "accessible forest land," an area of trees at least one acre in size and 120 feet wide. With other required specifications, the inventory samples only trees found in forests, while ordinarily excluding arboretums, ornamental plantings, and field breaks (Perry).

Information obtained from the Forest Service maps for Osage orange is cited for those states not represented on the maps depicting the Forest Inventory and Analysis Database.

Alabama

The Osage orange tree was introduced to the state from the Southwest and frequently cultivated for hedges. In Alabama it escapes from cultivation in the black belt and possibly also in the Tennessee Valley. These are the regions most nearly resembling its natural home in Texas. Robert M. Roland, an early botanist, reported in 1928 that he had seen the tree growing apparently wild in Pickens, Sumter, and Perry counties (Harper 151).

Alaska

The northern location and below-freezing winters of Alaska cannot be tolerated by Osage orange, and growth in a forest setting accounts for the omission of the tree from the Forest Inventory and Analysis Database.

Arizona

Occurrences of Osage orange in Arizona do not qualify for inclusion in the Forest Inventory and Analysis Database.

Arkansas

The tree is most frequently found in open situations in the southern part of Arkansas, especially the southwestern (Moore). As a rule. the Osage orange does not occur as a forest tree throughout the state (Bucholz and Mattoon). The tree grows in every county of Arkansas (Clark), but its favorite environment is in open situations or in semi-open woods in the southern part of the state ("Osage-Orange, "*Fayetteville County Democrat*).

An area near President Bill Clinton's hometown of Hope is known as the bois d'arc wildlands (Diebel A21).

The trees lent their name to Bois d'Arc Reservoir, a fishing mecca in the region.

California

Introduced Osage orange hedgerows are common in rural sections of California (Metcalf).

One book on the trees of Santa Barbara, dismisses Osage orange as "rarely cultivated in this region, where it has no popular uses." Locations are given for small trees in Fanceschi Park and larger ones in Montecito (Van Renesselaer).

A later book about Santa Barbara trees identified a single tree in Franceschi Park, two trees on Riven Rock Road, and others on the north side of Schoolhouse Road (Muller, Broder, and Beittel 133). Although isolated clusters of Osage orange trees growing in California have been identified, the trees do not qualify for inclusion in the Forest Inventory and Analysis Database.

Colorado

The Osage orange trees found in Colorado are not sufficient in number for the Forest Inventory and Analysis Database. However, the Denver Botanic Gardens published a book including the Osage orange as an exotic tree in Colorado (Zeiner).

Connecticut

The Osage orange is rare in Connecticut, escaping from cultivation into roadsides and neglected places. Trees were identified in Waterford, East Haven, Waterbury, and Kent. Regional names are Osage orange, bois d'arc, Osage apple, mock orange, mock apple, and bow-wood (Connecticut Botanical Society 154).

Delaware

Osage orange hedgerows were reported as common in Delaware in 1900 ("Fruits and Vegetables." *Report of the Commissioner of Agriculture for Year 1859* 51). As early as 1869, hedges in New Castle were described as "incredibly old).

Florida

Osage orange is uncommon and sporadic in northern Florida (Duncan,). The tree is found in northern Florida in waste places or fence rows only in the vicinity of Tallahassee and Marianna (Kurz and Godfrey 118). Northwestern Florida is the beginning of the Gulf coast plains, where Osage orange grows well in the rich loose bottom soil (Wulff 217).

In this region Osage orange was listed among the Pleistocene flora on the grounds that the definite and abundant occurrence of the tree "point without question to the prevalence of a much warmer climate than now prevails" (Wulff 184).

When Harry Gray of Deerfield Beach wrote to a Fort Lauderdale newspaper asking where he could obtain Osage orange seeds or plants, he was told, "The tree does not appear to be for sale in Florida, according to several wholesale source guides. It will not grow here in South Florida because we do not have enough of the winter chill period that it requires (Haehle 3E).

Georgia

The Osage orange is found occasionally in various habitats throughout the state (Duncan). Favorite habitats of the tree are in alluvial pastures or fencerows (Radford, Ahles, and Bell 391). In 1933, a botanist who discovered a tree with three large shoots in a swamp in Dooly County estimated it to be at least fifty years old, and he wondered if it were possible that the tree might be native to a few swamps in Georgia and the Gulf States (Coker and Totten 172). The range of Osage orange in Georgia has been characterized as "uncommon and sporadic" (Godfrey, Robert, *Northern Florida and Adjacent Georgia and Alabama*).

Hawaii

Osage orange does not grow in Hawaii in concentrations sufficient to qualify for the Forest Inventory and Analysis Database.

Idaho

Idaho does not have enough trees in forest habitats to meet the standards of the Forest Inventory and Analysis Database.

Illinois

Although not a native plant in the state, Osage orange is found throughout Illinois as a hedge or windbreak, but as a general rule, it is not a forest tree (Jones, George). The state became closely identified with the tree after Jonathan Baldwin Turner of Illinois College began experiments with Osage orange hedges in the 1830s. Trner promotion of Osage orange made it the favorite hedge. Hedgerows could still be seen in 1987 in all but nine of Illinois' 102 counties (United Press. "Osage Orange Growing Scarce in Illinois" pt. 1, p. 1). Success of barbed wire fences did not replace Osage orange hedges until the Bessemer process made good steel wire possible ("Horse-High, Bull-Strong, and Pig-Tight" 221-22, 230).

Osage orange trees once surrounded nearly every farm field in Illinois as "life palace guards, defying penetration and protecting the soil within their perimeters." The hedges sheltered millions of pheasant chicks, crows, rabbits, and other animals" (Lyons).

Indiana

Osage orange was introduced in Indiana for hedge fences. Since land has become so valuable, its use for hedges has been discontinued (Deam, Charles *Flora of Indiana*). The tree has been but little used for forest planting (Division of Forestry Publication No. 13, Indiana).

A map designates significant stands of Osage orange in sixteen Indiana counties located in all sections of the state (Deam, Charles, *Flora of Indiana* 394)

In Indiana a state Department of Conservation concluded that Osage orange had only rarely been found as an escape plant (Publication No. 13 166). An Indiana botanist recorded these impressions of Osage orange: "I recall that I studied two lines of large trees that were planted on each side of a deserted lane in the Ohio River bottoms in Perry County. The line of trees was about a quarter of a mile long and the trees were mostly 10-14 inches in diameter near the base. I estimated that on the ground there were no less than 24 bushels of fruit and I assumed that the trees fruited almost annually. Yet I did not find a single seeding and I do not believe any were dug up. I made no special inquiry to ascertain the cause of the failure of reproduction" (Deam, Charles, *Flora of Indiana* 393-98).

Iowa

In the late 1860s and early 1870s, Osage orange hedge fences were at a fever heat in Iowa. Seed was shipped from Texas to the Midwest, where it sold for five dollars a pound (Iowa State College and Iowa Experiment Station. *Farming in Iowa*). The tree was not hardy in northern Iowa (Odenwald and Turner).

According to reports from county agricultural societies, Osage orange hedges had been planted in nearly thirty counties between the first ones in 1848 until 1859 (Hewes and Jung 195).

As an enticement to investigate free lands of Iowa, an 1860 promotional volume told potential immigrants, "As the settlements extend away from the timber, the wire fence and the hedge will be resorted to, both of which are practicable here, as in other and older portions of the state. The Osage Orange will thrive here, but will require perhaps some winter protection the first year or two" (Fulton 11).

In 1867, *The Handbook of Iowa* discussed the lack of fence material in the state and the many solutions investigated to remedy the problem. Prospective residents were told, "Among all these experiments the Osage orange hedge may be set down as the most successful. The only drawback upon its perfect success is the fact that the hard winter on the bleak prairie is sometimes too tough for it. This objection, which is not now a very serious one, will diminish as the country becomes better cultivated and more filled up with groves (Blanchard 26).

When prairie farmers gained a majority, they influenced the modification of laws so that experimental fences became legal through their vote in counties where they controlled the elections (Gue 101-02).

As land has become more valuable in Iowa, Osage orange planting has ceased, but escaped trees grow in all parts of the state, especially in Ohio River bottoms (*Woody Plants of Iowa* 449).

Kansas

Beyond its presumed natural distribution in eastern Texas and small areas of Oklahoma and Arkansas, the Osage orange has been planted widely and generally throughout Kansas, and has proven itself hardy in the state. The tree is concentrated in the southeastern and eastern parts of Kansas. (Kansas State Board of Agriculture. *Trees in Kansas* 62).

As early as 1856, the author of *The Kanzas Region: Forest, Prairie, Desert, Mountain, Dale, and River* reasoned, "Trees [in Kansas] are not so interspersed as to be found upon every quarter section. For enclosures, the Osage orange will, however, remedy this deficiency. Indigenous in Louisiana and Texas, it takes to the soil and cities of Illinois kindly; and must, therefore, thrive in Kanzas (Greene 144).

In 1867, the state offered a cash bonus of $2 for every twenty rods of hedge planted and sustained for five years (*Kansas. A Guide to the Sunflower State*). An increase in population during the 1870s resulted from a "wet cycle in 1878, return to business prosperity from 1877 onward, and technology's replace of the living fences with barbed wire in the late 1870s" (Davis, Kenneth). The Osage orange is more commonly known in Kansas as hedge or hedge apple and, in some areas of the state, bois d'arc (Stephens, H. A.). A unique practice in the LaCross area of Kansas was the use of limestone posts instead of Osage orange for stringing barbed wire (Howes, Charles C. 92).

In 1875 a statistical survey in Kansas revealed that state-wide averages for types of enclosures were rail in first place, hedges in second, board in third, wire in fourth, and stone in fifth (Hewes 519). Between 1865 and 1875, a dramatic increase in hedges almost doubled their number, making it the leading fence in the state, with about forty-nine percent of the total. Throughout eastern and central Kansas, Osage orange was the usual plant of choice for thousands of miles of hedge planted in the 1860s and 1870s (Davis, Kenneth 123). In 1882, hedge was the chief type of fence in Kansas and dominating in all of the counties where fences were inventoried except for two with rail fences leading and one with stone fences in majority use in another (Hewes 522, 524). Barbed wire did not become the major type until 1882 or the state leader until 1885 (Hewes 525).

Osage orange was one of six trees sent from the Bessey Nursery in Halsey, Nebraska, for planting in the Kansas Reserve in 1906. The Forest Service explained its effort n 1908 with a larger acreage and the title of the Kansas National Forest (Droze, *Trees, Prairies, and People* 34).

Kansas is the only state known to have made a census—or even an estimated census—of its tree inhabitants. The number of trees within the state's 86,276 square miles is estimated at 225,000,000, but the number of Osage orange trees is unknown although high (Teale 274).

An Osage orange of championship caliber grows on Campanile Hill on the campus of Kansas University. Its trunk circumference, total height, and limb spread make it the largest of its kind found in the state, according to records kept by the Department of Forestry at Kansas State University (Winingham 1, 3).

Kentucky

Not many Osage orange hedges remained in the state in 1973, but the species escaped and may be a thorny pest on roadsides, in pastures, and in other open places. Most common in the Bluegrass region, it is known across the state as Osage orange, hedge apple, bois d'arc, bodark, and bow wood (Wharton and Barbour 520).

Louisiana

The Osage orange tree in northwestern Louisiana is perhaps a native plant, but it is so widely cultivated in the state that determining its original range is not possible (Brown, Clair A. *Louisiana Trees and Shrubs*). Although debates continue about whether the tree is native or naturalized in the state, Louisiana botanists now believe that Osage orange was apparently introduced (Brown, Clair, *Commercial Trees* 42). On river plantations living bois d'arc hedges survive as significant landmarks (Dorman 38).

The common name of the tree in Louisiana is bois d'arc, but it is also called Osage orange, hedge apple, and horse apple (Thomas 148).

Maine

Phillip Rutherford grew up surrounded by native Osage orange trees in Roxton, Texas. He took pride in a nearby family estate with an Osage orange hedge that survived to be almost one hundred. When he took a college teaching assignment in Maine, he never spotted the familiar tree during the ten years he lived in the northeastern state.

It is not surprising that little printed material exists about the Osage orange in Maine, which is part of the region north of Boston where the tree could not survive winter kill (Rutherford).

Maine is not included in the Forest Inventory and Analysis Database.

Maryland

State botanists recognize Osage orange as not native to Maryland. It is found in coastal and midland zones of the state, with frequent escape from cultivation, but the tree is not hardy in the mountain zone (Shreve, Crysler, Blodgett, and Bexley 327; Howe 74). Isolated trees grow in eastern woods as far east as Maryland (Hylander 103).

Massachusetts

Books about trees in the northeastern United States report that the Osage orange does not survive the winters above Massachusetts. In the 1896 *Report of Trees and Shrubs Growing Naturally in the Forests of Massachusetts*, there is no mention of Osage orange. Rare in Massachusetts, the tree has been reported growing in towns including Danvers, Wakefield, and Springfield (Seymour).

A significant general statement about the presence of Osage orange trees in the northernmost tiers of states was, "Occasionally adventive or persistent in our range but probably no where fully established (Gleason, *Northeastern United* States). Massachusetts, frequently mentioned as the northeastern limits of Osage orange, as in the following statement: "It is hardy as far north as Massachusetts" (Fett 258).

Although Massachusetts experiments with hedging started soon after 1812, the living fences were primarily viewed from a negative English perspective (*The Fence* Sec. 14, p. 1*)*.

Michigan

The Osage orange tree, a native of the South, is hardy throughout Michigan. One of the state guides to trees classified it as a desirable ornamental tree and useful for hedges (Otis 133).

A state champion Osage orange tree in Michigan grows near the edge of Coloma in Berrien County (http//www.msue.msu.imp/moduf/102.12 December 2009).

Minnesota

The tree does not qualify as winter hardy in Minnesota (Odenwald, and Turner; Michaelson 100; Van Dersal 163). The state had no concentrations of trees to justify its inclusion in the Forest Inventory and Analysis Database,

Mississippi

The favored habitat for Osage orange is in alluvial pastures or fence rows (Radford, Ables, and Bell 301). Concentrations of the tree were surveyed in the east central portion of the state for the Forest Inventory and Analysis Database.

Missouri

Osage orange grows in the majority of Missouri's counties. Common habitats within the state for the tree are in low alluvial woods; in valleys along streams, borders of woods, pastures, fence rows; and in thickets (Steyermark 563). In southwestern Missouri the Osage orange thrives in pasture and fence rows as a hardy thorny tree resistant to drought (Rafferty, *Ozarks* 146).

Osage orange seeds brought $40 a bushel in the 1870s (Rafferty *Ozarks* 146). In Missouri the Osage orange posts are described as "nearly indestructible." If a post fails early, it is not uncommon to hear an oldtimer forgive it with, "That post was just cut under the wrong rising of the moon." In 1890 Osage orange posts were selling for about $3 each for a four-inch-diameter line post seven feet long or $10 for a seven-inch, nine-foot corner post. Larger ones—the kind you set with immortality in mind—naturally cost more" (Grace 52-53).

The dates of the earliest planting of Osage orange hedges in Missouri were recorded in 1867 by the Missouri State Board of Agriculture. Areas included Holt County (northwest Missouri) in 1851, Cass County (west-central) about 1851, Greene County (southwest) about 1856, and Grundy (north-central) about 1856 (Hewes and Jung 198).

Montana

Osage orange fails to be included in the Forest Inventory and Analysis Database for Osage orange. Montana has also been designated as a state where the tree is not winter hardy, and thus it is not used in windbreaks (Michaelson 100; Van Dersal 163).

Nebraska

Osage orange was introduced into Nebraska by early settlers who planted it as a hedge fence now seen in nearly all parts of the state. Although severely tested by the hot summers and the cold, dry winters of central to western Nebraska, it ensures a remarkable range of habitat conditions. Some counties in Nebraska had as many as 1,000 miles of Osage orange hedge in 1880 (Baltensperger, 51). Terrain influences the pattern of the hedges, and in sections of the state with rolling and hilly surfaces, the hedges are shaped to conform with the land, bending around hills and gullies (Baltensperger 212).

Osage orange is found in almost all parts of Nebraska, where it has been planted as a hedge and along fence rows (Pool 109). Thousands of miles of Osage orange trees that were once cultivated in hedges no longer function as living fences. Nevertheless, they remain as one of the most prominent landmarks of the rural landscape along the fields and the roads in southeastern Nebraska

(Baltensperger 210). Hedging began as early as 1857 or 1858 in Nebraska (Hewes 503). The tree is now seen in very nearly all parts of the state (Hewes and Jung). By 1871 Osage orange hedges were though to be equal to post and rail and to board fences as the three leading types of enclosures in Nebraska (Hewes 510).

Although Osage orange can endure a remarkable range of habitat conditions, the hot summers and cold dry winters of central to western Nebraska test it very severely. It does not do well in the northern or western portions of the state or in the sandier soil (Pool 102). In Nebraska the typical hedgerow occupies about three acres per mile, and shelterbelts consume as much as five times that acreage (Baltensperger 211).

Bob Brandt, a banker in Unadilla, has increased his state's number of champion trees by identifying giant flora such as the largest Osage orange. Following a tip from a bank customer, Brandt found the champion in a cluster of trees about four miles southeast of Table Rock. Brandt believes the tree may be 150 years old ("Banker Locates Champion Tree in Nebraska" 3).

Nevada

The Osage orange is occasionally planted in western Nevada (Billings 71). Nevada is not part of the Inventory and Analysis Database for Osage orange.

New Hampshire

As a state north of Massachusetts in the winter-kill zone, the Osage orange does not survive the winters in New Hampshire. The state does not have Osage orange trees in forest settings and is not included in the Forest Inventory and Analysis Database.

New Jersey

In celebration of Arbor Day's 125th anniversary in May 1977, Montgomery, New Jersey, organized a tour to showcase trees that had witnessed the history of the community. One of the trees honored was an Osage orange in Montgomery Park. It was planted in the mid-nineteenth century by farmers who wanted it to become a living fence. It did not disappoint them (Grey 043).

New Mexico

In New Mexico the Osage orange, also known to state residents as bois d'arc, is found on waste ground and in arroyos, probably mostly on limestone soils. The distribution of the tree is plotted in four central counties and in one of the southernmost counties (Martin and Hutchings 524, 526).

New York

In New York State, the Osage orange is usually a much smaller tree than elsewhere, often a large shrub. Preferring rich moist bottom lands in its native Southern habitat, the Osage orange, in the east, grows under a variety of conditions as a hedge plant. The tree was once classified as a plant with "no commercial importance" in New York State (Brown, H. P., *Commercial Woods* 209).

A venerable Osage orange attracts much attention in Manhattan's Central Park. Neil Calvanese, Central Park horticulturist, recorded these remarks about his Osage orange trees: "The finest example (and the oldest) is located on the center drive adjacent to Wollman Rink. At Wollman Rink the tree is female and bears fruit the size of grapefruit, which are apparent in the fall. The tree may predate the park which would make it at least 132 years old [in 1991]. The tree was most likely planted as a small sapling" (Calvanese, Neil. Letter to Fred Tarpley, May 23, 1991). Check Peet and Calvanese sources.

A 1903 guide to trees and shrubs in Central Park stated that near the 72nd Street gate "a fine old osage orange spreads out its shining canopy of sun-glinted leaves (Peet 134).

An Osage orange stands in Brooklyn's Prospect Park, located in Nethermead, the park's second large meadow space. It is one of the oldest trees in the Park (Dunning C11).

In 1858, *Moore's Rural New-Yorker* printed statements by its editor who had inspected hedging. He wrote, "Hundreds of thousands of acres on the western prairies have been enclosed with Osage orange hedge by the owners, as a matter of speculation, solely to add to the value of the land when sold. We have seen miles of this hedge planted that will be a total failure. Indeed not one rod in a hundred of the many thousands we saw at the West will ever make a hedge worth having (*The Fence* sec. 1, p. 2*)*.

In 1862, the Farmers' Club discussed hedges at the state fair in Rochester. E. Cornell made observations about hedges he had observed in Europe. In France, he thought there was not enough fencing to suit American needs. In England, he thought there was too much hedging although " . . . hedge evidently destroys the value of the land for several feet on each side. . . . the necessary trimming is expensive and troublesome, and without it the hedge is valueless."

North Carolina

The range of the Osage orange is widespread in North Carolina (Radford, Ables and Bell 390). On the North Carolina side of the Great Smoky Mountains National Park, the Osage orange persists at Smokemont and in the Visitor Center area along the Oconaluftee River (Stupka).

North Dakota

The Osage orange is not a winter hardy tree in North Dakota (Odenwald and Turner; Van Dersal 163).

After repeal of the Tree Culture Act, one final effort at furthering plains forestry preceded the Great Depression of the 1930s. In 1929, the Forest Service's Lake States Forest Experiment Station in St. Paul, Minnesota, established a survey of the tree-growing potential of the North Dakota Sand Hill region (Droze).

Ohio

Although widely distributed in Ohio and believed to be in every county of the state, Osage orange is considered a naturalized tree although it is sometimes spontaneous from seed (Braun 138-39). Rows of Osage orange hedge trees bear testimony to the farmer who was either too busy or dislike the task of trimming the hedges at the proper time. The habitat in Ohio is in dry soils, along fence rows, and in open fields (Vannorsdall 201). The greatest concentration of Osage orange trees will be found along the Ohio River in southwestern Ohio (Stephens 237).

The campus of Miami University in Oxford cherishes several near-champion trees including a that botanists prize as one of the best in the state (Chichester).

For more than thirty years, the Cincinnati Soil and Water Conservation District has been searching for big trees. In 1997 the target of the search was for the largest bois d'arc in Clermont County, Ohio. Owner of the biggest tree is recognized at the district's annual meeting ("Tristate A.M. Report." *Cincinnati Enquirer.* 27 July 1997 B02).

Oklahoma

Osage orange is found primarily in eastern Oklahoma. Common names for the tree in Oklahoma are Osage orange, bow d'arc, hedge apple, and mock orange. (Durrell' McCox 39). The tree can be found in six of the state's seven topographical districts but not in the Short-grass Plains of the Western Panhandle (Bell 3, 8).

Osage orange is listed among the flora extending from the Ozark Plateau, especially in river-bottom land (Wulff 414). In Oklahoma Osage orange is well established east of Interstate 35 and south of Interstate 40 (McCox 39).

Among the birds of Oklahoma, the loggerhead shrike is indebted to Osage orange trees as home for one-third of its nests built in Southwestern Oklahoma. A study of nesting habits was made from 1985 through 1988 (*Wilson Bulletin*. 104.1 95-104).

A picture postcard is sold in Webbers Falls, Oklahoma, claiming that the gigantic, stalwart Osage orange growing the banks of the Arkansas River is said to be "the largest of its kind in the United States." The only measurement given is 15'8" in circumference, By comparison, the Osage orange tree growing at the Patrick Henry home, mentioned often as the national champion has these measurements: circumference, 24' 6"; height 51'; spread, 92'. The age of the Oklahoma tree has been estimated at more than 225 years, making it at least twenty-three years older than the Louis and Clark Expedition.

When Walter Webber, a Cherokee Indian chief, operated a trading post here in 1849, the tree was said to be fully grown. The tree now overlooks traffic on the new Arkansas River channel.

Oregon

The presence of Osage orange in Oregon is not sufficient for inclusion in the Forest Inventory and Analysis Database. A national guide to woody plants recognizes Osage orange as growing in Oregon (Schopmeyer 525).

Pennsylvania

The Osage orange has been introduced into practically every part of Pennsylvania as a hedge or ornamental tree. Less exacting in soil than most of the state's trees, the Osage orange still chooses the best soil when it has a choice. It is occasionally found in swamps. (Illick 159; Li 141). In the southeastern counties of Pennsylvania, shortage of wood for fences became acute before 1840, and there was much interest in living fences. between 1850 and 1880, Nurserymen recommended Osage orange as the "best defensive hedge plant; it is also highly ornamental." Many of those who used it regretted their choice. The tree was described as viciously thorny, occupying too much land, requirirng much soil moisture, and demanding too much time to keep it within bounds of the hedge (Fletcher 70).

Rhode Island

The U.S. Forest Service survey of trees in a forest setting does not include Rhode Island in its Forest Inventory and Analysis Database for the Osage orange.

South Carolina

The Osage orange is widespread in the extreme northwestern and southernmost regions of South Carolina (Radford, Ables, and Bell 390).

South Dakota

The small Osage orange trees in South Dakota are not usually over six meters tall (twenty-one and a half feet). In the southern part of state, the tree is found at roadsides and waste places (Van Bruggen 168). They occasionally escape from cultivation and reproduce at roadsides and waste places (Van Bruggen 168)

Only small Osage orange trees grow in the states. The tree is not considered winter hardy in South Dakota (Michaelson 100; Van Dersal 163).

Tennessee

Although Osage orange is not a native tree in Tennessee, it has been widely planted for hedges and for ornamental trees. The tree is well distributed over the state. Common names applied in Tennessee are Osage orange, bois d'arc, and mock orange (*Forest Trees of Tennessee*). On the Tennessee side of the Great Smoky Mountains National Park, the tree persists in the immediate vicinity of former home sites in the Sugarlands and along Parsons Branch (Stupka 54).

Texas

Northeast Texas and portions of Arkansas and Louisiana along the Red River have been identified as the only native habitat of the Osage orange since the most recent ice age. It appears that the approach of the Bois d'Arc Creek to its mouth at the Red River in northern Fannin and Lamar counties in Texas could be the center of the largest stands of the tree that attracted Indian traders in the early nineteenth century.

Because some of the most impressive native growths of Osage orange were located in Northeast Texas, the *Galveston News* and the *Texas Almanac* ran frequent articles advocating the use of the tree as a hedge ("Osage Orange." *Dallas Morning News.* 22 Oct. 1944, sec. 4).

Most Texans know the tree as bois d'arc or horse apple, but other common names are understood, even they may not be used (Cox and Leslie 148; Bray 63).

In transcribing minutes of the Cat Spring Agricultural Society, founded in 1856, a Brenham, Texas, conservationist, found numerous references to bois d'arc trees that the farmers were planting as living fences (Krueger.).

Texas claims the distinction of having provided the setting for the turning point in convincing ranchers that barbed wire would contain their cattle without inflicting injury. On Military Plaza in San Antonio in 1878, Bet-a-Million Yates demonstrated the superiority of barbed wire. Sales increases followed immediately.

Two years earlier Osage orange hedges were gaining popularity on large ranches. In 1874 Capt. Richard King, owner 150,000 acre King Ranch, began fencing in 1871. Now he had an enclosed pasture of 70,000 acres. Osage orange was the most popular material for hedging, and several ranchers were building hedges of that tree while a few were building sod fences (Gard 207). Which one?

In a 1904 manual on wood published in London, Gainesville, Texas, was identified as a major shipping for Osage orange wood sawn into lumber and posts (Bray 63).

A controversial grove of Osage orange trees is found at Bois d'Arc Springs in Big Bend National Park. Several U.S. Forest Service checklists and maps of native habitats claim this locale although it is located four hundred miles from the long-established habitat in Northeast Texas. Local botanists in the Big Bend area are convinced that the Bois d'Arc Springs trees were planted by Comanche Indians who had brought the seed into the region from other locales (Peattie 180). ???

Near the George W. Bush presidential library site on the Southern Methodist University, remnants of ancient bois d'arc hedges mark Lovers Lane, Hillcrest, and other streets. Lovers' Lane was exactly that and arched bois d'arc trees romantically entwined above the lane (Greene, A. C.). According to an article in the *Dallas Morning News* in 1989, both Highland Park and University Park, independent communities surrounded by Dallas, treasure gnarled bois d'arc trees surviving many urban modifications to the area. The trees were planted by settlers in the 1850s as fence rows.

In San Antonio the Osage orange trees are recognized as having been introduced from northeastern Texas and planted for shade and hedges (Mackensen 16).

In the Trans-Pecos region of Texas, where the Osage orange grows, it is always found at Indian camping grounds or caves near a water source such as seeps, springs, and creeks. Historians and botanists claim these trees were seeded from "horse apples" carried by Indian tribes (Simpson).

The most likely habitat in East Texas for Osage orange trees is moist bottomlands (Nixon). In 1989 the champion Osage orange in Texas grew in the back yard of the home of Joe Mahone, 300 Frost Street, New Boston, Texas. The handsome tree held the Texas title in 1970. The state champion tree changes as trees with larger dimensions are discovered, nominated, and confirmed. Earlier, Osage Its measurements were 196" circumference, 40' tall, and 80' crown spread (Texas Forest Service, *1989 Texas Big Tree Registry* 8*)*.

The New Boston tree replaced another specimen which held the title in 1955 in DeKalb only fifteen miles away (*Texas Forest News* May 1955).

For a time, a tree near Redland in Angelina County was the champion. Trees in Marshall and south of Old Waverly in San Jacinto County also made claims to the designation as Texas' largest Osage orange (*Texas Forest News* January/February 1948).

Of all the trees in Eisenhower State Park on Lake Texoma, Osage orange inspired more questions at the reception desk than any other in the recreational area. Betty Thomas, the genial lady at the park office, observed that some visitors did not know what to call the tree, but many others had a variety of regional monikers. "Those who got tangled in its sharp thorns on the tree branches invented a few other names," Betty Thomas said (Cardwell). Visitors unfamiliar with the exotic fruit of the tree once mistook a disintegrating globule as the grisly wrinked remains of a human brain. When the concerned and agash visitors reported their discovery to the park manager, they were given an informative short course about the fruit of Osage orange tree and its resemblance to human anatomy.

Utah

Utah did not meet the criteria for sufficient stands of Osage orange to qualify for inclusion in the Forest Inventory and Analysis Database.

Vermont

Sufficient growths of Osage orange in Vermont did not meet standards of the U.S. Forest Service for inclusion in the Forest Inventory and Analysis Database

Virginia

The Osage orange, introduced from Texas and Arkansas, is found distributed throughout Virginia, but it does not as a rule occur as a forest tree. Growing chiefly in open fields, along fence rows, and as a pure hedge fence, the tree is used for shade, hedges, and as living fence posts (Guyton and Swope; Jones; Chapin 44). Favorite habitats of escape trees are alluvial pastures and fence rows (Radford, Ables, and Bell 381).

Common names for the tree heard in Virginia are bowdarc, hedge apple, and mock orange (Jones, Chapin).

Washington, DC

The most striking tree, according to a chronicler of Washington, DC, trees is the Osage orange growing on the grounds of the Soldiers' and Airmen's Home in the northwest part of the city (Chouks-Bradley).

The national capital, claiming to be a city of trees, takes pride in the hundreds of rolling acres of the Soldiers' and Airmen's Home. Considered to be the most striking of some the oldest and most beautiful trees is an ancient Osage orange on the grounds of the military home near the Lincoln Cottage (Choukas-Bradley 48-49).

Washington State

Osage orange is a very rare naturalized tree in Seattle, Washington. A guide to trees in that city comments, "Like its mulberry tree cousin, it's more beloved by kids than adults (Jacobson, 243). Sufficient numbers of the tree in one location did not qualify for inclusion in the Forest Inventory and Analysis Database, but a national guide to woody plants recognizes that the tree is found in Washington (Schopmeyer 525) A Forest Service check list of trees identifies Osage orange as growing in southeastern Washington (Little, *Check List* (1953:230).

The Osage orange tree is not shown in Washington forest settings for the Forest Inventory and Analysis Database.

West Virginia

Osage orange is listed as a tree found in West Virginia as a non-native plant that has escaped from cultivation (Brooks 239; Ore). Planted widely in West Virginia as hedges, the Osage orange is known as hedgeapple throughout the state. The tree thrives in alluvial pastures or fencerows (Radford, Ahles, and Bell 391). During World War I, Osage orange was a source of dye for olive-drab uniforms, and an extraction plant was located at Cass in Pocahontas County (Strausbaugh and Core 312).

Wisconsin

In Wisconsin Osage orange is more or less a curiosity despite the fact that it was occasionally used along roadsides as a hedge (*Wisconsin Trees*). In 1853, the Osage orange tree was recommended to farmers as the best hedge plant to prove hardy as far north as Wisconsin, even though doubts lingered. Winter-kill was a constant concern in this northern state. In 1851 attention was called to an Osage orange tree, in the Milwaukee garden of Lewis Potter. The tree had stood the test of over ten winters (*Transactions of the Wisconsin State Agricultural Society 1853*).

The following champion Osage orange trees in Wisconsin were reported in 1980 with their locations and dates of recognition: Pleasanton, Kenosha County, on the Weller farms (1963); Bayview Apartments, Madison, Dane County (1971); and Boerner Botanical Gardens, Hales Corners, Milwaukee County (1961) (Allison 44).

A book cataloging Wisconsin trees in 1970 included Osage orange as a tree growing in the state (Shonefelt 9). The seven counties in the southeastern corner of Wisconsin included Osage orange as one of the trees found in that area (*Deciduous Trees* 68).

Wyoming

As in most western states, Wyoming is not included in the Forest Inventory and Analysis Database for stands of the Osage orange in a forest setting.

Puerto Rico and Virgin Islands

Maclura tinctoria, but not Osage orange, is listed in *Trees of Puerto Rico and the Virgin* Islands (Little, Woodbury, and Wadsworth). An accompanying note explains that Maclura tinctoria is related to Osage orange and is sometimes placed in the same genus (Little, Woodbury, and Wadsworth 108).

Cautionary Note

As valuable and informative as the books are about the trees of America, the states, and regions, caution must be taken in accepting some of the opinions. Occasionally a practice is continued that was initiated by early botanists describing Osage orange and who transmit dubious information. An example is the following statement: "Apparently no bird or native mammal ever eats them [fruits of Osage orange] or carries them away (Gleason and Cronquist, *The Natural Geography of Plants* 44). Many printed sources and eyewitness accounts disagree with the declaration in the book written by Gleason and Cronquist. The publication date is always a factor to be considered.

Distribution of Common Names

An attempt was made in 1927 to show the distribution of common names for the Osage orange in the various states. The following names were identified: *Osage orange* (Massachusetts, Rhode Island, New York,

New Jersey, Pennsylvania, Delaware, Virginia, West Virginia, North Carolina, South Carolina, Georgia, Alabama, Mississippi, Louisiana, Texas, Kentucky, Missouri, Ohio, Illinois, Kansas, Nebraska, Iowa, Michigan; *bois d'arc* (Louisiana, Texas, Missouri); *bodeck* (Kansas), *mock orange* (Louisiana), *bow-wood* (Alabama), *Osage apple tree* (Tennessee), *yellow-wood* (Tennessee), *hedge* (Illinois), *hedge plant* (Iowa, Nebraska), *Osage* (Iowa) (Sudworth 117).

Outside the United States
Australia

At Steve LaValley's "botanic ark" in Warragul, Australia, sixty miles east of Melbourne, plants have been gathered from all over the world. Since 1981, LaValley has collected rare plants including a North American Osage orange (Scott*)*.

In Victoria, Australia, Osage orange was planted experimentally in state forests in 1935, but the trees did not survive rabbit damage. Osage orange is commonly grown as a low windbreak and stock-proof hedge in warmer lowland districts with rain falls fown to sixteen inches a year (Streets 431).

Canada

The Osage orange is not a native in the province, but tree has s become naturalized in some localities and is hardy in southern Ontario despite its origin in the southern United States (White, J. H. 68).

Although Osage orange may not survive a severe winter in the Ottawa area, the residents are experimenting with the plant as hedges, fully aware that they will need pruning each spring and that their thorns are brutal. The tree is dismissed with this statement: "The tree is of no special merit in the Ottawa area as an ornament, and its utilitarian aspect has not been fully explored" (Harshberger 64).

Osage orange does not grow well in the cool, wet climate of Vancouver, and there is often tip die-back (Stanley). Residents of Vancouver view the Osage orange as an unusual American tree with warty fruit (Hosie).

China

Cudrania, the only recognized hybrid of Osage orange is native to China, Korea, and Japan but is sometimes planted in the United States (Smith, "Aspects of the Autecology",1-2). This tree closely allied to Osage orange differs in its three-lobed leaves with more prominent veins and in its flowering on the current season's shoots. Native to China, it is used as food for silkworms (*Trees of Britain & Europe* 806).

England

The Osage orange tree crossed the Atlantic Ocean for an early introduction to England. In 1846, a tree with ripened fruit was reported growing in London (Browne). Because female trees do not begin to bear fruit until they are ten years or older, the description was a clue to the age of the tree.

In 1880 a correspondent of the London *Journal of Horticulture* took to England a fruit of the Osage orange from St. Louis. He called his import an Osage orange apple, declaring, "It had a delicious scent, but was quite uneatable" ("Osage Orange as a Fruit.")

Because of the scarcity of male and female trees adjacent to one another, the fruit of the Osage orange was classified as "rare" in 1971 (Mitchell 260).

Europe

The British editor of a multiple-volume work on *Trees and Shrubs Hardy in the British Isles* said of Osage orange that he had seen it used as hedges in Central Europe (Taylor 641). First imported in Europe and sold at a premium price as a curiosity, the tree never became a popular ornamental tree because it did not fit that mold in a formal sense (Baumgardt 47).

In a 1971 volume, the Osage orange fruit was said to be ". . . common on the Continent, rare in England because it needs male and female trees adjacent. . . (Mitchell 260). Osage orange sometimes grows as hedges or ornamental plants in southern Europe (Polunin 65). .

France

In 1846, Osage orange trees grown from American seeds and cuttings were reported to be bearing ripened fruit in Lyons Clairvaux, and Monpellier (Brown,). The first flowering of Osage orange trees in France was reported in 1835. The flowers were reported in the Luxembourg Garden in Paris and the King's Garden in Nueilly (*Gardener's Magazine* 11 (1835): 315).

Germany

The Osage orange from America was introduced to Germany in the nineteenth century. On June 15, 2010, the Botanical Garden KIT in Karlsruhe, Germany, was offering for sale a packet of six color pictures of Osage orange trees in Germany. The set included closeups of flowers, fruits, and leaves as well as a distant view of a mature tree (Wikipedia.org/wiki/File:Maclura_pomifera_003.JPG. Retrieded June 23, 2010.

Italy

An Osage orange tree introduced to Italy from America was reported growing in Monza in 1846 (Browne). An item on the Osage orange published in *The Farmer & Gardener* in Baltimore on January 30, 1888, stated, ". . . the Royal Garden of Botany and Agriculture at Turin, reports that the leaves of this tree are a substitute for Mulberry as food for Silk Worms," drawing attention to a valuable potential use of the tree.

Japan

Cudrania, the only recognized hybrid of Osage orange, is native to China, Korea, and Japan. (Smith, Jeffrey 2).

Korea

The solitary acknowledged hybrid of Osage orange is Cudrania, a native tree of Korea, China, and Japan. It is sometimes planted in the United States (Smith, Jeffrey 2). The small tree, reaching a height of fifty feet, with axillary thorns and small, spherical red edible fruit about one inch in diameter, has been crossed successfully with the Osage orange (Graves).

Mexico

Osage orange trees are cultivated in an agricultural region within the state of Chihuahua in northern Mexico (*Flora Taxonomica Mexicana*).

Netherlands

Specimens of Osage orange are reported growing in the Netherlands (Smith, Jeffrey 10).

New Zealand

Describing the Osage orange trees growing in New Zealand, a gardening columnist had this opinion about its curious fruit: "They may look like green-coloured oranges but the fruit of the Osage orange. . . are not edible." Nursery catalogues list the Osage orange, and the female tree consistently attracts seasonal interest with its unusual fruit ("Gardening." New Zealand *Nelson Mail*).

Portugal

Specimens of Osage orange are reported growing in Portugal (Smith, Jeffrey 10).

Rhodesia

In Southern Rhodesia, cultivation of the Osage orange tree has been successful on a small scale, but further trials have recommended to explore its potential here (Streets 431).

Romania

Specimens of Osage orange are reported growing in Romania (Smith, Jeffrey 10).

Russia

Specimens of Osage orange are reported growing in Russia (Smith, Jeffrey 10).

Southern Europe

Osage orange is sometimes grown as hedges and ornament in southern Europe (Pohmin).

Switzerland

Specimens of Osage orange are reported to be growing in Switzerland (Smith, Jeffrey 10).

Osage orange trees, no doubt, have been naturalized in many other counties of the world, but no mention of the plants in additional nations were found in botanical sources consulted in this research.

Osage Orange Hedge and Gateway
Southern Cultivator, 1864

14
A Tree by Any Other Name

Wherever the Osage orange has been introduced to a locale where another language is spoken, new names for the tree are likely to be adopted. The scientific appellation, *Maclura pomifera,* is universal, but common names vary and multiply. Perhaps the most surprising discovery in the game of matching names with languages is that of *bois d'arc.* French speakers in America encountered the tree in Louisiana and bestowed the name of *bois d'arc* meaning "wood of the bow." In France, however, that name is not linked to the Osage orange tree. Speakers of French will translate the name as "wood of the bow," but they have other names for the tree and not associate *bois d'arc* with *Maclura pomifera.* The following names were collected to illustrate how other countries and other languages identify the trees that speakers of English commonly call Osage orange.

Native American Tribes

Alabama

Alabama: *itto kamo, ittokamo ma, kama*. These words are translated into English as "bois d'arc," "Osage orange," or whatever termed the speaker uses in referring to the tree. Between 1980 and 1998, compilers of the Alabama dictionary conducted research on the Alabama-Coushatta reservation in Texas (Syestine, Cora, Heather K. Hardy, Timothy Montler. Austin: U of Texas P, 1993.

Caddo

Caddo: *bois d'arc*. Ann Penrod, director of the Caddo nation museum, explained that the word used by the Caddo tribe is the French American word *bois d'arc*. She knew of no other word adapted by Caddo people.

Cherokee

Cherokee: *galowegadi* (yellow gun). Ed Fields of the Cherokee Nation headquarters staff, said the meaning of the word for Osage orange refers to the use of the word for bows in tribal hunting, serving the same purposes as guns.

Chickasaw

Chickasaw: *itti' lakna'* .Only 'bois d'arc" is listed as the English name of the tree in this dictionary. A separate term for the bois d'arc fruit is *itti' laknani'*. (Pamela Munro and Catherine Wilmond. *Chickasaw: An Analytical Dictionary*. Norman: U of Oklahoma P, 1994.

Choctaw

Choctaw: *krili lakna, kuti lakna (kutih lakna itti* (thorn "yellow tree"). Billy Curtis, who is an instructor in the Choctaw language program at Southeastern Oklahoma State University in Durant; provided these translations. The words are the same as those recorded in 1852 in *English and Choctaw Definer*, which was compiled by Cyrus Byington).

Comanche

Comanche: *eh-te-hou-pe*. Wahnne Clark, a Comanche historian, reported after conferring the Sam DeVenney, the premier Comanche linguist, this word for the Osage orange tree in his language.

Creek

Creek: *'to-lane, ito lani* ("yellow wood"). The Creek language word for Osage orange was located in a Creek dictionary.

Navajo

When yellow dye from Osage orange trees was important to the Navajo, the word for the source of the dye was not recorded in the major Navajo dictionaries. Today the use of synthetic dyes gives members of the tribe even less incentive to use a native word for Osage orange. After a search of several Navajo dictionaries and telephone calls to the Navajo nation and to rug weavers suggested as language informants, the Navajo word for Osage orange has not yet been discovered. Because the tree does not thrive on tribal lands, the dye was always imported, leaving little cause for having a word in the native language.

Osage, Southern Indians

Osage and other southern Indians tribes: *ayac* (Womack 2).

Tewa

Tewa: *p'etsejiy* (from *p'e* "stick or plant") and *tse* ("yellow"). The wood was considered better for making bows and arrows than any which grew in the Tewa country. The Tewa brought the wood from eastern areas, or it was obtained from the Comanche Indians or other eastern tribes (Robbins, Harrington, and Freire-Marreco 68).

Names in Non-Indian Languages

The words used to refer to the Osage orange tree reported below were collected from various foreign language dictionaries and native speakers of the target languages.

Chinese

A word for Osage orange does not appear in major English-Chinese dictionaries. The search will continue with Chinese-speaking botanists.

French (Canada)

In Francophile Canada the following common names are used for Osage orange: *bois d'arc, oranger des Osages, Osage orange.*

French (France)

In France the following names are used for the Osage orange: *Maclura orange, maclura epineaux, macluier orange, murier des osages, oranger des osages.*

German

Names used for Osage orange trees in German-speaking countries are the following: *Maclura, Gelbas Holz, Orangenartige, Osage Pom, Osage Apfel, Osage Dorn, Milchorangenbaum,* and *Pomeranzengelbe Maclura*

Italian

In Italy names used for the tree are *Maclura Braziletto giallo, Osage orange, and Sandalo giallo.*

Japanese

A word for Osage orange is not listed in major English-Japanese dictionaries. Japanese botanists will be consulted.

Russian

While Osage orange is known to have been naturalized in parts of Russian, an English word is not listed in English-Russian dictionaries. The search will continue among Russian botanists fluence in English.

Spanish (Mexico)

Spanish names in Mexico for the Osage orange tree are *amarillo, moradilla, moral, naranjo chino, naranjo de Luisiana, palo amarillo, palo de arco, palo duro.*

Spanish (Spain)

In Spain the names for Osage orange in the national language are *naranjo de Louisiana, oranger des Osage, and Osage orange*

Spanish (United States)

In the United States, Spanish-speakers are most likely to call the Osage orange tree *naranjo chino*

Inscription Rocks, Bois d'Arc Springs
Photography Arlan Purdy

15
What Next for Osage Orange?

During the estimated three billion years of life on planet earth, many major temperature shifts have affected plants and animals. Thousands of years ago during the last thermal rise. Osage orange and other warm-climate species expanded their range as far north as Canada. Wild pigs enjoyed migrating to Pennsylvania. But plants and animals that could not adapt to the warmer temperature became extinct. When termperatures dropped, Osage orange was pushed southward to a small area traditionally identified as stretching along the Red River in present-day northeast Texas and southeastern Oklahoma. The rising and falling temperatures made all the difference. Some flora and fauna were unable to adjust to the thermal shift. Their earthly tenure ended with extinction (Owen 34). The Osage orange not only survived, but it later found new missions: arming Indians with powerful elastic bows, fencing the prairies with living fences, feeding hungry hords of silkworms in a valiant effort to sustain American silk mills, dying military uniforms, and tautly holding the barbed wire that supplanted its reign as the ideal hedge. Today the tree entices scientists to detect the yet-undiscovered potential of its chemical uniqueness.

As an example of Americana, Osage orange was viewed by one naturalist as standing beside "the log cabin and apple butter, essential for awhile but soon replaced" (Baumgardt 47).

The tree's future unfolds steadily with surprising applications of the Osage orange tree. At present much interest centers on the potential of the tree as a treatment for cancer. With time, additional information will come to light, revealing new insights into the human interaction with the Osage orange tree.

For example, on May 24, 1984, a letter was presented to the Thomas Jefferson Collection at the University of Virginia. The three donors identified themselves as descendants of Dr. Samuel Brown, the recipient of the letter. The donors were from Lindon, Kentucky,; Prospect, Kentucky; and New York, New York.

Jefferson had written to Dr. Brown from Monticello on April 29, 1814. Jefferson was asking Dr. Brown to send seeds and cuttings of the Osage orange tree from Kentucky to a European friend, as the doctor had done earlier for other acquaintances of Jefferson.

In the letter the former president wrote, "I have just received from a European friend, Mr. Correa de Serra, a reqauest to engage some friend on the Mississippi to send me a young branch or two of the Bow-wood, or bois d'arc of Louisiana, pressed in brown paper with their leaves, and both the male and female flowers, also some of the fruit, either dry, or in a mixture of 1/3 whiskey and 2/3 water. The dry no doubt can come most conveniently by mail. Also in the proper season :re ripe seeds. Can I get the favor of you to execute the commission? Mr. Correa is now at Philadelphia, setting out on a visit to Kentucky. He is perhaps the most learned man in the world, not in [blotted],, but in men and things. And a more amiable and interesting one I have never seen. Altho' a stranger to no science, he is fondest of Boarc. Should you have gone to to Kentucky as your last letter seemed to contemplate, take him in your bosom, and recommend all the attention to him by which our brethren of Kentucky can honor themselves". (University of Virginia Thomas Jefferson collection, accession number 10594).

Historians already knew Mr. Correa as a Portuguese diplomat who delivered the first Osage orange cutting to England, but other information provided by Jefferson's letter was previously unknown.

Scientific discoveries, unearthing of historical documents, and continuous adaptations by the tree itself indicate that the world does not yet have a definitive perspective of the tree that continuously commands attention. Who knows what information will come to light from letters and documents made public after discoveries are made in family papers by generous donors?

The evolution and rebound of Osage orange, or whatever a region calls the tree, is something to behold. Perhaps those who conjured the name of "wood eternal" have glimpsed its future.

Thomas Jefferson Signature
Letter to Dr. Brown

The Hedge

Like the lines of the human face, hedges betoken much, and if read aright are seen to have no slight connection with the history of the country. Yet few of us, it is to be feared, have ever bestowed a thought upon their origin, their varieties, and their meaning; or, if at all, only, perchance when we have stood upon some hill heaved high above the land, between the flat blue plain of the sea on one hand and the undulating earth on the other, the crests of whose solid billow are crowned by copses and woods rising among a network of thin green lines of hedgerows.

Living Age
February 14, 1903

Bois d'Arc Creek
Photograph by Arlan Purdy

Afterword

Wood Eternal is a lifelong work with more than twenty-five years of intensive research. Some of my earliest childhood memories in Leonard, Texas, were of the bois d'arc trees in the neighborhood and the summer fun of making hats from the lustrous leaves pinned together with thorns from the trees or enjoying improvised bowling with horse apples sent rolling along the sidewalks to topple standins for ten pins.

Serious interest in the tree began at East Texas State Teachers College when I interviewed Dr. L. D. Parsons, head of the chemistry department and wrote a feature article for the *East Texan*. Dr. Parsons, a Northeast Texan who completed his doctorate at Vanderbilt University, told me about his research to convert horse apples into a money crop. He sought ways of drying and enriching the fruit of the bois d'arc tree to make it appetizing food for livestock. He explained how disappointed he was when his major professor discouraged him from writing a dissertation on the potential of horse apples. "The fruit of Osage orange is only a season crop, after all," the professor said, dismissing the research topic.

Dr. Parsons slept on the discouragement, and the next morning he thought, "Well, cotton is only a seasonal crop, but that doesn't stop serious research." He reported that rebuttal to his major professor and then began work on his dissertation. After that interview, I began to see the tree in a different light. After I outlined a fall celebration of the tree in Commerce, Texas, in 1986 and became founding director of the Bois d'Arc Bash for five years, I started collecting oral and printed information about the tree. Wherever I traveled, I made time to visit libraries and photocopy any material I could find about the tree that was becoming an obsession with me.

Collected material came from three trips to the Library of Congress, research in about two hundred Texas libraries and two hundred more throughout the United States, as well as in England, France, Mexico and Canada. The library research and interviews with botanists, chemists, farmers, and folk with Osage orange information produced material that eventually filled twenty-five loose leaf notebooks with some 5,000 pages. Years passed, and it became harder and harder to find books that I had not previously inspected for bois d'arc information.

The advent of online archives for periodicals and the availability of nineteenth century publications on microforms multiplied the number of pages in the collection. Online databases for periodicals provided at least two hundred useful articles each year when I entered *Osage orange* as the keyword, and another one hundred when I entered *bois d'arc*. Recently I registered for Google alerts for the words *Osage orange* and *bois d'arc*. Daily reports from fifteen or so online links for each word brought to my computer screen information I would never have found otherwise.

As I developed the reputation as someone possessed by the tree, friends, colleagues, and students began to send or slip under my office door clippings, articles, and notes about bois d'arc. Sometimes the name of the publication, the date, and the page numbers were missing, as well as the name of the anonymous donor. Efforts were made to retrieve missing bibliographical information, and for any not recovered, I am truly remorseful.

When I resorted to interlibrary loan, I was able to read many theses and dissertations or receive photocopies of microforms, books, and periodicals, often with blotches from the printer cartridges or vital bibliographical material beyond the margins of the photocopy machines. Of the thousands of books scanned for words about Maclura, only the scientific volumes always had indexes. For *Wood*

Eternal I sought complete documentation so that the reader would know that most of the misinformation came not from me but from the sources cited.

To all of the librarians who guided me to these sources and to authors of material in my bois d'arc collection, I am deeply indebted.

Equal gratitude is extended to all who shared their bois d'arc tales with me or showed me their bois d'arc relics or favorite trees and described undreamed of uses of the trees. As I began to write articles about the tree and to speak at historical and linguistic conferences, my correspondence files bulged with a wealth of personal experiences and research reported by mail.

One of the great research adventures was in collecting the words for Osage orange or bois d'arc from Native American languages. Through the years I had collected a few words from tribal dictionaries. When I read about a recent annual Indian crafts show in Arlington, Texas, that was attracting artisans from forty-five different tribes, I devised a short interview form and headed for the crafts show. Although I talked with members of about thirty tribes, I came away with no Indian words for the target tree. Most potential informants had heard of the tree, but they did not know what their Native American language called it.

Using a more academic approach, I found two university libraries in Oklahoma with special collections of tribal dictionaries. I discovered only six dictionaries with the Indian words for Osage orange I needed, most of them already in my collection.

Deciding to use the modern research tool of online research, I Googled *Osage orange* and *bois d'arc* but found no glossaries with these words. I did locate telephone numbers for some of the Indian nations, but their dictionaries rarely listed the words I needed. Sometimes on the fourth telephone call, a tribal member had been located who could provide the name. That search will continue until I have found the names of the tree used among Indians where the Osage orange thrives.

What has been attempted in *Wood Eternal* is the most comprehensive book ever written about an intriguing tree. Additional information will be welcomed.

Fred Tarpley
4540 FM 1568
Campbell, TX 75422
Fred_Tarpley@TAMU-Commerce.edu
Telephone: 903-886-6498

Works Cited

Adrosko, Rita J. *Natural Dyes and Home Dyeing.* New York: Dover, 1971.

Abraham, Doc, and Kathy Abraham. "Ask the Gardeners. Q&A. *Christian Science Monitor* 29 April 1986.

Acheson, Sam. "Battling Mud with Bois D'Arc." *Dallas Morning News* 15 Jan. 1968.

Agricultural Report. 1870. Washington, DC: Department of Agriculture.

Aker, Scott. "A Report Card on Osage Orange." *Washington Post* 29 Jan. 2004: H07.

Allison, Bruce, ed. *Wisconsin Champion Trees.* Madison: Wisconsin Books, 1980.

American Farmer 1818-19.

American Monthly 1818-19.

Anderson, David A, and William A Smith. *Forests and Forestry.* Danville, IL: Interstate Printers, 1976.

Anderson, Paul J., Walter C. Muenscher, Clara J. Weld, Jessie I. Wood, and G. Hamilton Martin. *Checklist of Diseases of Economic plants in the United States.* U.S. Department of Agriculture Bulletin 1366. Washington, DC: Government Printing Office, 1928.

Andrews, A. E. "Wood for Archers." *American Forests.* Oct. 1940: 46-47

Arkansas. A Guide to the State. New York: Hastings House 1941.

Associated Press. "Bowmakers Still Make Them Like They Used To." *Dallas Morning News* 11 Nov. 1984.

Associated Press. Iowa State University. Ames, IA.

Associated Press. "Osage Orange Growing Scarce in Illinois."

Atwell, Lionel. "Bow Camp." Jan. 1992: 38-40.
Atwell, Lionel. "The Gift of a Bow." *Field & Stream.* 1 Apr. 1997: 66).
Azpieitia, Antonio Aguirre. *Atologia Vegetal.* Barcelona: Ediciones Omega, 1974.
Baerg, J. *The Western Trees.* 2nd ed. Dubuque, IA: William C. Brown, 1973.
Baggett, Dennis. "No Hedging on Bois d'Arc. Readers Root Out Strong Bond, Memories of Tough Trees." *Dallas Morning News.* 3 Dec. 1995.
Bailey, L. H. *The Standard Cyclopedia of Horticulture.* Vol. 2. New York: Macmillan, 1950
Baker, Richard St. Baarbe. *Green Glory. The Story of the Forests of the World.* London: Lutterworth Press, 1948.
Baltensperger, Bradley H. *Nebraska. A Geography.* Boulder, CO: Westview Press, 1995. ??
Bancroft, Hubert Howe. *The Native Races.* Vol. 1. San Francisco: History Company, 1886.
"Banker Locates Champion Tree in Nebraska." *Northwestern Financial Review.* 2.89 (1 Nov. 2004): 33.
Barnes, Burton V., and Warren H. Wagner, Jr. *Michigan Trees. A Guide to the Trees of Michigan and the Great Lakes Region.* New York: U of Michigan P, 1981.
Barton, James D. and James P. Barnett. "Osage Orange: A Small Tree with a Big Role in Developing the Plaints." Research Paper SO-285. New Orleans: Southern Forest Experiment Station, March 1995.
Basalla, George. *The Evolution of Technology.* New York: Cambridge UP, 1988.
Bates, Carlos G. *The Windbreaks as a Farm Asset.* Farmers' Bulletin 788. Washington, DC: U.S. Department of Agriculture.

Bates, Marston. *The Nature of Natural History.* Princeton: Princeton UP, 1950.

Baumgardt, John Philip. *Horticulture.* 10:1 (Oct. 1972): 26, 47.

Bean, W. J. *Trees and Shrubs Hardy in the British Isles.* 8th ed. Vol. 2: D-M. London: John Murray, 1973.

Bell, Robert E. ed. *Prehistory of the Osage Orange.* Orlando: Academic Press, 1984.

Bell, W. B. Jack. Interview about his father's career as "Bois d'Arc King of Texas" by Esther MacMillan, Institute of Texas Cultures, 11 March 1983.

Bennish, Steve. "The Bowyer's Art." *Dayton Daily News.* 1 Sept. 2003: B7).

Benson, Henry C. *Live Among the Choctaw Indians.* Cincinnati: L. Swormstedt & A. Poe, 1860.

Benson, Lyman. *Plant Classification.* Boston: Heath, 1957.

Bernatzky, A. *Tree Ecology and Preservation.* New York: Elsevier Scientific, 1978.

Berry, Mike. "Kansas Town Wows to Defend Barbed-Wire Title." *Dallas Morning News* 15 Feb. 1990: 22A.

Bettendorf, Elizabeth. "Environment Artist Creates a Raft for Wildlife." Springfield, Illinois *State-Journal.* 27 Apr. 1997: 14.

Betts, Edwin M. *Thomas Jefferson's Garden Book- 1766-1828.* Philadelphia: American Philosophical Society, 1993..

Billings, W. D. *Nevada Trees.* Bulletin 94. 2nd ed. Reo: Agricultural Extension Services U of Nevada, 1954.

Blanchard, Rufus. *Handbook of Iowa.* Chicago: Blanchard & Oram, 1867.

"Bois d'Arc." *Texas Almanac.* Dallas: A. H. Belo, 1961. p. 125.

"Bois d'Arc Chemicals." *Dallas Morning News* 28 Apr. 1942: Sec. 2.

"Bois d'Arc Fence Reigned till Barbed Wire's Advent." *Dallas Morning New* 10 Dec 1989.

"Bois d'Arc for Paving." *Dallas Morning News* 16 Nov. 1899: 3.

"Bois d'Arc Still a Treasure." Unknown Texas newspaper.

Boom, B. K., and H. Kleijn. *The Glory of the Tree*. New York: Doubleday, 1966.

Botanical Gazette. Vol. 17, 1892.

Botanical Gazette. Vol. 19, 1894.

Boulger, G. S. *Wood*. London: Edward Arnold, 1908.

Bourcier, Paul G. "'In Excellent Order'": The Gentleman Farmer Views His fences, 1790-1860." *Agricultural History* 58.4 (Oct. 1984): 546-84..

Bradford, Carol. "Here's a Guide to What Trees Not to Plant." *Syracuse Herald American* 28 Apr. 1996. 11.

Branwell, Marilyn. *International Book of Wood*. New York: Simon and Schuster, 1976.

Braun,E. Lucy. *The Woody Plants of Ohio*. Columbus: Ohio State UP, 1961.

Bray, William T. *Forest Resources of Texas*. Washington, DC: Government Printing Office, 1904.

"A Brief History of the Wood of the Osage Orange tree." *Textile Colorist*

Britton, Nathaniel, Lord, and Addison Brown. *Illustrated Flora of the Northern United States, Canada, and the British Possessions*. Vol. 3. New York: Charles Scribner's, 1896.

Brooks, L. B. *West Virginia Trees*. Parsons, WV: Agricultural Experiment Station, West Virginia University, 1922 (reprinted 1972).

Brown, Clair A. *Commercial Trees of Louisiana*. Bulletin No. 20, 6th ed., 1992. Louisiana Office of Forestry.

Brown, Clair A. *Louisiana Trees and Shrubs*. Baton Rouge: Claitor's Book Store, 1966.

Brown, H. P. *Atlas of the Commercial Woods of the United States.* Bulletin of the New York State College of Forestry of Syracuse University, 1912.

Brown, H. P., A. J. Panshin, and C. C. Forsmith. *Textbook of Wood Technology.* Vol. 1. New York McGraw-Hill).

Brown, H. P. *Trees of New York State.* New York: Dover, 1975.

Browne, D. J. *Trees of America Native and Foreign..* New York: Harper, 1846.

Buccholtz, Brad. "Sawdust Memories." *Austin American-Statesman* 4 July 2004: El.

Bucholz, John T., and Wilbur R. Mattoon. *Common Forest Trees of Arkansas.* Fayetteville: U of Arkansas.

Burch, Bonnie. "Class Offers Tips on Holidays Ornaments." *The Tennessean* 25 Sept. 1997: 11W.

Burchard, Hank. "Fence Sitting." *Washington Post.* 7 June 1996: N51.

Burnett, Edmund Cody. "The Passing of the Old Rail Fence: A farmer's Lament." *Agricultural History.* 22.4 (January 1948):11-32.

Burton, James D. "Osage-Orange." FS-21. Washington DC: Department of Agriculture Forest Service, Jan. 1976.

Burton, James D., and James p. Barnett. "Osage-Orange: A Small Tree with a Big Role in Developing the Plains." Research Paper So-285, Southern Forest Experiment Station, New Orleans. March 1995.

Butler, Robert L. *Wood for Wood-Carvers and Craftsmen.* London; Thomas Roseleaf, 1974.

Butterfield, W., H. *Making Fences Walls and Hedges.* New York: McBride, Nast, 1914.

Byington, Cyrus. *English and Choctaw Definer.* New York: S. W. Benedict, 1852.

Cain, Stanley A. *Foundations of Plant Geography.* Facsimile of 1944 ed. New York: Hafner 1971.

Calvanese, Central Park horticulturist. Letter to Fred Tarpley, May 23, 1991.

Campos, Carlos. "Bombs Away." *Atlanta Constitution* 21 Sept. 1995. 1:3.

Cardwell, Paul O. "'Bo-dark' Draws Interest." *Sherman Democrat*. 3 Sept. 1991.

Carmody, Dierdre. "New York Again Tree City U.S.A. Pays Homage to Its Finest Specimens." *New York 'Times* 27 Apr. 1985: 27; "Great Tree Hunt." *New York Times* 13 Jan. 1985.

Carriel, Mary Turner. *The Life of Jonathan Baldwin Turner*. Urbana: U of Illinois P, 1951.

Carey, James, and Morris Carey. "Wood Can Be a Good Alternative Hear Source." Associated Press. *The Columbian* 25 Jan. 1998.

Cassidy, Frederic, ed. *A Dictionary of American Regional English*. Cambridge: Belknap Harvard, 1985.

Cater, Ruth Cooley. *Tree Trails and Hobbies*. Garden City: Garden City Books, 1950.

CBS "This Morning." 2 Sept. 1997. Martha Stewart interview. "Tips on Using Natural Dye to Dye Your Fabrics Successfully."

Cerny, Denise. "Bulbs, Perennials Show. Signs of Life." *Grand Rapids Press* 4 Apr. 1996: 17.

Chichester, Kathy. "Miami Adds to Leafy Ceiling." *Cincinnati Enquirer* B03

Choukas-Bradley, Melanie. *City of Trees. The Complete Field Guide to the Trees of Washington, DC*. rev. ed. Baltimore: Johns Hopkins UP, 1981, 1997.

Chrysler, Forrest Shreve, Frederick H. Blodgett, and F. W. Beasley. *The Plant Lore of Maryland*. Baltimore: Johns Hopkins Press, 1910.

Clark, Wahnne. Comanche word for Osage orange: eh-te hou-pe (bow wood). Email 6 June 2010

Clifton, Robert T. *Barbs, Prongs, Points, Prickers, and Stickers*. Norman: U of Oklahoma P, 1970).

Clopton, John R. "Antioxidant Material from the Osage Orange." *Journal of the American Oil Chemical Society* 30: 156-59.
Cochran, James Madison. *The Value of Bois d'Arc Timber.* Bonham, TX: Baptist Trumpet, 1896.
Choukas-Bradley, Melanie. *City of Trees. The Complete Field Guide to the Trees of Washington, DC.* rev. ed. Baltimore: Johns Hopkins UP, 1981, 1997.
Clopton, John R. "Antioxidant Material from the Osage Orange." *Journal of the American Oil Chemical Society* 30:156-59.
Clopton, John R., and Ammarette Roberts. "Osage Orange, a Potential Source of Edible oil and Other Industrial Raw Materials." *Journal of the American Oil Chemical Society* 26 (1848): 470-72.
Cochran, James Madison. *The Value of Bois d'Arc Timber.* Bonham, TX: Baptist Trumpet, 1896.
Coker, William Chambers, and Henry Roland Totten. *Trees of the Southeastern United States.* Chapel Hill: U of North Carolina P, 1945.
"Collin County, the Way It Was" radio series for 1977 Bicentennial. "The Bois d'Arc Tree" by Mike Apsey. Script from McKinney Public Library. Photos of bois d'arc grave markers.
Collingwood, G. H., and Warren D. Brush. *Knowing Your Trees.* Rev. and ed. by Devereux Butcher. 1974.
Collingwood, G. H. "Osage-Orange." *American Forests.* October 1939.
Commissioner of Agriculture, 1868 report. Washington, DC: Government Printing Office, 1868.
Commissioner of Agriculture. 1869 report. Washington, DC: Government Printing Office, 1969.
Commissioner of Agriculture. 1872 report. Washington, DC: Government Printing Office, 1872.
Compton, Jim E. Letter to Tex Peacock, *Texas Highways.* 23 July 23 1995.

Connecticut Botanical Society. *Catalogue of the Flowering Plants and Ferns of Connecticut.* State Geological and Natural History Survey. Bulletin No. 14.

Connelley, William E. *History of Kansas. State and People.* 2 vol. Chicago: American Historical Society, 1928.

Conrad, James H. *A Brief History of the Bois d'Arc Tree.* Commerce, TX: Commerce Bois d'Arc Bash, 1994.

Constantine, Albert Jr. *Know Our Woods.* New York: Scribner's, 1959.

Conzatti, Cassiano. *Flora Taxonomica Mexicana.* Vol. 1. Mexico, DF: Conseljo Nacional de Ciencia y Tecnologia, 1988.

Coombes, Allen J. *Trees.* New York: Dorling Kindersley, 1992.

Copier, Leslie. "A Design I History: 'Osage Orange' by John Steuart Curry." M.S. thesis, U of Wisconsin-Madison, 1977.

Core, H. A., W. A. Cote, and A. C. Day. Syracuse: Syracuse UP, 1976.

Correll, Donovan Stewart, and Marshall Conring Johnston. Renner: Renner Research Foundation, 1970.

Coues, Elliott, ed. *the History of the Lewis and Clark Expedition by Meriwether Lewis and William Clark.* 3 vol. New York: Dover.

Coulter, John M. "Botany of Western Trees." *U.S. National Herbarium.* Vol. 3. 1891-1904.

Coulter, John M. *The U.S. National Herbarium.* Vol. 2. Washington, DC: Government Printing Office, 1891-94.

Coulter, John M., Charles R. Barnes, and J. C. Arthur, eds. *The Botanical Gazette.* Vol. 19. Madison, WI: Published by the Editors, 1894.

Cox, Paul W., and Patty Leslie. *Texas Trees. A Friendly Guide.* San Antonio: Coma, 1988.

Crawford, Hewlette S., Clair L. Kucera, and John H. Henreich. *Ozark Range and Wildlife Plants.* Washington, DC: U.S. Department of Agriculture, 1959.

Crenshaw, Holly. "Festivities Branch Out Arbor Week." *Atlanta Constitution.* 12 Feb. 1998: E 11.

Crowley, T. E. Letter to W. Walworth Harris, Greenville, Texas. 25 Sept. 1967.

"Current Extent of Osage orange (Maclura pomifera) in the Forest Inventory and Analysis Database (FIADB 3.0." 3 March 2010.

Curtis: Choctaw informant

Curtis, Carlton C., and S. C. Bausor. *The Complete Guide to North American Trees.* New York: Perma Giants, 1950.

Dale, Thomas R. *100 Woody Plants of Louisiana.* Monroe: Herbarium of Northeast Louisiana University, 1988).

Danhof, Clarence H. "The Fencing Problem in the Eighteen Fifties." *Agricultural History* 18.4 (Oct 1944: 168-87.

Darby, John. *Botany of the Southern States.* New York: A. S. Barnes, 1855.

Davidson, Mary Frances. *The Dye-Pot."* Gatlinburg, TN: Author, 1967.

Davidson, Mary Matilda. *Bombyx Mori. A Manual of Silk Culture.* Kansas City, KS: published by the author, 1881.

Davidson, Mary Matilda. *Silk, Its History, Manufacture, Culture.* Juncture City, KS: J. B. Wadleigh. 1885).

Davis, Kenneth S. *Kansas: A. Bicentennial History.* New York: W. W. Norton, 1976.

Davis, Walt. Interview about Charles Goodnight's original chuckbox in the Panhandle-Plains Museum and aoubt Davis' childhood experiment with Osage orange. 9 June 2010.

DeMorse, Charles. Letter form McKinney. *The Clarksville* [Texas] *Standard.* 1 May 1853.
Deam, Charles C. *Flora of Indiana.* Indianapolis, IN: William B. Burford, 1940.
Deam, Charles C. *Trees of Indiana.* Fort Wayne: Fort Wayne Printing, 1931.
Deciduous Trees. Southeastern Wisconsin. Milwaukee, WI: Milwaukee County Park Commission, 1977.
Dean, Willa Mims. *Diamond Bessie.* Dallas: Mathis Van Nort, 1949.
Debates and Proceedings of the Congress of the United States. Ninth Congress, Second Session. Washington, DC: Gales and Seaton, 1852.
Deciduous Trees. Southeastern Wisconsin. Milwaukee, WI: Milwaukee County Park Commission, 1977.
Dictionnaire des Sciences Naurelles. 7: 517-78 Paris: 1823.
Diebel, Linda. "'Watermelon Capital' Wows Tourists." *Toronto Star* 34 Oct. 1992: A21.
Dirr, Michael A. *Manual of Woody Landscape Plans.* Champlain, IL: Stripes, 1983.
Division of Forestry Publication No 13. 1st rev. State of Indiana Department of Conservation, 1931.
Dormon, Caroline. *Forest Trees or Louisiana.* Baton Rouge: Division of Forestry, Louisiana Department of Conservation, 1941.
Douglas, C. L. "Cattle Kings of Texas." *Fort Worth Press* 18 May 1935.
Douglas, David. *Journal Kept by David Douglas During His Travels in North America. 1823-1827.* New York: Antiquarian Press, 1939.
Droze, W. H. "Changing the Plains Environment: The Afforestation of the Trans-Mississippi West" in *Agriculture in the Great Plains. 1876-1936.* Thomas R. Weaver, ed. *Agricultural History.* 51.1 (January 1977).

Droze, W. H. *Trees, Prairies, and People*. Denton: Texas Woman's University, 1977.

Duncan, Wilbur H. *Guide to Trees, Shrubs, and Wood Vines of Northern Florida and Adjacent Georgia and Alabama*. Athens: U of Alabama P, 1962.

Duncan, W. H., and Marion B. Duncan. *Trees of the Southeastern United States*. Athens: U of Georgia P, 1988.

Dunning, Jennifer. "Sunday Walk to Scale Heights of Prospect Park." *New York Times*. 5 Feb. 1982.

Durrell, Glen R. *Forest Trees of Oklahoma*. 5th rev. ed. Oklahoma City: Division of Forestry, 1939.

Eads, Nola McKay. "Church Wagon: online material retrieved 9 May 2010.

Earll, Alice Morse. *Old-Time Gardens*. New York: Macmillan 1928.

"Early History of Osage Orange." *Meehans' Monthly* 7 (Jan. 1847): 4.

Eifert, Virginia S. *Tall Trees and Far Horizons*. New York: Dodd, Mead, 1968.

Elias, Thomas S. *The Complete Trees of North America*. New York: Knopf, 1980.

"Elk Falls Reinvents Itself Via Some Clever Marketing.: Minneapolis/St. Paul *Star-Tribune* 3 Sept. 1995: 2G.

Ellias, Thomas S. *Trees of North America*. Van Norstrand, 1980.

Elliott, R. S. *Report of the Commissioner of Agriculture for the Year 1872*. Washington, DC: Government Printing Office, 1872.

Elliott, R. S. *Forest Trees for Kansas*. Lawrence, 1871.

Elliott-Tenort, Debra. "Group Firm on Osage Mound Goals." Memphis *Commercial Appeal* 30 Jan. 1997. CC1.

Elmer, Robert P. *Archery*. New York: Putnam's, 1925).

Emerson, George B. *A Report on the Trees and Shrubs Growing Naturally in the Forests of Massachusetts.* Vol. 1. Boston: Little, Brown 1878.

Evans, Charlotte. "Time Was When the Wild West Danced to the 'Devil's Rope'" Smithsonian July 1991: 75.

Evans, Glen. "Notes form 18;38 Surface in Land Case." Cox News Service. 19 Jan. 2005.

Everett, Dick. *The Sod House Frontier 1854-1890. A Social History of the Northern Plains from the Creation of Kansas and Nebraska to the Admission of the Dakotas.* Lincoln, NB: Johnsen, 1954.

Everett, Thomas. *Living Trees of the World.* New York: Doubleday, n.d.

Everett, Thomas. *The New York Botanical Garden Illustrated Encyclopedia of Horticulture.* Vol. 6. New York: Garland, 1981.

"Evolutionary Analogies." *The Economist* 16 Feb. 1991: 10-11.

Farmer, Nancy. "Hot Stuff? Crackling Fire Can Soothe the Mind, but Take Precautions Before You Light Up.' Louisville *Courier-Journal* 4 Oct. 1995: 7N.

Farish, Jennifer. "Former Home of One of Mississippi's Statesmen Targeted for Restoration." Associated Press 31 May 2004.

Federal Writer' Project. *Kansas.* New York: Viking, 1919.

Feltwell, John. *The Story of Silk.* New York: St. Martin's Press, 1900.

The Fence. A Compilation of Facts, Figures and Opinions. Worcester, MA: Press of Moyes, Snow and Company, 1879.

Fernald, Merritt Lyndon. *Gray's Manual of Botany.* New York: American Book Company, 1950.

Fett, Ephriam Porter. *Shelter Trees in War and Peace.* New York: Orange Judd, 1943.

"Firewood Facts Keep You from Getting Burned." Louisville *Courier-Journal*. 2 Feb. 1998: 10C.

Fitzerald, John C. ed. *The Writings of George Washington. 1745-1799*. 39 vol. Westport, CT: Greenwood Press, 1940.

Fletcher, Stevenson Whitcomb. *Pennsylvania Agriculture and Country Life. 1840-1940*. Harrisburg: Pennsylvania Historical and Museum Commission, 1933.

Flexner, Stuart Berg. Listening to America??

Flora Taxonomica Mexicana. Vol. 1. Mexico, DF: Cosejo Nacional de Ciencia Technologia, 1988.

Flore Canadienne. Vol. 1. Basse-Ville: Joseph Darveau, 1862.

Flores, Dan L. *Caprock Canyonlands*. Austin: U of Texas P, 1990.

Flores, Dan L. "The Ecology of the Red River in 1806. Peter Custis and Early Southwestern Natural History." *Southwestern Historical Quarterly*. 88 (July 1984): 33.

Flores, Dan L. *Jefferson and Southwestern Exploration. The Freeman and Custis Accounts of the Red River Southwestern Exploration*. Norman: U of Oklahoma P, 1984.

Flores, Dan L. *Journal of an Indian Trader. Anthony Glass and the Texas Trading Frontier. 1790-1870*. College Station: Texas A&M UP, 1985,

Forbes, Thomas. *New Guide to Better Archery*. Harrisburg, PA: Stackpole, 1960.

Forest and Inventory and Data Base, U. S. Forest Service.

Forest Trees of Illinois. How to Know Them. Springfield, 1934. p. 58.

Forest Trees of Oklahoma. Publication 1. Oklahoma Planning and Resources Board, 1939.

Forest Trees of Tennessee. Nashville: Department of Conservation, 1943.

Forest Trees of Texas. Bulletin 20. 8ᵗʰ ed. College Station: Tessa Forest Service, 1971.

Foster, Steven, and James A. Duke. *Medicinal Plants.* Boston: Houghton Mifflin, 1990.

Foster, J. H., and Harry E. Krausz. *Tree Planting Needed in Texas.* Bulletin 2 Department of Forestry. College Station: A&M College of Texas. 3.1 (10 Jan. 1917: 11.

Foster, William C. *The LaSalle Expedition to Texas. The Journal of Henri Joutel 1684-1687.* Austin: Texas State Historical Association.

Frank, Charles E. *Pioneer's Progress. Illinois College, 1829-1779.* Urbana: Southern Illinois UP, 1979.

"Fruits and Vegetables." *Meehans' Monthly.* 10 (October 1900): 51.

Franklin, Benjamin. *The Papers of Benjamin Franklin.* Ed. William W. Labaree. New Haven, CT: Yale UP, 1959.

Freas, Dorothy D. "Osage Orange." *Natural History* 60.1 (1951): 48.

Fugatt, Barry. "Bois d'Arc Trees Prized for Toughness, Used for Benches." *Tulsa World* 2 Nov. 1996: D1.

Fulton, A. R. *The Free Lands of Iowa. Sioux City Land District.* Des Moines, IA: Mill, 1860.

Galloway, Joseph I. "War Casualty Prompts Unusual Love Story." *Tulsa World.* 26 Oct. 2003: G2).

Gard, Wayne. "Before Barbed Wire." *Cattleman*

Gard, Wayne. *The Chisholm Trail.* Norman: U of Oklahoma P.

"Gardening." New Zealand *Nelson Mail.* 27 May 2004,

Gardener's Magazine 1 (1826): 356.

Gardener's Magazine 11 (1835): 312; 315

Gardens and Trees 20 Dec. 1893: 524.

Gee, Benjamin. *History of Iowa.* Vol. 4, 1866 to 1903. New York; Century History.

Giles, Janice Holt. *Johnny Osage.* Boston: Houghton-Mifflin 1960.
Gleason, Harry A., and Arthur Cronquist. New York: Columbia UP, 1964.
Gleason, Harry A., and Arthur Cronquist. *The Natural Geography of Plants.* New York: Columbia UP, 1967.
Gleason, Henry A. *Illustrated Flora of the Northeastern United States and Adjacent Canada.* Vol. 2, 1952.
Glover, Jack. *The 'Bobbed" Wire Bible."* Sunset, TX: Cow Puddle Press, 1977.
Godfrey, Ed. "Turkey Hunting Is All About the Call." Oklahoma City *Oklahoman* 16 April 2003.
Godfrey, Robert K. *Trees, Shrubs and Woody Vies of Northern Florida and Adjacent Georgia and Alabama.* Athens: U of Georgia P, 1941.
"Goodnight, Charles." *New Handbook of Texas.* Austin: Texas State Historical Association, 1996.
"Goodnight-Loving Trail." *New Handbook of Texas."* Austin: Texas State Historical Association, 1996.
Gorer, Richard. *Trees and Shrubs.* London: David & Charles, 1976.
Grace, Jim W. "The Ornery Osage Orange." *American Forests* Nov. 1990: 51-52.
Grae, Ida. *Nature's Colors: Dyes from Plants.* London: Collier Books, 1974.
Graves, Arthur Harmount. *Illustrated Guide to Trees and Shrubs.* Rev. ed. New York: Harper & Row, 1956.
Great Plains Agricultural Council. *Windbreaks: What Are they Worth"* Proceedings of the 34th Annual Meeting of the Forestry Committee. Publication 106, 1982.
Greeley, William B. *Forests and Men.* Garden City, NY: Doubleday, 1941).
Green, Charlotte Hilton. *Trees of he South.* Chapel Hill: U of North Carolina P, 1939.

Greene, A. C. "Bois d'Arc Fences Reigned Till Barbed Wire's Advent.' *Dallas Morning News* 1 Dec. 1989.

Greene, A. C. "Group Got Lost on Way to Forge Indian Treaty." *Dallas Morning News* 19 May 1991: 42A.

Greene, Max. *The Kanzas Region: Forest, Prairie, Desert, Mountain, Dale, and River."* New York: Fowler and Wells, 1856.

Greer, James K. *Dallas:*

Gregg, Josiah. *Commerce on the Prairies.* Ed. Max L. Moorhead. Norman: U of Oklahoma P, 1954.

Grey, Alicia. "Town's Tour Focus on Trees." *Newark Star-Ledger* 27 Apr. 1997: 043.

Grimm, William Carey. *The Trees of Pennsylvania.* New York: Stackpole and Peck, 1950.

Gue, Benjamin F. *History of Iowa.* Vol. 3, From 1866 to 1903. New York: Century History Company, n.d.

Guyton, Oscar W., and Fred C. Swope. *Trees and Shrubs of Virginia.* Charlottesville, VA: U of Virginia P, 1981.

Haas, Ann Johnston. "Branching Out. Two UC Professors Give Fallen Trees New Life as Furniture." *Cincinnati Enquirer.* 1996.

Haehle, Robert. "Growing Concerns." Fort Lauderdale *Sun-Sentinel* 18 Apr. 1997: 3E.

Hall, Gordon. "Bois d'Arc Among Most Tolerant Trees." *Dallas Morning News* 9 Aug. 1985.

Hamilton, T. M. *Native American Bows.* York, PA: Shumway, 1972).

Hancock, John. "The Osage Orange Hedge." *Prairie Farmer* 9 (1849): 189.

Hansen, Thor. "Drawing on an Ancient Art, One Austin Bow Maker Still Makes Them Like They Used To." *Austin American Statesman* 27 Nov. 1984).

Hardcastle, Ron. Oral history interview, Institute of Texan Cultures, San Antonio. 3 Aug. 1985).

Hardin, James W., and Jay M. Arena. *Human Poisoning from Native and Cultivated Plants*. Durham, NC: Duke UP, 1974.

Harold, D. *Keys to the Woody plants of Iowa in Vegetative Condition. Studies in Illinois History* 17.8 (19 Feb. 1940).

Harper, Roland M. *Economic Botany of Alabama. Catalogue of the Trees, Shrubs, and Vines of Alabama, with Their Economic Properties and Local Distribution.* Part 2. University, Al: 1928.

Harrar, E. S. *Hough's Encyclopedia of American Woods.* New York: Robert Speller, 1971.

Harrar, Ellwood S., and J. George Harrar. *Guide to Southern Trees.* 2nd ed. New York: Dover, 1962.

Harrington, Daniel D. *Keys to the Woody Plants of Iowa in Vegetative condition.* Iowa City: Iowa State University, 1934.

Harris, Paul. "Green, Slimy Horse Apples. Bois d'Arc Tree Apples Are Worthless." *Commerce, Texas, Journal* 20 Oct. 1993.

Harrison, Waldrop. Waldrop Harrison papers. Waldrop Harrison Public Library, Greenville, Texas.

Harshberger, John W. *The Botanists of Philadelphia and Their Work.* Philadelphia: 1899.

Harshberger, John W. *Phytogeographic Survey of North America.* New York: Hefner, 1958.

"Hawk Mountain to Teach Owl Spotting." *Allentown Morning Cal.* 17 Oct. 1977: B5.

"The Hedge." *Living Age* 24 Feb. 1903: 405-11.

"Hedges—Osage Orange." *The Farmer and Gardener* 5 (25 Dec. 1838): 29.

Hendee, David. "Nebraska City Set for Jefferson. A Bronze Sculpture Would Honor the President Who Sent Lewis and Clark West. Legacy in Bronze." Omaha *World Herald* 2 Nov. 2004: 18.

Hewes, Leslie. "Early Fencing on the Western Margin of the Prairie." *Annals of the Association of American Geographer.* 71.4 (Dec. 1981: 499-527.

Hewes, Leslie, and Christian L. Jung. "Early Fencing on the Middle Western Prairie." *Annals, Association of American Geographers* 71.4 (1981): 177-201).

Hicks, Ray R., Jr., and George K. Stephenson, eds. *Woody Plants of the Western Gulf Region* Dubuque, IA: Kendall/Hunt, 1978.

Hill County Historical Commission. *A History of Hill County, Teas. 1853-1980. Hillsboro*: Hill County Historical Commission, 1980.

Hill, Deborah B. "Living Fences." In Moll, Gary, and Sara Ewe-neck, eds. *Shading Our Cities.* Washington, DC: Island Press, 1989.

Hodge, Floy Crandall. *A History of Fannin County.* Hereford, TX: Pioneer Publishers, 1966.

"Home Furnishings Fit for a Museum." *San Francisco Chronicle* 26 Aug. 1992.

Hoopes Josiah. *The Book of Evergreens.* New York: Orange Judd, c. 1850.

Hora, Bayard, ed. *Oxford Dictionary of Trees of the World* New York: Oxford UP, 1981.

"Horse-High, Bull-Strong, and Pig-Tight." *The Living Museum.* Illinois State Museum, Springfield. (1955):221-222; 230).

Hosie, R. C. *Native Trees of Canada.* 7th ed. Ottawa: Canadian Forestry Service, 1959.

Hough, Romeyn Beck. *Handbook of the Trees of the Northern States and Canada East of the Rocky Mountains.* New York: Macmillan, 1947.

Hougham, Paul C. *The Encyclopedia of Archery.* New York: A. S. Barnes, 1958.

http.//www. Windsor plywood.com.world of woods/northamerican/Osage Orange.

Howard, Alexander. *A Manual of the Timbers of the World.* London: Macmillan, 1948.
Howe, Hollis. *Our Common Trees How to Know and Use Them.* Baltimore: Natural History Society of Maryland, 1942.
Howes, Charles C. *This Place Called Kansas.* Norman: U of Oklahoma P, 1952.
Huang, Chien Li. Pharmacy Thesis, College of Pharmacy, Butler University, Indianapolis, Indiana, June 1957.
Hume, Paul. "Big D: column. Bois d'Arc Trees. *Dallas Morning News* c. 1956.
Hunter, Carl G. *Trees, Shrubs & Vines of Arkansas.* Little Rock, AR: Oxard Society Foundation, 1980.
Hunter, John D. *The Indians of North America.* London: Longman, 1824.
Hunter, John D. *Manners and Customs of Several Indian Tribes Located West of the Mississippi.* Minneapolis, MN: Ross and Haines, 1947).
Hutchings, Ross E. "Wood-of-the-Bow." *Nature Magazine* January 1934: 38-39.
Hutchings, Ross I. *This Is a Tree.* New York: Dodd, Mead, 1964.
Hutton, Jerry. Interview about bird house refuges on Osage orange trees. 10 June 2910.
Hyatt, Harry Middleton. *Folk-Lore form Adams County Illinois.* Memoirs of the Alma Egan Hyatt Foundation, 1965.
Hylander, Clarence J. *Trees and Trails.* New York: Macmillan, 1952.
Hylander, Clarence J. *The World of Plant Life.* 2nd ed. New York: Macmillan.
Illick, J. S. *Pennsylvania Trees.* Bulletin 11. 4h ed. Pennsylvania Department of Forestry, May 1923.
Imlay, Gilbert. *Topological Description of the Western Territory of North America.* 3rd ed. New York: Augustus M. Kelley, 1797, reprinted 1969.

Independence Hall Association. "St. Peter's Church." Philadelphia, 1995, 1996.

Iowa State College and Iowa Experiment Station. *Farming in Iowa. 1846-1946.* Ames, : Iowa State College Press, 1946.

Jackson, Donald, ed. *Letters of the Lewis and Clark Expedition 1783-`1854.* Urbana: U of Illinois P., 1962

Jacobson, Arthur Lee. *Trees of Seattle. The Complete Tree Finder's Guide to the City's 740 Varieties.* Seattle: Sasquatch Brooks, 1989.

"Jelly, Cotton Gin Waste, Staring with Poultry, Osage Oranges and Armadillos." *Countryside and Small Stock Journal* Nov.-Dec. 1992: 22-23).

Johnson, Hugh. *Route to the Trees of Our Forests and Gardens.* New York: Simon and Schuster, 1973.

Johnson, Michael, and Sharon Johnson. Interview about choice of Osage orange for hanging children's swing. 15 June 2010.

Johnson, Mildred Price. "Texas Trees." Article from unidentified publication in vertical file at Baylor University.Dames, I: University Press, 1945.

Johnson, Patricia. "Dan Phillips Not Only Builds Delightful, Affordable Houses from Other People's Discards. He's Also Been Known to Finance Them for Buyers." *Houston Chronicle Texas Magazine.*

"Jonathan Turner Focal Point of New Play." Springfield *State Journal-Register* 11 May 1995.

Jones, Chapin. *Common Forest Trees of Virginia.* 4th ed. Charlottesville, VA: Forestry Service. December 1928.

Jones, George Neville. *Flora of Illinois.*

Jones, George Neville, and George Damon Fuller. *Vascular plants of Illinois.* Urbana: U of Illinois P and Illinois State Museum, Springfield, 1955.

A Journal of Travels into the Arkansas Territory During the Year 1819. Ed., Savoie Lottinville. Norman: U of Oklahoma P, 1980.

Joutel, Henri. *The LaSalle Expedition to Texas. The Journal of Henri Joutel 1684-1687.* Austin: Texas State Historical Association, 1988.

Kamdem, Donathien Pascal. "Fungal Decay Resistance of Aspen Books Treated with Heartwood Extracts." *Forest Abstracts Journal.* Jan. 1993: 30-32.

Kansas: A Guide to the Sunflower State. New York: Viking Press, 1939.

Kansas State Board of Agriculture. *Trees in Kansas.* Topeka, 1928, p. 63.

Keeler, Harriet L. *Our Native Trees.* 8th ed. New York: Charles Scribner's, 1912.

Kennicott, John A. *Horticulturist* 7 (1852): 374.

Kieran, John. *An Introduction to Trees.* Garden City, NY: Doubleday, 1966.

Killam, Steve. "My Memories of a Christmas as a Kid." Cox News Service 23 Dec. 2003.

King, Julius. *Telling Trees.* New York: William Sloane, 1953.

Hylander, *Trees and Trails.* New York: Macmillan, 1952.

Kirkegaard, John. *Trees Shrubs Vines and Herbaceous Perennials.* Boston: Bullard, 1912.

Kirshman, Cindy. "Earthworks Art Sways with Its Dimensions." *Chicago Tribune* 3 Apr. 1987

Krell, Alan. *The Devil's Rope. A Cultural History of Barbed Wire.* London: Reaktion Books, 2002.

Krueger, Ernest P. "Bois d'Arc Trees Make List." *American Farmer* Jan. 1958.

Labarre, Leonard, ed. *The Papers of Benjamin Franklin. Vol. 4.* New Haven: Yale UP, 1961.

LaTour, Kathy. "The Patriots, Working for East Dallas." *Dallas Morning News* 17 Dec. 1978.

Laurence, C. Walker. *Trees An Introduction to Trees and Forest Ecology for the American Naturalist.* Englewood Cliff, NJ: Prentice-Hall, 1984.

Lawrence, Eleanor, ed. *The Encyclopedia of Trees and Shrubs.* Chancellor Press, 1985.

Lawrence, Eleanor, ed. *The Illustrated Book of Trees and Scrubs.* New York: Gatley Books, 1985.

Leet, Judith. *The Botanical Paintings of Esther Heins.* New York: Harry N. Abrams, 1987.

Lemke, Janet. *Shake Them ' Simmons Down.* N.p.: Lyons & Burford, 1996.

Levi, Pita. "Harvest of the Hurricane. The Exotic Victims of Kew Are Transformed into Furniture." *Times* Newspapers Ltd., 1990.

Levison, J. J. *Studies of Trees.* New York: John Wiley, 1914.

Lewis, Isaac M. *The Trees of Texas.* Bulletin of the University of Texas. 15 Apr. 1915.

Lewis, Lloyd. *John S. Wright. Prophet of the Prairies.* Chicago: The Prairie Farmer Publishing Company, 1941.

Lewis, Walter H., and Memory P. F. Elvin-Lewis. *Medical Botany.* New York: Wiley, 1977.

Li, Hui-lin. *Trees of Pennsylvania, the Atlantic states and the Lake States.* Philadelphia: U of Pennsylvania P, 1972.

Little, Elbert, Jr. *Check List of Native and Naturalized Trees of the United States.* Agriculture Handbook No 41. Washington, DC: U.S. Government Printing Office, 1953.

Little, Elbert L., Jr. *Checklist of United States Trees (Native and Naturalized).* Agriculture Handbook No. 541. Washington, DC: Forest Service, U.S. Department of Agriculture, 1979.

Little, Elbert L., Jr., Roy O. Woodbury, and Frank H. Wadsworth. *Trees of Puerto Rico and the Virgin*

Islands. Vol. 2. Agriculture Handbook No. 449, Washington, DC: Forest Service, U.S. department of Agriculture, 1974.
Little, R. D. *H. J. Conn's Biological Stains.* Baltimore: Williams & Williams, 1969.
"Losz Exhibit Spotlights Adams' Life." *The Tennessean* 17 Oct. 1997:13W.
Loudon, J. C., ed. *Gardener's Magazine.* London: Longman, Rees, Orne, Brown, and Green, 1850. "Maclura aurantiaca of Nuttall." 1 (1826): 356-57.
"Louisiana Trees." Baton Rouge: Louisiana State University Agricultural Center, 1994.
Louisville *Courier-Journal.* 4 Oct. 1995: 7N.
"Low-Input Framers Proving as Profitable as Conventional Ones. The Fruits of Osage Orange, Alas, Aare Useless as Food." *Countryside and Small Stock Journal* July 1992: 58.
Lowman, Al. Ron Hardcastle interview at Texas Folklife Festival. 3 Aug. 3 1984. San Antonio: Texas Institute of Cultures Library.
Lundell, Cyrus Longworth. *Agricultural Research at Renner 1944-66.* Renner: Texas Research Foundation, 1967.
Lyons, Mike. "Tales of the Osage Orange (or Bois d'Arc) in Illinois." *Paris News,* Paris, Texas, 25 Apr 1987.
Lytle, Jerry. Interview about bois d'arc wood collection and "Forever Sticks." 12 July 2010.
Mackensen, Bernard. *The Trees and Shrubs of San Antonio and Vicinity.* San Antonio: Published by the author, 1909.
McCallum, Henry D., and Frances T. McCallum. *The Wire That Fenced the West.* Norman: U of Oklahoma P, 1965.
McClure, C. Boone. "History of the Manufacture of Barbed Wire." *Panhandle-Plains Historical Review* 31 (1958): 3.

McCox, Doyle. *Roadside Trees and Shrubs of Oklahoma.* Norman: U of Oklahoma P, 1981.

McCree Tree. Fred Tarpley collection of papers from Texas Historical Association, Crosby County Historical Commission, and *Amarillo News.*

McCurdy et. al., 1972.

McDaniel, Joseph C. "New Developments in the Osage Orange." *Plants and Gardens* 28:4 (March 1973): 45.

McKee, Victoria. "Windfalls for English Furniture Makers." *New York Times* 21 Nov. 1990: C5.

McKelvey, Susan Delano. *Botanical Exploration of the Trans-Mississippi West. 1790-1850.* Jamaica Plain, MA: Arnold Arboretum of Harvard Univeristy, 1955.

McLean. *Papers Concerning Robertson's Colony in Texas.* Vol. 8. David Crockett to His Daughter Margaret and Her Husband, Wiley Flowers. 9 January 1836: Vol. 12, Item 6;18. Fort Worth: Texas Christian Univeristy, 1974-93.

MacMillan, Esther. Interview with W. A. "Jack" Bell about his Father's Careers as "Bois d'Arc King of Texas." Institute of Texan Cultures, San Antonio. 11 March 1983.

Main, Thomas. *Directions for the Transplantation and Management of Young Thorn or Other Hedge Plants.* City of Washington: A&G Printers, 1807.

Maino, Evelyn, and Frances Howard. *Ornamental Trees.* Berkeley: U of California P, 1972.

Makins, F. K. *The Identification of Trees & Shrubs.* London: J. M. Dent, 1936.

Malone, Dumas. *Jefferson and His Time: Sage of Monticello.* Boston: Little, Brown, 1981.

"Man or Myth. The Real Truth About George Washington." Brochure from Mount Vernon

Ladies Association of the Union sent to Fred Tarpley by John P. Riley, archivist, 12 June 1990.
Marsh, Barbara. "The Way Work Ought to Be Hands-On." *Los Angeles Times-*. 15 Sept. 1997:B2, B14.
Master Tree Finder. Warner Books, n.d.
Martin, William C., and Charles R. Hutchings. *A Flora of New Mexico.* vol. 1. N.p.: J. Cramer, 1980).
Mathews, F. Schuyler. *Field Book of American Trees and Shrubs.* New York: G. P. Putnam's, 1915.
Mathies, Katharine. *Trees of Note in Connecticut.* Connecticut Daughters of the American Revolution, 1934.
Mattoon, Wilbur. *Forest Trees of Texas.* Bulletin 30. rev. College Station: Texas Forestry Service, 1943.
Max bois d'arc tree citation, Commerce, TX. For induction into American Forests Famous and Historical Trees.
May, Irving M., Jr. "A Historiography of Texas Agriculture."
Meehan, Thomas. *American Handbook of Ornamental Trees.* Philadelphia: Lippincott, Grambo, 1853.
Meehans' Monthly 4 (1984): 123.
Meehans' Monthly 5 (1895): 17.
Merris, Bob. Four-part series on Jonathan Baldwin Turner. Turner file, Illinois College Library.
Metcalf, Woodridge. *Introduced Trees of Central California.* Berkeley: U of California P, 1968.
"Metro Past." *Dallas Morning News* 15 March 1983.
Michaelson, M. *Freewood.* Mankato, MN: Gabfried Books, 1978.
Michener, James Papers. Center for American History, University of Texas at Austin.
Middleton, Harry. *Folk-Lore from Adams County, Illinois.* Memoirs of the Alma Egan Hyatt Foundation.
Miller, Howard A. *How to Know the Trees.* 3rd ed. Dubuque, IA: William C. Brown, 1978.

Milwaukee County Park Commission. *Deciduous Trees. Southeastern Wisconsin.* Milwaukee County Park Commission, 1977.

Mims, Willa Dean. *Diamond Bess.* Dallas: Mathis Van Nort, 1942.

Mitchell, Alan. *Trees of Britain and Northern Europe.* Boston: Houghton Mifflin, 1974.

Moerman, Daniel F. *Medicinal Plants of Native America.* Vol. 2. Ann Arbor: University of Michigan, 1986.

Mohlenbrock, Robert H., and John W. Thierel. *Trees.* New York: Collier, 1987.

Mohr, Charles. *Plant Life of Alabama.* Washington, DC: Government Printing Office, 1901.

Moll, Gary, and Sara Ebenreck. *Shading Our Cities.* Washington, DC: Island Press, 1989.

Moore, Dwight M. *Trees of Arkansas.* rev. ed. Little Rock: Arkansas Forestry Commission, n.d.

Morgan, Alan V. Osage orange.science/.uwaataerlooca/earth/qsi/t).

Morgan, Rhett. "Claremore Student a Finalist for Young Naturalist Award." *Tulsa World* 1 June 2004: A18.

Morton, C. V. "Freeman and Custis Account of the Red River Expedition of 1806." *Journal of the Arnold Arboretum* 48:431-59.

Mount Vernon Ladies Association of the Union. Letter to Fred Tarpley. 12 June 1990.

Muenscher, Walter Conrad. *Poisonous Plants of the United States.* New York: Macmillan, 1945.

Mullen, Katherine K. Richard C. Broder, and Will Beittel. *Trees of Santa Barbara.* Santa Barbara, CA: Santa Barbara Botanic Garden, 1974.

Mullenburg, Grace, and Ada Wineford. *Land of the Post Rock. Its Origins, History, and People.* Lawrence: UP of Kansas, 1975.

Mundell, Lynn. "An Alumnus Creates a 'Climbing Sculpture' for Haverford College." *Chronicle of Higher Education* 9 May 1990..

Munger, Susan H. *Common to This Country. Botanical Discoveries of Lewis & Clark.* New York: Artisan, 2003.

Munns, E. N. "The Distribution of Important Forest Trees in the United States." Miscellaneous Publication 287. Washington: U.S. Department of Agriculture, 1938.

Naughton, Gary C., and Stephen W. Capels. "Root-Pruning Osage orange Windbreaks." In *Windbreaks: What Are They Worth?* Great Plains Council Publication 106, 1982, p. 233.

Naughton and Capsis, p. 120.

"Nesting Ecology of the Loggerhead Shrike in Southwestern Oklahoma." *Wilson Bulletin* 104.1 (1992): 95-104.

Neville, A. W. "Backward Glances: Bois d'Arc Seed Were Valuable." *Paris News* 11 May 1942.

Neville, A. W. *The Red River Valley Then and Now.* Paris: North Texas Publishing Company, 1948.

New Handbook of Texas, The. 6 vol. Austin: Texas State Historical Association, 1996.

New York Times News Service. "Kew Storm Is a Windfall for Furniture." 29 Nov. 1990.

Nixon, Elray S. *Trees, Shrubs, & Woody Vines of East Texas.* Nacogdoches, TX: Bruce Lyndon Cunningham Productions, 1985).

"North Texas Bois d;Arc Is Unsurpassed Material for Wagon Spokes and Felloes." *Dallas Morning New.* 7 May 1893.

Nuttall, Thomas. *The Genera of North American Forests.* vol. 2 Philadelphia: D. Heartt, 1818.

Nuttall, Thomas. *North American Sylva.* Philadelphia: Robert Smith, 1835.

Odenwald, Neil, and James Turner. *Identification, Selection and Use of Southern Plants for Landscape Design.* Baton Rouge: Claitor.

Ogle, Jane. "Sweet Scents to Repel Pests." *New York Times* 1 June 1980: 74.

"1 Tree – 7,000 Photos!" Peter Ceren's Been Shooting His Orange Tree for 20 Years. But He Isn't Done Yet."

"150-Year-Old Bois d'Arc Log." *Dallas Morning News* 6 April 1912).

"Of the Leaves of the Maclura Aurantiaca as a Substitute for Those of the Mulberry, as Food for the Silk Worms." *Farmers' Register* 3: 1836).

"The Onery Osage Orange." *American Forests* Nov. 1990: 51-52, 76.

"Origin of Nightstick." *Dallas Morning News* 30 Oct. 1951.

Orndorf, Beverly. "The Trebuchet Changed Face of War Before Canon. Gravity Device Wrecked Walls." Richmond *Times-Dispatch.* 11 April 1996: E1.

"Osage Orange. An American Wood." Washington, DC: U.S. Department of Agriculture Forest Service, January 1976).

"Osage Orange." *Dallas Morning News* 22 Oct. 1944, Sec. 4.

"Osage Orange." http/www. msue.msu.edu/msue/imp/moduf/102. Retrieved 3 Dec. 2009.

"Osage-Orange." *Fayetteville County Democrat.* Lewisville, AR. Series from 1982.

"Osage Orange: Value of Scientific Facts." *Meehans' Monthly* 3 (1893): 102; 5 (1895):77.

"Osage Orange as a Fruit." *Meehans' Monthly* 10 (1900): 155).

"Osage Orange as Railroad Ties." *Meechans' Monthly.* 4 (1893): 102; 5 (1895): 77.

"Osage Orange Wood May Have Good Use. New Industry Possible of Development in Southwest as a result of War." *Dallas Morning News* 1 Jan. 1916.

"Osage Oranges Take a Bough; the First Shipment of Botanical Specimens Sent to President Jefferson Contained the Seeds of Thousands of Miles of Fences." *Smithsonian* 34.12 (1 March 2004).

Osborne, C. C. "Osage Orange." *The New Country Life* February 1912,

Otis, Charles Herbert. *Michigan Trees.* Ann Arbor: U of Michigan P, 1981.

Owen, Oliver S. "The Heat Is On. The Greenhouse Effect and the Earth's Future." *The Futurist.* Sept.-Oct. 1989: 34-38).

Palmer, E. Lawrence. *Fieldbook of Natural History.* Rev. by H. Seymour Fowler. New York: McGraw-Hill, 1975.

Pammel, L. B. *A Manual of Poisonous Plants .* Part 2. Cedar Rapids, IA: 1911.

Panhandle-Plains Museum papers.

Panshin, A. J., and Carl de Zeeuw. *Textbook of Wood Technology.* 4th ed. New York: McGraw-Hill, 1980).

Park Pride Atlanta and Susan Newell, Atlanta arborist. Information about Atlanta Memorial Park Osage orange tree.

Parker, Nathan H. *The Kansas and Nebraska Handbook.* Boston: John P. Jewett, 1857.

Parkhurst, H. E. *Trees, Shrubs and Vines of the Northeastern United States.* New York: Charles Scribner's, 1903.

Patterson, Jacqueline Memory. *Tree Wisdom.* New York: Thorsons, 1996.

Pearce, Michael. "Bowhunting [for White-tailed Deer]" *Outdoor Life:* 82.

Peattie, Donald Culross. *A Natural History of Western Trees.* Boston: Houghton Mifflin, 1953.

Peet, Louis Harman. *Trees and Shrubs of Central Park* New York: Manhattan Press, 1903.

Pennington, T. D., and Jose Sarukhan. *Arboles Tropicales de Mexico.* Oxford, UK: Commonwealth Forestry Institute, 1968.

Perry, Charles H. U.S. Department of Agriculture, Forest Service, Northern Research Station, St. Paul, MN. Letter to Fred Tarpley, 1 March 2010.

Petrides, George A. *A Field Guide to Western Trees.* Boston: Houghton Mifflin, 1998.

Petrides, George A. *Trees and Shrubs of Central Park.* New York: Manhattan Press, 1903.

Phillips, Richard. "Insect Wars. Science Battles an Old Bugaboo—Pesticide Immunity." *Chicago Tribune* 18 April 1987: Sec. 15. pp. 32-33.

Phillips, Roger. *A Photographic Guide to More Than 500 Trees of North America and Europe.* New York: Random House, 1978.

Pickering, Charles. *Chronological History of plants.* Boston: Little, Brown, 1879.

Pike, Doug. "Angry Ranchers Battling TPWD." *Houston Chronicle.* 1 Sept. 1993.

Pimentel, Richard A. *Natural History.* New York: Reinhold, 1963.

Plant Life of Alabama.

"Plants That Really Bug Garden Pests." *San Diego Union-Tribune* 15 March 1998: H-21.

Platt, Rutherford. *Discover American Trees.* New York: Dodd, Mead, 1968.

Platt, Rutherford. *1000 Questions About Trees.* New York: Dover, 1959.

Plowden, C. Chicheley. *A Manual of Plant Names.* London, UK: George Allen and Unwin, 1970.

Poage, W. R. *McLennan County—Before 1980.* Waco, TX: Texian, 1961.

Polunin, Oleg. *Trees and Bushes of Europe.* New York: Oxford UP, 1976.

Polunin, Oleg. *Trees and Bushes of Europe.* New York: Oxford UP. New York: A. S. Barnes, 1855.

Pool, Raymond J. *Handbook of Nebraska Trees. Botanical Survey of Nebraska.* New Series, Number 3, March 1919, 2nd ed. May 1929.

Pooley, William Vipond. *The Settlement of Illinois from 1830 to 1850.* Madison: U of Wisconsin, 1905.

Porch, Tom. "Bear Was on Target with His Dream." *Columbia Dispatch.* 9 Jan. 1998, 11F).

Porcher. *Resources of Southern Fields and Forests.* ??

Porter, Jack. "Famed Area Tree Near Death" *Amarillo Daily News. n.d.*

Porter, Larry. "Scavengers Turn Out Traditional Bows." *Omaha World Herald* 11 Feb. 1944: C3.

Powell, C. P. *Hedges Windbreaks Shelters and Live Fences.* New York: Orange Judd, 1922.

Powell, E. P. "The Making of a Hedge and Where to Put It." *Country Life in America May* 1903.

Preston, Richard J., Jr. *North American Trees* 3rd ed. New York: McGraw-Hill, 1975.

Primack, Martin I. "Farm Fencing in the Nineteenth Century." *Journal of Economic History* 30 (1960): 287-89.

"Prize for Bois d'Arc." *Dallas Morning News* 27 Dec. 1903.

Pyke, Marmi. "The Doctor Is In." Chicago *Daily Herald* 9 Sept. 2004: 1.

Radford, Albert E., Harry E. Ahles, and C. Ritchie Bell. *Manual of the Vascular Flora of the Carolinas.* Chapel Hill: U of North Carolina P., 1968.

Rafferty, Milton D. "The Limestone Fenceposts of the Smokey Hill Region of Kansas." 40-46.

Rafferty, Milton D. *The Ozarks Land and Life*. Norman: U of Oklahoma P, 1980.

Rafinesque, C. S. *American Manual of the Mulberry Trees*. Philadelphia: 1839.

Rafinesque, C. S. *Atlantic Journal*. 1.4 (1818): 146.

Rafinesque, C. S. *Atlantic Journal* 2.1(1818):118.

Rammelkamp, Charles Henry. *Illinois College. A Centennial History 1829-1929*. New Haven, CT: Yale UP, 1928.

Ramsey, Dan. *The Complete Book of Trees*. Blue Ridge Summit, PA: Tab Books, 1983.

Randall, Charles Edgar, and Henry Clepper. *Famous and Historic Trees*. 2nd printing. Washington, DC: American Forestry Association, 1976.

Raver, Anne. "What Horrifies Roaches and Grows on Trees?" *New York Times* 28 Nov. 1994.

Raynor, Vivien. "Sculpture Dominates a Show on S.I." *New York Time*. 7 May 1989: 26.

Radford, Albert, Harry E. Ables, and C. Ritchie Bell. *Manual of Vascular Flora of the Carolinas*. Chapel Hill: U of North Carolina P, 1968.

Regel, E. *Gartenflora*. Erlangen: Veriagr von Ferdeinand Enke, 1855.

Rehder, Alfred. *Bibliography of Cultivated Trees and Shrubs*. Jamaica Plain, MA: Arnold Arboretum of Harvard University, 1949.

Rehder, Alfred. *Manual of Cultivated Trees and Shrubs*. New York: Macmillan, 1940.

Reich art, Natalie, and Gilman Keasey. *Archery*. 3rd ed. New York: Ronald, 1961.

Rensselaer, Maunsell Van. *Trees of Santa Barbara*. rev. ed. Santa Barbara, CA: Santa Barbara, CA: Santa Barbara Botanic Garden, 1948.

"Osage Orange. An American Wood." Washington, DC: U.S. Department of Agriculture Forest Service, January 1976).

Report of the Commissioner of Agriculture for the Year 1860.

Report of the Secretary of Agriculture. 1891

Report of Trees and Scrubs Growing Naturally in the Forests of Massachusetts. Boston: Dutton and Wentworth, 1846.

Renwald, Kathy. "Colour Me Purpose." *Hamilton Spectator,* Ontario, Canada, 8 April 2004: G8.

Rice, Mary Louise. "The Role of the Osage Orange Hedge in the Occupation of the Great Plains." M.A. thesis, Knox College, Galesburg, IL 1936.

Rice, Charles. *Friendly Farmersville. 1845-1994.* Tyler: Tyler Print Shop, 1994.

Richard, Katherine K., Richard E. Broder, and Will Bettel. *Trees of Santa Barbara.* Santa Barbara: Santa Barbara Botanic Garden, 1974.

Richards, Gov. Ann. Proclamation: Commerce, Bois d'Arc Capital of Texas. 27 July 1994.

Richards, W. M. "Fencing the Prairies" *Heritage of Kansas* 4.2 (May 1960): 7-19.

Richmond, Robert W. *Kansas. A Land of Contrasts.* St. Charles, MD: Forum Press, 1974.

Richards,, W. M. "Fencing the Prairies." *Heritage of Kansas* 4.2 (1960).

Robbins, Wilfred William, John Peabody Harrington, and Barbara Freire-Marreco. *Ethnobotany of the Tewa Indians.* Washington: Government Printing Office, 1916.

Robinson, Gladys Reed. "Osage Orange Tree: Ornamental and Useful." *Horticulture*

"Rockwell's Son Shuns Americana for Gargoyles." *New York Times* 8 April 1980: Sec.1, p. 2.

Rogers, Julia Ellen. *Tree Crops. A Permanent Agriculture.* New York: Harcourt Brace, 1929.

Rogers, Julia Ellen. *The Tree Book.* New York: Doubleday, 1905.

Rogers, Julia Ellen. *Trees Worth Knowing.* N.p.: Nelson Doubleday, 1925.

Rogers, Patricia Dane. "Vintage Christmas Splendor." *Washington Post magazine.*

Rogers, Walter E. *Tree Flowers of Forest Park, and Street.* New York: Dover, 1935.

Ruede, Howard. *Sod-House Days.* New York: Cooper Square, 1966

"Rust, Carol. "Even Now, the Thong Lingers On." *Beaumont Enterprise* 22 Nov. 1986: 28A.

"Rustic Bentwood for the Garden."
http:...www,uon.lastate.Edu/ipm/hortnews/hnl19996 /5-2441'995.bent.

Rutter, Larry. "Farmer Preserves Historic Hedge Line." *Topeka Capital-Journal* 25 Sept. 2003.

Sargent, Charles Sprague, and Mary W. Gill. 2 vol. *Manual of he Trees of North America.* New York: Dover, 1933.

Sargent, Charles Sprague. *The Silva of North America.* Vol. 3. New York: Murrey, 1947.

Saunders, Charles Francis. *Edible and Useful Wild Plants.* New York: Dover, 1948.

SBE's List of Natural Pesticide Plant Seeds from Around the World. Retrieved from Natural Pesticides from Around the World. http//www.seedman com. 1 December 2009.

Schambach, Frank F. "Spiroan Traders, the Sanders Site, and the Plains Interaction Sphere: A Reply to Bruseth, Wilson, and Peritula." *Plains Anthropologist* 45 (2000): 7-32.

Schmeckebier, Laurence E. *John Steuart Curry's Pageant of America.* New York: American Artists Group, 1943.

Schopmeyer, C. S. *Seeds of Woody Plants in the United States.* Agriculture Handbook No. 450.

Washington, DC: Forest Service, U.S. Department of Agriculture, 1974.

"Science Fare." *Dallas Morning News* 26 May 1997: 10D.

Scott, David Clark. "He Collects One of Each. Natural Scientist Hopes to Bolster Diversity of Australian Landscape." *Christian Science Monitor.*

Seymour, Frank Conkling. *The Flora of New England.* Rutland, VT: Charles E. Tuttle.

Sharpe, Grant W., Clare W. Hendee, and Shirley W. Allen. *Introduction to Forestry.* 4th ed. New York: McGraw-Hill, 1976.

Shigo, Alex L. *A New Tree Biology.* Durham, NH: Shigo and Trees, 1988.

Shonefelt, R. D. *A Key to Wisconsin Trees.* Madison, WI: Department of Natural Resources, 1970.

Shreve, Forest, M. A. Crysler, Frederick H. Blodgett, and F. W. Bexley. *The Plant Life of Maryland.* Baltimore: Johns Hopkins Press, 1910.

Shumate, R. D. *Wisconsin Trees.* Madison: Department of Natural Resources, 1970.

Simon and Schuster's Guide to Trees. New York: Simon and Schuster, 1978.

Simpson, Benny J. *A Field Guide to Texas Trees.* Austin: Texas Monthly Press, 1988).

Smallwood, James A., Barry A. Crouch, and Larry Peacock. *Murder and Mayhem.* College Station: Texas A&M UP, 2004.

Smith, Alice. *Trees in a Winter Landscape.* New York: Holt, 1969.

Smith, Doug. "One Man's Calling: Minneapolis-St. Paul *Star-Tribune.* 1907: 10C.

Smith, Edward. *Account of a Journey Through North-Eastern Texas. Undertaken in 1849 for the Purposes of Emigration.* London: Hamilton, Adams, 1849.

Smith, J. Russell. *Tree Crops. A Permanent Agriculture.* New York: Harcourt, Brace, 1929.

Smith, Jeffrey Lynn. "Aspects of the Autecology of Osage Orange, *Maclura Pomifera* (Raf.) Schneid." M.S. thesis, Miami U, Oxford, OH, 1979.

Smith, Jeffrey L., and Janice V. Perino. "Osage Orange and Economic Uses." *Economic Botany..* 35:1: 24-42

Soltes, Fiona. "Ask and You Shall Receive Even If It's a Question about Silverfish." *The Tennessean,* Nashville 2 Dec. 1996: 8D.

Soltes, Fiona. "How to Keep a Fire in Our hearth." *Des Moines Register* 25 Jan. 1998: 3.

Solota, Justin A. "Posing Trees for Their Portraits Takes Its Own Technique." *Chicago Tribune* 2 Sept. 1988: sec. 7, p. 62+.

Spiegelman, Willard. "Dallas On (and Off) My Mind." *Parnassus: Poetry Review* 28 (1 Jan. 1995): 365).

Springfield, Rex. "Seedlings with Links to History Not All Equal." *Richmond Times-Dispatch* 5 June 1997:E-1

Spurlock, Lu. "Ex-meat Carver Turns Blade on Wood. Faces from the Past Inspire Sculptor." *Dallas Morning New.* 8 Sept. 1988. Metro sec., p. 1.

Spurrier, John. *The Practical Farmer.* Wilmington, DE: 1793.

Stafford, William. "The Osage Orange Tree." In Bruce, Erma. *Short Stories About Youth & Adolescence. Coming of Age.* Lincolnwood, IL: National Textbook Company. p. 175).

Stanley, Gerald B. *Trees of Vancouver.* Vancouver UBC Press, 1922.

State of Indiana. Department of Conservation. Publication No. 13. 1931.

State of Pennsylvania. Publication No. 12. Division of Forestry, 1933.

Steavenson, Hugh A., Henry E. Gearhart, and R. L. Curtis. "Living Fences and Supplies of Fence Posts," *Journal of Wildlife Management* 7.3 (July 1943): 257-61.: 1941.

Stemen, Thomas R., and W. Stanley Myers. *Oklahoma Flora.* Oklahoma City: Harlow, 1937.

Stephens, H. A. *Poisonous Plants of the Central United States.* Lawrence: Regents Press of Kansas, 1980.

Stephens, H. A. *Trees, Shrubs, and Wood Vines in Kansas.* Lawrence: UP of Kansas, 1969.

Stephens, H. A. *Woody Plants of the North Central Plains.* Lawrence, Manhattan,/Wichita: U P of Kansas, 1973.

Stephens, H. A. *Poisonous Plants of the Central United States.* Lawrence: Regents Press of Kansas, 1980.

Stephens, H. A. *Trees, Shrubs, and Wood Vines in Kansas.* Lawrence: UP of Kansas, 1969.

Stephens, Howard. Interviewed by Fred Tarpley, 20 Oct. 1995.

Stepp, Diane. "Heritage Days at Bulloch Osage Orange Festival Immerses Participants." *Atlanta Constitution* 30 Sept. 1993: H3.

Strausbaugh, P. D., and Earl L. Ore. *Flora of West Virginia.* 2nd ed. Grantville, WV: Seneca, 1978.

Streets, R. J. *Exotic Forest Trees in the British Commonwealth.* Oxford, UK: Clarendon Press, 1962

Stupka, Arthur. *Trees, Shrubs and Woody Vines of Great Smoky Mountains National Park.* Knoxville: U of Tennessee P, 1964

Steyermark, Julian A. *Flora of Missouri.* Ames, IA: Iowa State UP, 1963.

Stillwell, Norma. *Keys and Guide to Native Trees, Shrubs, and Woody Vines of Dallas County.* Dallas: Boyd Printing, 1939.

Straley, Gerald B. *Trees of Vancouver.* Vancouver: UBC Press, 1992.

Strausbaugh, P. D., and Earl L. Core. *Flora of West Virginia.* 2nd ed. Grantsville, WV: Seneca 1978.

Streets, R. J. *Exotic Forest Trees in the British Commonwealth.* Oxford, UK: Clarendon Press, 1962.

Stupka, Arthur. *Trees, Shrubs and Woody Vines of Great Smoky Mountain National Park.* Knoxville: U of Tennessee P, 1964.

Sudol, Valerie. "Legendary Explorers Also Stopped to Pick Flowers." *Star-Ledger* 20 Nov. 2003.

Sudworth, George B. *Check List of the Forest Trees of the United States. Their Names and Ranges.* Miscellaneous Circular 92. Washington, DC: U.S. Department of Agriculture, 1927.

Swanton, John R. *Source Material on the History and Ethnology of the Caddo Indians.* Norman: U of Oklahoma P, 1942, 1996.

Swineford, Grace, and Swineford Ada. *Land of the Post Rock. Its Origins, History, and People.* Lawrence: UP of Kansas, 1975.

Switzer, John. "Butcher Bird Sets Up Shop in Licking County." *Columbus Dispatch* 16 Aug. 1997.

Symonds, George W. D. *Tree Identification Book.* New York: Quill, 1958.

Syestine, Cora, Heather K. Hardy, Timothy Montler. *Dictionary of the Alabama Language.* Austin: U of Texas P, 1993.

Takhtajan, Armen. *Floristic Regions of the World.* Berkeley: U of California P,

Tarpley, Fred. Collection of student reports on Osage orange, East Texas State University, 1980s.

Tarpley, Fred. *Jefferson: Riverport to the Southwest.* Austin: Eakin, 1983.

Tarpley, Fred. "Orangeville." *1001 Texas Place Names.* Austin: U of Texas P, 1980.
Tax Appraisal District. Fannin County, Texas. Abstract, vol. 572, p. 37.
Taylor, Raymond L. *Plants of Colonial Days. A Guide to One Hundred and Sixty Flowers, Shrubs, and Trees in the Gardens of Colonial Williamsburg.* Williamsburg, VA: Colonial Williamsburg, 1952.
Teale, Edward Way. *Journey into Summer.* New York: Dodd, Mead, 1960.
"Texas Agriculture as Reflected in Letters to the *Southern Cultivator Prior to 1861.* Thesis, East Texas State.
Texas Almanac 1961. "Osage Orange." Dallas: *Dallas Morning News* 1961.
"Texas Champion Bois d'Arc Tree." *Texas Forest News.* Jan./Feb. 1948.
Texas Forest Service. *1989 Texas Tree Registry.* Lufkin: Texas Forest Service, 1989.
Texas Forest Service. *Famous Trees of Texas.* 3rd ed. 1984.
Texas Senate Bill 1519, 2006. Lower Bois d'Arc Creek Reservoir.
Thomas, Dale, and Dixie S. Scogin. *1001 Woody Plants of Louisiana.* Monroe, LA: Northeast Louisiana University, 1988.
Thomas Jefferson's Garden Book. Philadelphia: American Philosophical Society, 1944.
Thomas, Pete. "Tall Truths: Biggest Tree, Oldest Tree." Clipping without newspaper info.
Thorne, Frank. "Nature Ramblings: Technological Unemployment." *Science News Letter.* 26 July 1947).
Thurman, Nita. "Hiking tours Offer Rare Glimpse of Trinity. South Dallas Preserve's Fall Fling Shows Off City's Natural States." *Dallas Morning News* 9 Nov. 1997: 42A.

Tolbert, Frank X. "Old Inscriptions on a 'Hidden Cliff." *Dallas Morning News.* N.d.
Tolbert, Frank X. "About Mr. Crowley, 'Bois d'Arc Man.'" *Dallas Morning News* 4 Nov. 1963.
Tolbert, Frank X. "Old Inscriptions on a 'Hidden Cliff." *Dallas morning News* 11 Nov. 1976.
Totemeier, Carl. "Paintings Can Bar the Unwanted." *New York Times* 5 May 1995.
Toumey, James W. *Seeing and Planting.* New York: John Wiley, 1916.
The Traditional Bowyer's Bible. Vol. 1. Guilford, CT: Lyons Press, 200?.
Transactions of the Wisconsin State Agricultural Society. Vol. 3. Madison: Beriah Brown, 1853.
Tree Planting in he Great Plains Region. Farmers' Bulletin No. 1312. Washington, DC: U.S. Department of Agriculture, c. 1973.
"Tree's Company." *Commerce Journal.* 4 Sept. 1888: 5A.
Trees. Yearbook of Agriculture 1949. Washington, DC: U.S. Department of Agriculture, 1949.
"Trees with Eye-Catching Bark." *Dallas Morning News* 22 Dec. 1991: 14.
Trees Every Boy and Girl Should Know. Washington, DC: American Forestry Association, 1977.
Trees for Roadside Planting. Farmers' Bulletin 1482. Washington: U.S. Department of Agriculture, n.d.
Trees in the 21st Century. Based on the First International Aboricultural Conference. ABAcademic Publishers, n.d.
Trees of Britain & Europe. Collins Wildlife Trusts, 1999.
"Tricounty Report." *Cincinnati Enquirer* 27 July 1977: B02.
Turner, John S., and Michael J. Brodhead, eds. *A Naturalist in Indian Territory. The Journals of S. W. Woodhouse, 1849-50.* Norman: U of Oklahoma P, 1992.

Tynan, Chip. "Bark Won't Repel Ladybugs." *St. Louis Post-Dispatch* 19 Feb. 2005: 32.
United Press. Oklahoma. "Frosters' Blue Ribbon Downs Entries." 6 Apr. 1988.
U.S. Department of Agriculture. *Report of the Secretary of Agriculture 1891.* Washington, DC: Department of Agriculture, 1891.
U.S. Department of Agriculture. *Yearbook of Agriculture 1949.* Washington, DC: Department of Agriculture, 1949.
U.S. Department of the Interior. "Fencing Materials." *2003 Federal Information and News Dispatch.* 10 November 2003.
Van Bruggen, Theodore. *The Vascular Plants of South Dakota.* 2nd ed. Ames, IA: Iowa State University Press, 1985.
Van Der Linden, Peter J., and Donald R. Farrar. *Forest and Shade Trees of Iowa.* Ames: Iowa State UP, 1984.
Van Dersal, William. *Native Woody Plans of e United States.* Washington, DC: Government Printing Office, 1939.
Van Mullekom, Kathy. "Down the Garden Path." Albany *Times Union* 28 Jan. 1998: D8.
Van Renesselaer, Manunsell. *Trees of Santa Barbara.* rev. ed. Santa Barbara: Santa Barbara Botanic Gardens, 1948.
Vannorsdall, Harry H. *Trees of Ohio.* Wilmington, OH: Vannorsdall, 1958.
Vera, John. "No Post, No Fence." *Country Journal.* p. 74.
Vines, Robert A. *Trees, Shrubs and Woody Vines of the South Southwest.* Austin: U of Texas P, 1960.
Wagner, Warren H., Jr. *Michigan Trees. A Guide to Trees of Michigan and the Great Lakes Region.* Ann Arbor: U of Michigan P, 1981.

Walker, John Charles. *Plant Pathology*. 2nd ed. New York: McGraw-Hill, 1957.

Walker, Laurence C., and G. Loyd Collier. *Geography of the Sothern Forest Region*. Nacogdoches, TX: Stephen F. Austin State University, 1959.

Walking Elk, Phil. *The Art of Making Indian Bows and Arrows*. Norman: Phil Walking Elk, 1990.

Walsh, Sandra Holmes. "Locust Hill's Rich Heritage. Lewis Plantings Remain." Richmond *Times-Dispatch* 11 April 2004: S-4.

Wang, Shih-chi. "Heartwood Extractives of Maclura Pomifera and their Role in Decay Resistance." Doctoral dissertation, Michigan State University, 1977.

Ward, H. Marshall. *Trees*. Vol. 4. Fruits. Cambridge. Cambridge U P, 1908. Wardleigh.

Warder, John A. *Hedges and Evergreens. A Complete Manual for the Cultivation, Pruning, and Management of all Plants Suitable for American Hedging; Especially the Maclura, or Osage Orange*. New York: Orange Judd, 1857.

Washington, George. *Writings of George Washington*. Ed Chauncey Ford.

Washington Post. Article about Annual Page County Woodchoppers Ball & Virginia Championship Rail Splitting Competition) n.d.

Watkins, Brandon. "Doctor Pens Prescription for writing Instruments." *Tulsa World* 10 Jan. 1996: 1.

Watts, Mary Threilgaard. *Reading the Landscape*. New York: Macmillan, 1957.

Wayman, Dave. "All About the Osage Orange." *Mother Earth News* March/Apr. 1985: 121.

Weaver, j. E. *Prairie Plants and Their Environment*. Lincoln: U of Nebraska P, 1968.

Webb, Walter Prescott. *The Great Frontier*. Austin: U of Texas P, 1951.

Webb, Walter Prescott. *The Great Plains*. Boston: Ginn, 1931.
Weed, Clarence M. Our Trees. How to Know Them. Philadelphia: J. B. Lippincott, 1908.
Wedel, Waldo R. *Prehistoric Man on the Great Plains*. Norman: U of Oklahoma P, 1961.
Wendt, Lloyd, and Herman Kogan. *Bet a Million: The Story of John W. Gates*. Indianapolis: Bobbs Merrill, 1948.
Weniger, Del. "Catalpa (*Catalpa Bignonioides, Bignoniaceae)* and Bois d'Arc *(Maclura Pomifera, Moraceae)* in Early Texas Records." *SIDEA* 17:1 (1996): 231-42).
Werthner, William B. *Some American Trees*. New York: Macmillan, 1935.
Westbrook, Robert F. "State-Wide Service Test of Fence Posts. Twenty-Year Progress Report. Publication 110. Texas Forest Service Report, 1973.
Weston, Randy. "Plimoth Plantation workers Finish Making Historically Accurate Fence." Quincy *Patriot Ledger* 15 Feb. 1996.
Wharton, Mary E., and Roger W. Barbour. *Trees Shrubs of Kentucky*. Lexington: UP of Kentucky, 1973.
Whitcomb, Carl E. *Know It and Grow It*. Stillwater: Oklahoma State U P, 1975.
White, J. H. *The Forest Trees of Ontario and the More Common Planted Foreign Trees*. 4th ed. rev. by R. C. Hosie. Ontario: Ministry of Natural Resources, 1986.
White, Newman Icy, ed. *North Carolina Folklore*. 7 vols. Durham: Duke UP.
Wiggers, Raymond. *The Plant Explorer's Guide to New England*. Missoula, MT: Mountain Press, 1994).
Williams, Jerry. "Grow a Piece of History. These Trees Offer Presidential Roots." *Richmond Times-Dispatch* 9 Jan. 1996: G-10.

Williams, John. "The Unmistakable Bois d'Arc." *Texas Parks and Wildlife* December 1986.
Willis, j. C. *A Dictionary of the Flowering Plants and Ferns.* 7th ed. Cambridge, UK: University Press, 1966.
Wilson, Clyde N., ed. *The Papers of John C. Calhoun.* Vol. 17, 1843-1844.
Winberry, John. "The Osage Orange." *Pioneer America* 11:3 (Aug. 1, 1979):134-43.
Wineford, Gene and Ada. *Land of the Post Rock. Its Origin, History and People.* Lawrence: U P of Kansas, 1975.
Winer, Hollace. "Barbed Wire Machine Piques Interest at Show." *Fort Worth Star-Telegram.* 19 Jan. 1997.
Winingham, Don. "Champion Trees Put Down Roots in County." *Lawrence Journal-World* 18 Jan. 1984.
Winterringer, Glen S., Harry S. Ayhles, and Alice A. Flynn. *Vascular Plants of Illinois.* Urbana: U of Illinois P, 1955.
Wisconsin State Agriculture Society. *Transactions of the Wisconsin State Agriculture Society.* Vol. 3, 1952. Madison: Berian Brown, 1853.
Wisconsin Trees. Milwaukee: Milwaukee Journal, 1927.
Wodhouse, Roger. *Hayfever Plants.* Vol. 15. New Series of Plant Science Books. Walton, MA: Chronico Botanica, 1945.
Wohler, Pat. "10,000 Gather to Fete Lewis and Clark Heritage." *St. Louis Post Dispatch* 21 May 1996: 1).
Womack, Walter C. "A Survey of the Constituents of the Fruit of the Osage Orange (Maclura Pomifera)." M.S. thesis, East Texas State Teachers College, 1951.
Wright, Carl C. "Oranges. From Prairie Hedgerows to Today's Popular Juice." *Christian Science Monitor* 27 Sept. 1988: 21.

Wulff, E. V. *An Introduction to Historical Plant Geography.* Waltham, MA: Chronica Botanica, 1943.

www.choctawnation.com/history/people/original-enrollees/carnes-andrew-j/ Retrieved 20 June 2010.

www.waymarking.com/waymarks/WM192GT_Bois_darc_Edmond,_OK. Retrieved 21 June 2010.

Yearbook of the U.S. Department of Agriculture. 1904.

Yearbook of the U.S. Department of Agriculture. 1908.

Yearbook of the U.S. Department of Agriculture. 1915.

Wyman, Donald. *Hedges Screens & Windbreaks.* New York: Whittlesey House, 1938.

Young, Chris. "Tall Tales: The Owners of Starhill Forest Arboretum Share the Stories of Their Many Trees, Including the Peculiar Osage Orange." *Springfield Star Journal-Register,* Illinois. 1 Nov. 2003: 21).

Zeiner, H. M. *Exotics of Colorado—Osage Orange, Maclura Pomifera.* Denver: Denver Botanic Gardens, 1985.

Zim, Herbert C., and Alexander C. Martin. *Trees.* New York: Golden Press, 1956.

Index

Adams, John, 156
Alabama, 220
Alabama tribe, 250
Alaska, 220
American Farmer, 76
Ammunition, 163
Antioxidants, 163
Archery, 125, 128
Appeal of tree, 24
Arizona, 220
Arkansas, 220
Arrows, 164
Artificial limbs, 165
Art, 164
Atlanta Arbor Day, 145
Australia, 243
Awls, 166
Ball, T. E., 153
Barbed wire, 97, 103, 105-114, 117
Bark, 11
Barrel staves, 166
Barriers, 166
Baseballs, 166
Beame, Bois d'Arc, 160
Bell, Jack, 160
Bentwood, 207
Biblical hedge, 56
Big Max, 138
Bird house refuge, 166
Bird prey sanctuaries, 167
Bois d'arc, 9
Bois d'Arc Bash, 147
Bois d'Arc Creek, 26, 35
Bowling balls, 167
Bowls, 167
Bows, 167
Bowyers, 126
Boxes, 167
Branches, 11
Bridge floors, 168
Bridge pilings, 168
Britain, 53
Building pegs, 168
Bulloch Hall, GA, 145
Business names, 168
Caddo, 250
California, 221
Cancer treatment, 169
Cherokee, 250
Chickasaw, 250
Children's activity, 169
China, 244
Chinese, 252
Choctaw, 250
Chouteau, 8
Christmas switches, 169
Chuck wagons, 170
Cincinnatus, 81,
Coffins, 171
Colonial trees, 41
Colorado, 221
Comanche, 251
Commerce tree trunk, 137
Common names for Osage orange, 243
Community names, 171
Connecticut, 221
Costumes, 171
Creek tribe, 251
Crime detection, 172
Crockett, David, 152
Crowley, T. E., 158
Crutches, 173

Davis, Walt, 153
DeKalb, IL, 107
Debris catchers, 173
Decay resistance, 173, 206
Decorated mottles, 174
Decorations, 174
Delaware, 221
Descriptors, 22
Doerle, Bois d'Arc, 156
Duck/turkey calls, 174
Dunbar, William, 1
Durability, 21
Durable wood, 174
Dyes, 175
Ecology, 93,
Edmond, OK, 139
Ellwood, I. E., 110
Europe, 53
European explorers, 39
Fabric design, 178
Falloes, 178
Farmers' Register, 76
Fedges, 178
Fence posts, 98, 178
Fences, 55
Firewood, 178
Flights of fancy, 179
Flooring, 180
Florida, 222
Flowers, 15, 180
Folk remedies, 180
Folk superstitions, 180
Food, 181
Food processing, 181
Forever sticks, 182
Foundation blocks, 182
Fragrances, 183
France, 245
Franklin, Benjamin, 41

Freedman's Bois d'Arc, 135, 236
French (Canada), 252
Fruit, 16, 182
Furniture, 183
Garner, John Nance, 154
Gates, John Warne "113
Georgia, 222
German, 252
Germany, 245
Glass, Anthony, 45
Glidden, Joseph L., 107
Global range, 219
Glue, 185
Goodnight, Charles, 152, 170
Grave markers, 185
Haish, Jacob, 109
Hampden-Sydney tree, 140
Hanging limbs, 185
Hanzlick, Bud, 183-84
Hardcastle, Ron, 128
Hardness, 21
Hats, 186
Hawaii, 223
Hedge fences, 41, 55, 73
Hedges, 187
Henry, Patrick, 136, 150,
Horticulturist, 78
Hunter, John D., 48
Hutton, Jerry, 166
Idaho, 223
Illinois, 223
Illinois College, 143
Indian clubs, 286
Indian traders, 46
Indiana, 223
Insect repellent, 187
Iowa, 224,
Italian, 252

Italy, 245
Japan, 246
Japanese, 252
Jefferson, Thomas, 1, 35, 43, 256
Jessup Collection log, 138
Johnson, Michael and Sharon, 211
Kansas, 225
Kelley, Michael, 111
Kentucky, 227
Kewanee, IL, 134
Knife handles, 188,
Korea, 246
Lamar, L. Q. C., home, 139
Landmarks, 189
Landreth, David, 2
Latex, 107
Leather tanning, 190
Leaves, 13, 131
Lee, Col. Bob, 156
Lewis, Meriwether, 1, 38, 43, 155
Literature, 190
Longevity, 21
Louisiana, 227
Louisiana Purchase, 42
Lytle, Jerry, 138, 182
Maclura pomifera, 2, 6
McClure, William, 2
McCree's Tree, 136
Maine, 227
Maryland, 228
Massachusetts, 228
Mauls, 193
Medicine, 193
Meehans; Monthly, 100
Memories, 193
Mexico, 246

Michener, James A., 157
Michigan, 228
Mine timbers, 197
Minnesota, 229
Misinformation, 51
Mississippi, 229
Missouri, 229
Montana, 230
Moraceae, 6
Mottled decorations, 196
Mouthwash, 196
Musical instruments, 197
Names, 160, 171, 197
Names of tree, 2, 3, 7, 47; 93, 242
Native American names for tree, 249
Navajo, 251
Native habitat, 25, 29
Native tree, 27
Nature mimicked, 104
Naturists, 54
Naturalized tree, 27
Nebraska, 230
Neck yokes, 199
Netherlands, 246
Nevada, 231
New Castle, DE, 64
New Hampshire, 231
New Jersey, 232
New Mexico, 232
New York, 232
New Zealand, 246
Nightsticks, 199
Noah's ark, 149
North Carolina, 233
North Dakota, 233
Nuttall, Thomas, 2
Ohio, 234

Oklahoma, 234
Oregon, 235
Osage Indians, 251
Osage orange, 5, 8, 88, 115
Osage Orange Day, 143
Paintings, 202
Parkhouse, Joann, 160
Parsons, L. D., 259
Paving for streets, 200
Pennsylvania, 235
Pestle, 202
Photographic model, 202
Pins, 203
Plows, 203
Plows, 203
Policeman Clubs 204
Pollen, 16
Pomade balls, 204
Portugal, 246
Potential uses, 204
Prairie Farmer, 65
Prairies, 64
Prehistoric trade, 39
Projectiles, 205
Promoters, 53
Pronunciation, tree name, 4
Puerto Rico, 242
Pulley blocks, 206
Queen Victoria, 151
Radiocarbon-dating, 37
Railings, 205
Railroad ties, 206
Rainfesque, 1, 8
Rainwater, Hattie, 157\
Reservoir names, 206
Resistance to decay, 207
Rhode Island, 236
Rhodesia, 246
Romania, 247

Roosevelt, Franklin D., 119
Roots, 20
Rope, 207
Rose, Henry, 111
Rubber, 207
Russia, 247
Russian, 249
San Antonio, TX, 112
Sapwood, 13
Sayings, 207
Schambach, Frank., 30, 296
Sculpture, 208
Seed, 19, 81, 85
Sex, 11,
Shelterbelts, 119
Side effect of juice, 19
Silk, 132-135
Silkworm food, 208
Silkworms, 131
Smith, Edward, 54
Soap, 209
South Carolina, 236
South Dakota, 235
Southern Cultivator, 80
Southern Europe, 247
Southern Indians, 251
Souvenirs, 209
Spanish (Mexico), 253
Spanish (Spain), 253
Spanish (United States), 253
Speed bumps, 210
Starch, 210
Starhill Forest, IL, 135
Street names, 210
Strength, 21,
Stewart, Martha, 159
Swing limbs, 211
Switzerland, 247
Tannin wheel, 211

Tanning of leather, 211
Tarpley, Fred, 160
Taylor, Doris, 160
Telephone poles, 211
Tennessee 236
Tewa, 151
Texas, 237
Texas prize logs, 141
Thorns, 13, 94
Tobacco pipes, 211
Tours, 211
Tracking deer, 171
Travel trees, 212
Treenails, 213
Trellises, 213
Trimmers, 85,
Trunk, 11,
Trunnels, 213
Turner, Jonathan, 65, 70, 86, 95,
University of Virginia, 256
Uses of tree, 163
Utah, 239
Vermont, 240
Virgin Islands, 242
Virginia, 240

Wagon axles, 214
Wagon shafts, 214
Wagon tongues, 214
Wagons, 214
Walking canes, 215
Walking sticks, 215
War cubs, 215
War paint, 215
Washington, D.C., 240
Washington State 240
Washington, George, 57-64
Washington's dentures, 215
Weight, 20
Weninger, Del
West Virginia, 241
Whip handles, 216
Wind Shelters, 216
Windbreaks, 119, 216
Wire fences, 94
Wisconsin, 241
Witness trees, 32
Wood carvings, 217
Wright, John S. 65, 68, 86
Writing pens, 217
Wyoming, 242

Made in the USA
Lexington, KY
08 April 2015